IGCSE
Business Studies

Chris J Nuttall

CAMBRIDGE
UNIVERSITY PRESS

CAMBRIDGE UNIVERSITY PRESS
Cambridge, New York, Melbourne, Madrid, Cape Town, Singapore, São Paulo

Cambridge University Press
The Edinburgh Building, Cambridge CB2 2RU, UK

www.cambridge.org
Information on this title: www.cambridge.org/9780521750950

First published 2002
4th printing 2005

Printed in the United Kingdom at the University Press, Cambridge

A catalogue record for this publication is available from the British Library

ISBN-13 978-0-521-75095-0 paperback
ISBN-10 0-521-75095-4 paperback

Design, page layout and artwork Illustrations by Hardlines, Charlbury, Oxford.

Cover image by courtesy of 'Digital Vision'

Contents

Introduction

Welcome to the International GCSE in Business Studies!

This book is designed to help you as you progress through your course. It has been specially written to cover the University of Cambridge IGCSE Business Studies syllabus that you will be following. The syllabus is divided into sections, and the structure of the book reflects these, closely following the order of the syllabus.

How will this book help you?

Cambridge IGCSE Business Studies is an up-to-date and lively text, which uses an enquiry-based and active approach to the subject. It does not assume any prior knowledge of business, although as you progress you will probably find that many of the businesses that you come across in these pages are familiar.

Cambridge IGCSE Business Studies is divided into units to provide convenient and manageable bite-sized areas of learning. Each unit begins with learning outcomes and then has a brief introduction followed by a Business in context section, which presents a real world or realistic setting for the topic of the unit. Questions based on the Business in context will help you to understand the implications of the topic. There are revision questions and questions from past examination papers at the end of units 5, 17, 21, 31 and 34. These test the student's knowledge and understanding of the topics covered in the preceding units.

Units also contain Activities, which encourage you to think about, discuss or carry out activities to explore a topic for yourself.

The symbols that follow each question (>, >>, >>>) represent the level of difficulty of the question: > = level 1, >> = level 2, >>> = level 3.

Key terms are given in bold and explained in the margin, near where they are first used. At the end of each unit is a Summary of the work covered.

Model answers to the revision questions and to the questions at the end of the Business in context and Activity boxes are given in the Appendix.

What papers will you have to sit?

The International GCSE consists of three papers, of which paper 3 is optional:

Paper 1 contains short-answer questions and structured data-response questions; this paper is compulsory. Questions from past examination papers are given at the end of each Section.

Paper 2 will present a business situation or problem with questions arising from it; this paper is compulsory. Questions from a past examination paper are given in the Appendix.

Paper 3 consists of coursework and will be assessed by your school or college. You will have to submit a single piece of written work. Your coursework assignment should be related to a particular business situation or problem, and should take the form of a response to a clearly formulated question. Your assignment should be between 3,000 and 4,000 words in length, and will occupy about 20% of the course time for the subject as a whole.

If papers 1 and 2 are taken without the coursework option, each paper carries 50% weighting. If the coursework option is taken, papers 1 and 2 carry 40% weighting and paper 3 20% weighting.

All papers (except paper 3) are 1 hour and 45 minutes long.

How should you approach coursework assignments?

If you are taking the coursework option, you should discuss the topic question with your teacher so that you know what is involved. Don't start too early, or you won't have progressed in your course far enough. But don't leave it too late, either, or you will not have time to gather all the information you need.

When starting your coursework assignment you need to think about its purpose and how you are going to obtain the information you need. While this textbook and your teacher will help you gain the background knowledge required, you will have to do some of your own research. There are various sources of information you will find helpful in this. Your school or local library may be able to help, or you may be able to find some useful information on the Internet.

Sooner or later, however, you will have to contact a business organisation. Don't worry, you will probably find they are quite happy to help and supply you with the information you are looking for. Write a short, polite letter, explaining who you are, what you want to know, and why you want the information. Allow the business time to reply – it could be five or six weeks before they have time to attend to your request.

Do not start to actually write your assignment until you have enough information. If you start writing too soon you may find that you have to do it all over again when some new information comes to hand. But again, don't leave it too late or you will have to rush and not produce your best work. Try to allow yourself time to complete the assignment, put it aside for a few days, and then read through it to see that you are satisfied with it. Don't forget to check your spelling and grammar. If you have access to a computer, it is easy to use the spell and grammar checkers that come with most word-processing software.

How do you prepare for the exam?

Preparing for the exam takes time. Do not leave it until the last minute – or even the last few weeks. Effective revision is essential. Use the syllabus for guidance, go through past papers (such as the one included in the Appendix to this textbook), and use your own coursework and notes.

Break up the material you are trying to revise into manageable pieces. Remember that merely re-reading your notes or the textbook is not revising. Run through what you read in your mind and note down the key points. This will help fix the information in your memory.

One of the biggest obstacles to learning, and to revising in particular, is boredom. Try to vary your activities between note-taking, reading and doing some active research. And always try to build in some time for yourself. Remember that life is not just about studying (although it may seem like it at times).

Once again, welcome to the course. We hope you enjoy your studies, and wish you every success.

Chris Nuttall

1 The nature and purpose of economic activity

In this unit you will learn that economic activity is concerned with the ways in which the scarce resources of the earth are used to produce goods and services.

Businesses produce **goods** and **services**:

- Goods are things you can touch and use, or consume, such as clothes, food and books.
- Services are things that other people do for you, such as cutting your hair or selling you goods in a shop.

To produce goods and services businesses use resources or other goods that are made from resources that are found naturally occurring on or in the earth.

Goods
tangible products that can be touched and consumed

Services
things other people or businesses do for you

Business in context

Shell is one of the world's largest oil companies. The company makes products such as petrol and diesel from crude oil. Crude oil is unrefined oil that is found occurring naturally in deposits within the earth. To produce the petrol that people buy from garages Shell must first extract the crude oil from the earth. The company does this by drilling oil wells, many of which are under the sea.

Questions

1 What does Shell produce? (>)

2 Where can you buy Shell's product? (>)

3 What is Shell's product made from? (>)

Think carefully about the following products and answer the questions: (a) a loaf of bread (b) an oak coffee table and (c) this book.

1 What are the materials that each product is made of? (>)
2 Where do these raw materials come from? (>)
3 If society keeps using these raw materials will they eventually run out? Explain your answer. (>>>)

Scarcity, choice and the allocation of resources

Everything found on earth is finite, or in other words in limited supply. This is as true of resources, such as oil and the human labour required to operate the refineries that turn the oil into petrol, as it is of the money that is used to build the refineries, pay the wages of the employees, or used by customers to pay to fill their cars at filling stations.

The supply of some resources, such as air, is plentiful enough to satisfy everybody's needs. But the supply of most resources is not and, where this is the case, the resource is said to be scarce. This is so even though some resources, like trees or wheat, are renewable and replace themselves either naturally or through careful management.

Since the resources needed to produce goods and services are scarce, a choice must be made as to what to produce from them. For example, timber is used to make furniture and to build houses. However, a tree that has been cut down to produce furniture cannot also be used in the frame of a house. A choice has to be made between using the tree for furniture or houses.

Similarly, if you have $100 you can spend it on a mobile phone but you cannot also spend it on a pair of trainers. And the government cannot train additional doctors with the money it has already put into refurbishing schools.

Needs and wants

Need
something necessary to sustain life

Want
something chosen to satisfy a need or to make life more enjoyable

We all have **needs** that must be satisfied in order to sustain life. **Wants** are the ways in which we choose to satisfy our needs, and also to gain a level of satisfaction and enjoyment. For example, we need things like food and drink, shelter and clothing, but may choose to satisfy those needs with a burger or a pizza, a house or an apartment, and jeans or a suit, because these are the things we want. We also want refrigerators, radios and cars, because these things make life easier and more enjoyable, although they are not necessary to sustain life.

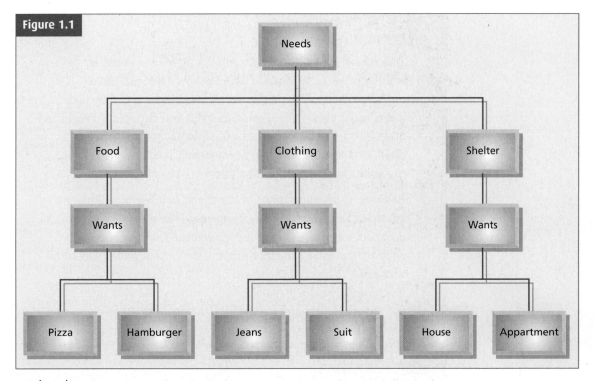

Figure 1.1

Needs and wants

While resources are scarce, however, people's needs and wants are potentially unlimited:

- In time, most things that you buy wear out and need to be replaced.
- Fashions and people's tastes change.
- As technology develops, new or improved products become available.

Demand and effective demand

When you want something, you create a demand for it. However, you cannot satisfy your want unless you have the money and are willing to pay for it. For example, while you may want a new pair of trainers you cannot satisfy your want unless you have the money to pay for the trainers, and are willing to spend it on them (you may prefer to spend the money on books or a sweater).

Even so, your demand for trainers will not be effective unless other people want trainers and are able and willing to pay for them, too. **Effective demand**, therefore, is created when enough people want something and are able and willing to pay for it. Demand is cumulative: the greater the number of people who want something and are able and willing to pay for it, the stronger the demand for it. The stronger the demand, the more likely a business or other organisation will supply the item demanded.

Effective demand
demand for a product that is backed up by an ability and willingness to pay for it

Throughout the world, the demand for petrol and diesel is enormous. Without petrol or diesel people could not travel anywhere in their cars, either on business or for pleasure, and goods could not be transported to shops and customers. People and other businesses are therefore willing to pay for the petrol and diesel that Exxon and other oil companies produce, even though they often complain about the price!

However, think about some of the things you buy regularly – for example clothes or food. The companies that make these products do so because there is an effective demand for them – enough people are prepared to buy them at their current prices. But think what might happen if the prices of these products increased. How much would you be prepared to pay for them? At what price would you reduce the amount you bought? At what price would you stop buying them altogether? What does this tell you about those companies and their products?

Allocating resources

Figure 1.2

Trainers | T shirt

Satisfying our wants from scarce resources involves a choice. For us as individuals, the choice is: which of our wants do we satisfy? If you want a pair of trainers and a T shirt, but only have enough money to buy one, you have to choose between them.

This choice, although it may be difficult, is fairly straightforward. When you consider that all the different wants of everybody in society have to be satisfied from scarce resources, however, choosing which wants should be satisfied is far more complex. It involves allocating resources to the satisfaction of those wants.

Cost and opportunity cost

We saw that if you want a pair of trainers and a T shirt but only have enough money to buy one of them, you have to choose between them. Both the trainers and the T shirt cost money – that is their financial cost. They also have an **opportunity cost** – the opportunity to purchase and enjoy the use of the other thing you would have liked to buy. If you buy the trainers, the opportunity cost of the trainers is the T shirt and the enjoyment you would get from it.

Every choice made by an individual or society, by the government or a business, involves an opportunity cost. If a government decides to spend an extra $100 million improving roads, the opportunity cost is spending it on other things such as schools or hospitals. The opportunity cost of society wanting more cars is the other things that could be produced using the extra labour and materials allocated to car production, such as houses or aeroplanes.

Opportunity cost
the cost of one item in terms of the next best alternative that must be foregone

The emergence of specialisation, the division of labour and exchange

Exchange in early societies

In the earliest societies, people had to produce everything they wanted for themselves. They had to grow their own food, build their own shelters and make their own clothes. The reasons for this were that there were not so many people alive as there are today, and with the tools (technology) available they could only produce what they required for their own needs.

As societies developed, however, so too did technology. New technology meant that one person could produce more than he or she needed. The result was that some people had a surplus of the goods they produced and found they were able to **exchange** this surplus for the surplus goods and services produced by other people.

Exchange
the ability to exchange one type of goods or services for another, normally using money as a means of exchange

People began to specialise in producing the goods and services they were best at producing, because they knew they could exchange them for other goods and services. **Specialisation** and exchange meant that society as a whole could produce more goods and services than when individuals had to produce everything they needed for themselves. Goods and services were also of a higher quality.

Specialisation
the tendency of an individual, business, region or country to produce certain goods or services

Money as a means of exchange

In the early days of specialisation, goods and services could only be exchanged by a system of barter, or swapping one product for another. The problem with this was that somebody who produced, say, cabbages and wanted a cart needed to find a person who not only produced carts but wanted cabbages and was prepared to exchange a cart for them. This introduced another problem: how many cabbages was a cart worth?

Money was developed to solve this problem. In the past, many things have been used as money: cattle, cocoa beans, maize, beeswax, shells, teeth, gold rings, iron swords and axe heads have all served as money. Most societies, however, have settled on the type of metal coin and paper note money familiar today.

Whatever is used as money, it must be accepted as a means of exchange for different types of goods. People who accept money in exchange for goods or services must be able to exchange it again for other goods or services. Money must also serve as a measure of value so that comparisons of the value of different goods and services can be made.

The development of firms and the division of labour

In the eighteenth century, the development of specialisation and of money as a means of exchange, coupled with developments in technology, gave rise to the growth of firms and the division of labour. A firm, or business, is able to specialise in one type of good or service because the owners of the firm can sell (exchange for money) their goods and services and buy those produced by other firms.

Similarly the employees of a firm (the people who work in the business) can specialise in one type of activity, such as accountancy or operating a computer, as they can exchange their labour for money to buy the goods and services they need. The specialisation of individual employees is known as the division of labour.

This is only one level of specialisation, as can be seen in Figure 1.3. Each level depends on the principle of exchange and on money as both a means of exchange and a measure of value.

Figure 1.3

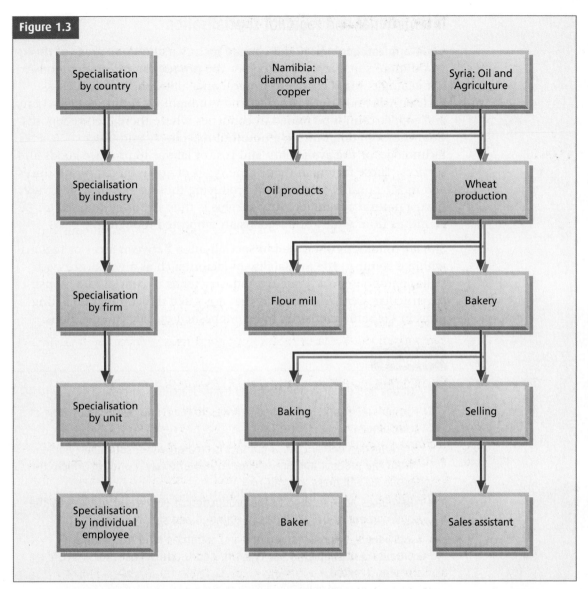

Levels of specialisation. At the highest level, countries may specialise in the production of goods for which they have a natural advantage (such as an abundance of natural resources). Within a country, industries specialise in types of goods (level 2). Individual businesses within an industry specialise in different stages of production, for example production and retailing (level 3), and a firm may have different units (e.g. factories or branches) to manufacture different parts of the product (level 4). Finally, people employed by a business will specialise in the type of work in which they have the greatest skills or abilities (level 5)

International and regional specialisation

Geographical, geological and climate factors make some areas of the world more suitable than others for the production of certain goods. For example, tea is grown in tropical and subtropical areas such as eastern Asia and South America and is bought by countries elsewhere, and copper cannot be mined in countries where there are no deposits. Countries also differ in the amount of machinery and other technology, or the availability and cost of labour to produce goods and services. These factors influence the types of goods a country produces, and most countries specialise in producing those goods in which they have a natural advantage. Any surplus is then exported to (sold to) countries from which other goods are imported (bought).

Similar conditions often lead to specialisation between areas or regions within a country. The availability of factors such as a workforce with skills appropriate to a particular industry tends to concentrate industries in particular areas. The result is that it is often difficult for competing firms in the same industries to be established outside those regions.

Summary

- Goods and services are produced using scarce resources.
- Businesses supply goods and services to meet the needs and wants of consumers.
- An effective demand for a product is created when sufficient people want the product and are willing and able to pay a price at which the producer will make a profit.
- Resources are allocated to the production of goods and services by the government or by the forces of demand and supply.
- Individuals, businesses, regions and countries tend to specialise in producing or supplying the types of goods and services for which they are most suited.
- Money allows individual employees and businesses to exchange their services or the goods they produce for other goods and services.

2   *What is business all about?*

In this unit you will find out about the people involved with business and the different reasons business organisations exist. You will see how these can sometimes change over time.

Many different groups of people are interested in the activities of a business. These are called the stakeholders of the business. Each group of stakeholders may have its own **objectives** for the business. The **purpose** of a business organisation is to meet the objectives of its stakeholders through the production of goods or the provision of services that are wanted by people in society. The success of a business is measured by the extent to which it achieves these objectives.

Objectives
goals or targets set by a business or its stakeholders which they seek to achieve through the activities of the business

Purpose
the purpose of a business is to provide goods or services; this enables the business to fulfil the objectives of its stakeholders

Business in context

Mission Statement: Local government

Our mission statement is "Striving for excellence – working with and for our communities".

Our values are to strive for excellence in:
- Focussing on our customers' needs
- Being honest, open and accountable
- Providing equality of opportunities
- Developing our employees
- Making best use of resources
- Working in partnership

Mission Statement: Neptune Shipping Agency Ltd

Our mission: To be the most successful company supplying Freight Forwarding Services.

Our aims: Service and value for money – Customer care – Environmental commitment – Employment standards

Mission Statement: International Energy plc

We are passionately committed to:
- Leading in our field
- Operating at the highest levels of efficiency
- Investing for the future
- Stimulating the personal development of employees
- Working for shareholders and satisfying customers
- Protecting and improving the environment in which we operate

Questions

A mission statement is a statement of the general purpose and aims of a business. Read the three mission statements above.

1 What product or service does each of the businesses provide? (>)

2 Who is affected by the activities of each business? (>)

3 What are the main purposes of each business? (>)

4 Suggest other purposes each business is trying to fulfil, not included in its mission statement. (>>)

5 Explain why each business was established. (>>>)

Who are the stakeholders?

Stakeholders
people who have an interest in the performance and activities of a business: shareholders, managers, employees, trade unions, creditors, suppliers, customers, the government

Stakeholders are individuals and groups involved with a business or with an interest in the activities of a business. They include:

- consumers
- employees
- managers
- owners
- financiers
- the community as a whole
- the government.

Some stakeholders, such as employees and managers, are internal (inside the business) while others, such as consumers and financiers (people and businesses that provide finance or loans for the business), are external (outside the business). Each group of stakeholders has its own objectives and exerts influence over the business in order to achieve these:

- Consumers – the main areas of interest for consumers are quality of product and value for money; they have influence over a business because they can take their custom elsewhere.
- Employees – the main areas of interest for employees are working conditions and pay; they have influence over a business because they can produce poor work, strike, or leave to find employment elsewhere.
- Managers – the main areas of interest for managers are the success of the business, power and payment for themselves; they have influence over a business because they are responsible for planning the activities of the business and for its day-to-day running.
- Owners – the main areas of interest for the owners of a business are the success of the business and the amount of profit the business makes: the higher the profits of a business, the more the owners receive; they have influence over the business because they have the final power to take decisions on the activities of the business.
- Financiers – the main areas of interest for those with a financial interest in a business are how secure is the money they have invested in or loaned to the business, and the return they are receiving; they have influence over the business because they can withdraw their financial support, causing the business to curtail its activities, and possibly even close down.
- The community as a whole – the main areas of interest for the community are social and environmental matters such as pollution, noise and destruction of the environment; they have influence because they can organise pressure groups to lobby the business itself, other groups of stakeholders, and the government.
- The government – the main areas of interest for the government are the well-being of all sections of society, including employees, consumers, the community as a whole, and environmental issues; it has influence over the business because it can legislate on matters of concern, restricting the activities of businesses or compelling them to behave in certain ways. The government also has an interest in the success of businesses in the country, and may support business through grants and subsidies, by promoting exports abroad and by restricting imports.

Stakeholders can increase their power by forming alliances. For example, suppose a textile company disposes of its waste in a local river. This pollutes the river and kills fish, but is an effective and cheap way to get rid of the waste. The community objects to the damage to the environment and wants the textile company to stop the pollution. Since the final customers of the cloth produced by the textile company are members of the community, the company's own customers, such as clothing and fabric manufacturers, are concerned that their own businesses might suffer if they are seen as supporting a business whose activities damage the environment. They therefore threaten to take away their custom. The owners of the textile company are afraid that the company will lose customers and support the other stakeholders in changing the company's policies on the disposal of waste.

Sometimes the objectives of different stakeholder groups conflict. For example, traditional farming methods are increasingly being changed in response to new technology. Machinery can now enable one person to do the work that was previously done by several. This has reduced the cost of farming, leading to lower prices for customers while maintaining the farmers' profits. Obviously, this benefits both the farmers and their customers. However, it conflicts with the interests of farm workers, who may lose their jobs.

The widespread use of cash dispensers has led to a reduction in employment in banking resulting in reduced personnel costs and increased profits for the banks. This is to the advantage of the banks' shareholders (owners – see Unit 7) who see their dividends increasing. However, it conflicts with the interests of bank employees who may lose their jobs.

Where the objectives of different stakeholder groups conflict, a compromise must be reached.

What is the purpose of business?

The purposes or objectives of a business largely depend on whether the business is a private enterprise established to make a profit for its owners, a non-profit-making organisation such as a charity or voluntary organisation, or a public enterprise set up to provide a service to the community. In some circumstances the objectives of a business may conflict or change over time.

Figure 2.1

Employees look for better wages and salaries

Customers want low prices and high quality

Shareholders want bigger profits

Local communities want to preserve their environment

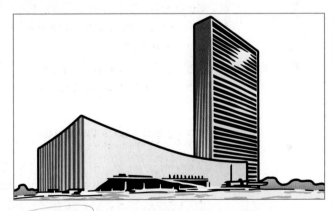

The government wants businesses to grow and to boost the economy

Stakeholders' objectives

Private enterprise

Making a profit

One of the main objectives of private enterprises (businesses owned by private individuals) is to make a profit. All business activity costs money, and businesses must pay their costs out of the income they receive from selling their goods and services. The profit a business makes is the amount by which its income exceeds its costs. Part of the profit of a business must be paid to the government in business or corporation tax. The remaining profit may be:

- kept by the owners of the business as a return on the money they have invested in the business
- distributed among the employees of the business, perhaps as a bonus in recognition of their efforts
- retained within the business to pay for new equipment, fund expansion, or just to meet future emergencies
- used to pay back loans.

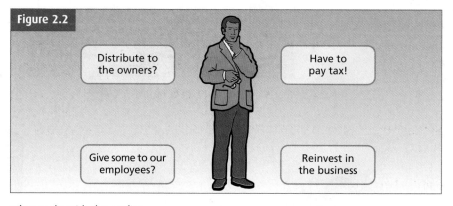

Figure 2.2

Distribute to the owners?

Have to pay tax!

Give some to our employees?

Reinvest in the business

What to do with the profit?

Increase sales revenue

The sales revenue of a business is the amount it receives from selling its goods and services. As we have seen, the excess of sales revenue over costs is profit. By increasing sales revenue without a corresponding increase in costs, a business can generate a higher profit.

Gaining and enlarging market share

The market for a product consists of the total value of sales of that product. Markets can be regional, national or international in scope. Obviously, to be successful, a business must gain a share of the market in which it operates. The larger the share of the market that a business has the better, since a larger share of the market means more sales and greater profits. A prime objective of many businesses is therefore to gain and enlarge their market share.

Growth

As businesses grow they are able to enjoy economies of scale (see Unit 5). This means that they are able to produce their goods or services for a lower average cost, increasing their profit. Businesses can grow by increasing sales, leading to increased production, taking on more employees, and perhaps even opening new factories or sales outlets, or by taking over or merging with another business, so that the combined business produces more goods and sells them at a more competitive price to more customers than either of the original businesses.

Provide employment

Small businesses are often set up in order to provide employment for their owners. This may then be a main objective for many small businesses.

In larger businesses the owners may not be employed in the business. No business can survive without employees to produce the goods or services, and to run the business, however. All businesses, whatever their size or product, must provide employment.

Public enterprise

Public service organisations provide services, such as education, health and national security, which are considered essential to the welfare of society. Some public services, such as museums, may not be provided if people had to buy the service individually. Other public services, such as national defence, must be provided to everybody in a society, or not at all – it is impossible to provide an army to defend some people and not others. The government usually takes over the provision of public services, which are paid for out of tax revenues.

Non-profit-making organisations

Non-profit-making organisations include charities and voluntary organisations. They may be national, such as Voluntary Action Network India, or international in scope, such as the Red Cross. Charities and voluntary organisations are set up to fulfil a perceived social need or to provide help to a specific section of the community.

Funds are raised through donations from the general public, other business organisations and governments. Any surplus, after the running costs of the organisation have been deducted, is used to support the charity's cause or reason for existence. Charities and voluntary organisations do not make a profit.

Changing and conflicting objectives

Sometimes the different objectives of a business may conflict. For example, a major concern is conservation of the environment. Most businesses share this concern and try to behave in an environmentally friendly way. A cement factory may therefore decide to burn a fuel that does not pollute the atmosphere rather than a chemical fuel that does cause pollution, even though the chemical fuel is cheaper and more efficient. While this helps the cement factory to achieve its objective of being environmentally friendly, however, the additional cost of the fuel, and the poorer performance of the factory hinders the factory from achieving its objective of maximising profit. The objectives conflict and the factory must make a business decision about the action it should take on burning fuel.

2.2 *Activity*

1   If you were a director of the cement factory, would you recommend burning the chemical or the non-pollutant fuel? Justify your recommendation. (>>>)

Summary

- Stakeholders are people and groups who are interested in the activities of businesses.
- Stakeholders try to influence the behaviour of businesses in order to achieve their own objectives.
- Businesses have objectives they are seeking to achieve.
- The objectives of a business may change and conflict over time.

3   *What part does the state play?*

In this unit you will learn why governments are involved in the economy and that the amount of government involvement depends on the political views of society.

Governments try to influence the economy of a country for several reasons:

- to make sure that essential goods and services are produced and made available to those sections of the community who need them
- to prohibit or control the production of goods and services considered undesirable or harmful to society, such as drugs
- to regulate the activities of producers and suppliers in order to protect the interests of consumers
- to help disadvantaged sections of the community by redistributing income through taxation and welfare benefits
- to help producers and suppliers by providing grants and subsidies and improving trading conditions.

Business in context

The government was in a dilemma. The latest statistics showed that more people in the country were smoking, and the incidence of deaths from lung cancer was increasing. This was not good news. The minister looked at the figures.

Soon the anti-smoking lobby would be calling for the government to introduce measures to reduce the number of smokers in the country. That would be countered by the campaigners for freedom to choose.

And then there was the health cost to consider: the minister had calculated that if everybody gave up smoking, the government could make a further reduction in tax. That would benefit everybody, smoker and non-smoker alike.

But the minister also had to consider the country's industry: the tobacco industry was a major employer and exporter. Any action now to reduce smoking in the country could harm employment and even drive the tobacco companies abroad.

It seemed that there were three things the government could do:

- increase the tax on cigarettes and tobacco in an attempt to reduce smoking – that would upset the campaigners for freedom to choose and the tobacco industry;

- put on a national television advertising campaign to educate people about the dangers of smoking – at least people could choose for themselves whether to smoke or not, but that would not be enough for the anti-smoking lobby;
- nothing – after all, was it the government's job to tell people whether they could or couldn't smoke?

All of the alternatives would upset somebody. The minister had to choose.

Questions

1 What is the problem that is troubling the minister? (>)

2 Why do you think the government has to deal with the problem? (>>)

3 Explain in your own words the three options for action that the minister has outlined. (>>)

4 Which course of action do you think the government should take? Justify your answer. (>>>)

Market, planned and mixed economies

Planned economy
an economy that is controlled by the state

Market economy
an economy that operates according to the forces of demand and supply, without interference by the state

Mixed economy
an economy that is partly left to the forces of demand and supply, and partly controlled by the state

The extent to which a government tries to influence or control the economy of its country depends on the political views of the government. At one extreme, in a **planned** or centralised economy the government will try to exert complete control over the economy and activities of business. At the other extreme, in a fully **market economy** the government will prefer to leave regulation of the economy to the forces of supply and demand. Between these extremes are **mixed economies** in which government influence and the forces of supply and demand all have a part to play.

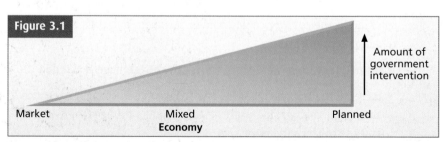

Market, mixed and planned economies

The planned or centralised economy

In a planned or centralised economy the government or the state decides what is produced, how it is produced and who receives it. The government allocates the resources of the country, including labour, to the production of specific goods and services. There is little or no competition because businesses and industry is owned and run by the government. Planned economies also avoid waste and duplication, such as advertising virtually identical products. However, the large number of administrators needed to do the planning and make decisions can be just as wasteful as some of the activities of the market economies.

The market economy

In a market economy customers choose the goods and services they want, and producers decide what they are going to supply based on what products will give them the most profit. Resources are thus allocated according to the forces of supply and demand without any government control or interference.

For this to happen people must be willing and able to buy the goods and services they want at the prices charged by producers – in other words there must be effective demand for the goods or services. In addition, the prices charged by producers must be sufficient for them to make a profit – there is no point in producing goods for $12 each and only being able to sell them for $10.

3.1 *Activity*

Read the section above on the market economy.

1 Suggest arguments for and against a market economy. (>>)
2 Do you think that a market economy is an effective way of providing the goods and services wanted by society? Explain your answer. (>>>)

The mixed economy

In practice most economies are somewhere between a market economy and a planned economy. A mixed economy is a balance between leaving the economy to the forces of supply and demand, and government control. The emphasis on government control or the forces of supply and demand varies from country to country.

Planned economies avoid duplicating expensive resources such as offices of different banks

3.2 *Activity*

Consider the country in which you live.

1 Do you think it has a market, planned or mixed economy? Give reasons for your answer. (>)

2 Compare your country's economy with that of another country with which you are familiar. (>>>)

Why does a government want to influence the economy?

There are three main areas of an economy that a government tries to influence:

Unemployment
the level of people without jobs who are both seeking and willing and able to accept suitable employment

Inflation
a general rise in the level of prices

Economic growth
an increase in the value of goods and services produced by a country and sold at home and abroad

- Unemployment: if **unemployment** is high the government has to pay more out in unemployment benefits. This means there is less to pay for other services provided by the government. In addition, unemployed people have less to spend on non-essential goods and services, so unemployment can lead to a reduction in demand for these.
- Inflation: a continuing rise in the general level of prices. The more expensive goods and services are, the less people can afford to buy. High **inflation** resulting in high prices can lead to increased unemployment, as less labour is required to produce fewer goods and services.
- Economic growth: the more goods and services a country produces using available factors of production, the better off the people in that country are. Increasing production can lead to **economic growth**. To achieve this, governments try to stimulate demand (both at home and abroad) for their country's goods and services, and encourage business to meet that demand.

What is the business cycle?

National economies often seem to go through cycles of buoyancy and decline (boom and bust), known as the business cycle. There are four clearly identifiable phases in the business cycle:

- Recession – falling demand leads to cuts in output, rising unemployment and businesses making losses and even closing down.
- Recovery – demand begins to increase, possibly due to government fiscal and monetary policies. Output increases and employment levels rise. Sometimes recovery can be a slow process as business confidence slowly returns.

- Boom – as business and consumer confidence strengthens, demand continues to increase and businesses create more jobs, increasing wages to attract employees, and invest in capital equipment. High employment and demand leads to inflation.
- Downturn – increased costs due to high wages and inflation lead to lower profitability and discourage continued growth. Demand falls, possibly due to government action to curb consumer spending. Output again decreases in response to falling demand possibly leading eventually to higher unemployment and another recession.

How does a government influence business and the economy?

A government's economic policies fall into four broad categories:

- **fiscal policies**, which are to do with how the government raises and spends its money
- **monetary policies**, which are to do with the amount of money there is in the economy
- legislation, including consumer protection, environmental protection, marketing and trading legislation, and employee protection
- policies on **nationalisation**, competition and international trade.

Fiscal and monetary policies are discussed in Unit 32, while consumer, environmental, marketing and trading, and employee legislation is discussed in Unit 34. Here we will look at nationalisation, competition and trade.

Nationalisation

In some countries, governments take over the provision and running of certain industries and services themselves. These may be paid for either wholly or in part by the government out of taxes. The actual industries and services vary from country to country, but usually include one or more of the following:

- defence services
- transport, such as the national railway system
- power and energy, including coal, electricity and gas
- postal services
- national broadcasting.

There may be other services that are provided and run by the government in your country.

Fiscal policies
government economic policies based on how the government raises and spends its money

Monetary policies
government policies based on controlling the amount of money in an economy

Nationalisation
taking ownership and control of an industry or business by the government

An industry or service that is taken over by the government is called a nationalised industry. In other words it has been taken into ownership by the state, or nation. The main reasons for nationalising some industries are:

- Industries such as defence must be provided for the nation as a whole or not at all and cannot just be provided for those who pay for them.
- Only a government with access to huge financial resources can provide the necessary investment in, for example, rolling stock (trains and carriages), rail systems, stations and so on for industries such as railways, both to provide these in the first place and to ensure the system is adequate and safe.
- Industries such as power and energy are considered essential to the operation and well-being of the nation, and therefore too important to be left to private enterprise.
- Nationalising large industries with many employees can be a way of maintaining levels of employment.
- Control of industry is often part of a government's political policies.

Privatisation
returning a government-owned industry or business into private ownership

In recent years, however, there has been a trend in many countries for nationalised industries to be returned to private ownership, rather than to continue being owned and run by the government. This is called **privatisation**. Privatisation usually occurs because nationalised industries may become too large and inefficient. Very large organisations are slow to react to the changing needs of society, because they have huge, cumbersome and expensive administrations. There is little incentive for nationalised industries to operate efficiently or cost-effectively, since the government will always make up any losses. In addition the services provided by nationalised industries may be costly. In terms of type and quality, services are often what the industry wants to provide, rather than what the customer requires.

3.3 *Activity*

1 Identify any of the following industries that have been nationalised in your country: public transport (rail and/or road); energy supplies (coal, electricity, gas, oil etc); water supplies; banking and other financial services; health. (>)
2 Have any industries listed in question 1 been privatised again after having been nationalised? (>>)
3 Explain the reasons behind the nationalisation or privatisation of industries in your country. (>>>)
4 Identify any industries in your country that you feel should be nationalised or privatised. Justify your answer. (>>>)

Competition

Most governments are keen to encourage competition between businesses. This is because they believe that competition means that businesses have to attract customers by offering better quality products, keener prices, a wider variety of products designed to meet what consumers want, and better customer service (such as advice and after-sales service). In some countries anti-competitive practices such as price-fixing or restricting the choice of customers are prohibited by law. Mergers that might result in a monopoly that could be against the interest of consumers (where the resulting business is so large that it can control the market by setting prices and standards of service and quality) are investigated and may be prevented.

3.4 Activity

1   Does the government of your country encourage or discourage competition in business? (>)
2   What methods does your government use to encourage or discourage competition? (>>)
3   You have been asked by the government of your country to take part in a survey on competition. Write a letter to the minister responsible for competition outlining and explaining your views on competition in business. Use examples to show why you believe competition is a benefit or disadvantage to consumers and businesses. (>>>)

International trade

Exports
goods and services sold to other countries

Imports
goods and services bought from other countries

All countries depend on other countries for supplying some of the goods and services their societies need. **Exports** (goods and services sold to other countries) bring money into the exporting country while money paid for **imports** (goods and services bought from other countries) goes out of a country. The amount by which a country's exports exceed imports, or vice versa (known as the balance of trade), therefore affects its income and wealth: the more exports exceed imports, the stronger the country's economy. By opening up foreign markets, with the possibility of increased sales, international trade also provides opportunities for businesses to grow, while the increased competition from foreign businesses leads to improved goods and services at competitive prices, with more choice for consumers.

Governments can encourage exports and limit imports in several ways. Import taxes and tariffs (additional taxes or restrictions imposed) increase the price or restrict the quantity of imports, making domestic products more attractive to consumers. Many international agreements promote international trade and competition by limiting tariffs on imports. Such agreements may be local, within a group of countries such as the Southern Africa Customs Union (SACU), and the Gulf Cooperation Council (GCC), or global, such as the agreements of the World Trade Organisation. Exports may be encouraged by promoting the country's goods and services abroad (through events such as trade fairs), subsidising production of goods for export, and controlling the exchange rate.

Exchange rate
the rate at which the currency of one country can be exchanged for the currency of another

The **exchange rate** is the rate at which one currency can be exchanged for another. This determines the comparative cost of goods in different countries. For example, if 1 dollar ($) exchanges for 3.5 Saudi riyals (SR) ($1:SR3.5), $1 purchases imports from Saudi Arabia worth SR3.5. If the exchange rate changes to $1:SR3, $1 now only buys SR3 of imports from Saudi Arabia. Imports from Saudi Arabia are now therefore more expensive compared to the same goods and services produced in countries trading in dollars. Customers in those countries will tend to buy home-produced goods and services because they are cheaper. To keep exports competitive, therefore, most countries try to maintain a fairly low exchange rate of their currency against others.

Summary

- All governments become involved in the economy and business of their country in order to influence unemployment, inflation and economic growth.
- The amount of involvement of a government in the economy depends on the political views of the government.
- The main methods of influencing an economy available to a government are fiscal policies, monetary policies, legislation and policies on competition and trade.

4   How is business organised?

In this unit you will learn that some businesses are owned by private individuals or groups while other businesses are owned by local or national governments. Businesses owned by private individuals or groups are in the private sector; businesses owned by local or national governments are in the public sector. You will also learn about the three different levels of business activity.

Some businesses are owned by private individuals, while others are owned by the state. Businesses owned by private individuals are in the **private sector**. Businesses owned by the state are in the **public sector**.

Private sector
the sector of business consisting of businesses owned by private individuals or groups

Public sector
the sector of business consisting of businesses owned by the state

Business in context

Bus services are necessary in many communities. They can provide convenient means of travel at the right times and they can reduce pollution and traffic congestion. Rahim's bus service links several small communities with a local town, which is the place of work for many and the site of many schools, the college, and the main shopping and leisure area. Before Rahim, a private firm, took over, a year ago, the bus service was run by the state.

Most buses are full in one direction and almost empty in the other, depending on the time of day. In the last year the costs of running the bus service have increased sharply and gradually the service has become less reliable, the buses more uncomfortable and the attitudes of the drivers less friendly. Some morning and evening services have been cancelled and the fares have been increased.

Questions

1. How has the ownership of the bus service changed? (>)

2. What are the main problems faced by the bus service? (>)

3. What are the problems caused to users of the bus service? (>)

4. How might the problems you identified in questions 2 and 3 be connected with the change in ownership of the bus service? (>>)

5. Who do you think should own and run the bus service: Rahim or the state? Give reasons for your answer. (>>>)

Private sector businesses

Incorporated business
a business that has been established as a legal entity separate from its owners

Limited liability
a restriction on the liability of the owners of a business for the affairs of the business

Unincorporated business
a business that has not been set up as an entity separate from its owners

Unlimited liability
the liability of the owners of a business for the entire affairs and debts of the business

Private sector businesses are owned by individuals, either on their own or in groups. The aim of most private sector businesses is to make a profit by providing the goods and services that they produce. The owners of the business receive either the whole or a share of the profit of the business as a reward for investing their money, and often time and other resources, in the business.

Businesses in the private sector may be either incorporated or unincorporated. **Incorporated businesses** are set up as legal entities in their own right. The owners of an incorporated business have **limited liability**. This means that if the business gets into difficulties and is unable to pay its debts, the owners of the business are not held personally liable, although if the business has to close and its assets sold in order to pay its debts, the owners may lose the money they put into the business.

Unincorporated businesses have no legal existence separate from their owners, and the affairs of an unincorporated business are considered to be the same as the personal affairs of its owners. The owners of unincorporated businesses have **unlimited liability**. This means that the owners of the business are legally responsible for all the affairs of the business. If the business gets into difficulties and cannot pay its debts, the owners of the business are held personally liable for those debts. If necessary the personal possessions of the owners – including their houses – may be sold in order to pay the debts.

The question of limited or unlimited liability is therefore an important consideration when deciding what type of business to set up. We look in more detail at the types of business organisation that are found in the private sector in Units 6 and 7.

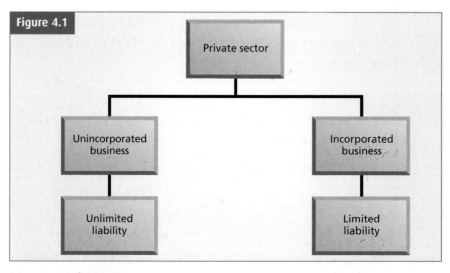

Private sector businesses

Public sector businesses

Public sector organisations are owned and run by local or national government on behalf of everybody in the community. They include government departments, such as welfare, health and defence, and nationalised industries and public corporations, such as state-owned car manufacturers, national radio and television networks, and postal services.

The main purpose of businesses in the public sector is to provide goods and services that are considered too important for the security of the country or the general welfare of society to be left to market forces and firms in the private sector.

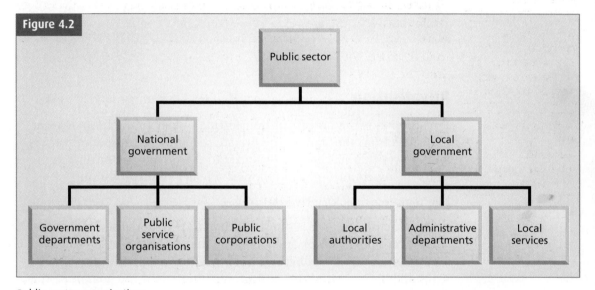

Figure 4.2

Public sector organisations

Nationalisation

Nationalisation is the process of taking over the ownership of businesses or industries by the state. A nationalised industry is an industry that has been taken over by the state.

There are many reasons for nationalisation:

- Political – governments of planned economies tend to take over the ownership and running of all businesses.
- National security – certain key industries, such as power, transport and defence, may be considered too important to be left to private enterprise.
- Failing industries – these may be nationalised in order to increase levels of investment and maintain employment.
- Natural monopolies – industries such as power, water and transport that require a national network and co-operation are often nationalised.

- Providing a service to the public – industries such as health and education may not be available to everybody in society if left to private enterprise where the profit motive may mean that only those who can afford to pay can get the service.

4.1 *Activity*

1 Find out what industries in your country are nationalised. (>)
2 Give reasons why the industries you identified in question 1 were nationalised. (>>)
3 Suggest other industries in your country that you think are appropriate for nationalisation. Give reasons for your suggestions. (>>>)

Privatisation

Privatisation is the process of transferring ownership of businesses or industries from the state to the private sector. A privatised industry is an industry that has been transferred to the private sector. In recent years, many countries have followed a policy of privatisation.

The main reasons for privatisation are:

- Too much power – it is often felt that large nationalised industries have too much power and can bring the country to a standstill through strikes or reductions in service provision.
- Competition – with little or no competition, and the guarantee that the government will continue to provide funds, nationalised industries may become complacent, providing poor services at a high cost.
- Government interference – governments may interfere too much with the running of nationalised industries, causing difficulties for management that lead to inefficiencies.
- Investment – nationalised industries may suffer from under-investment at times if the government feels the money should go elsewhere.

4.2 *Activity*

1 Find out if any previously nationalised industries have been privatised in your country. (>)
2 Why were they privatised? (>>)
3 What do you think have been the positive and negative consequences of privatising those industries? Give your reasons. (>>>)

Industrial sectors

Everything you buy starts out as a metal or mineral deposit in the earth, as a growing plant, or as an animal living on the land, in the air, or swimming in a river or the sea. Changing it into a useful product and getting it into a shop where you can buy it is a long process that involves businesses in different industrial sectors.

Business in context

Do you like chocolate? Have you ever stopped to think about just what goes into making the bar of chocolate that you can buy in a shop and eat before you get home?

To see how a bar of chocolate is made, we will look at the process involved in producing a bar of Cadbury's milk chocolate – one of the world's most popular brands of chocolate.

The process of producing a bar of Cadbury's milk chocolate starts with farmers in America growing and harvesting cocoa beans. The raw beans are then shipped in cargo vessels to the UK, where they are transported by road or rail to Cadbury's factory at Chirk. Here the beans are processed and turned into cocoa butter. This is then sent by road to the milk factory in Herefordshire.

At the milk factory, cooked full-cream milk and sugar are added to produce chocolate 'crumb'. This is pulverised between heavy rollers, other ingredients added and the chocolate moulded into bars. Finally, the bars are wrapped, packed into cases and delivered to retail outlets for sale to customers.

Questions

Look carefully at Figure 4.3.

1   How many different stages of production are there? (>)

2   How many different business organisations are involved in the process, assuming that each time the product is moved from one location to another, a different transport company is used? (>)

3   Explain how businesses at different stages of the production process are interdependent, basing your answer on Figure 4.3. (>>>)

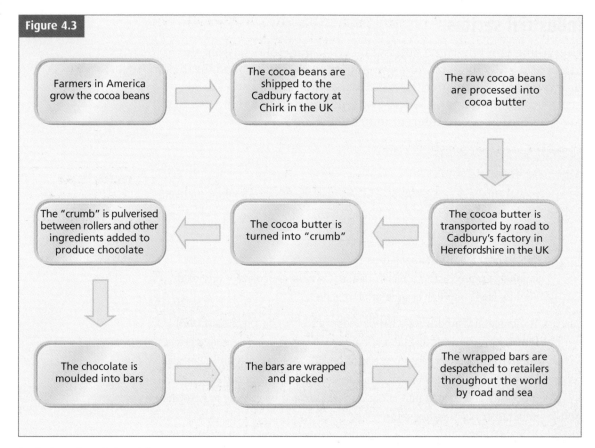

Figure 4.3

Farmers in America grow the cocoa beans	→ The cocoa beans are shipped to the Cadbury factory at Chirk in the UK	→ The raw cocoa beans are processed into cocoa butter
The "crumb" is pulverised between rollers and other ingredients added to produce chocolate	← The cocoa butter is turned into "crumb"	← The cocoa butter is transported by road to Cadbury's factory in Herefordshire in the UK
The chocolate is moulded into bars	→ The bars are wrapped and packed	→ The wrapped bars are despatched to retailers throughout the world by road and sea

Producing a bar of chocolate

Primary sector businesses

Primary sector
the sector of industry that produces unrefined raw materials

Businesses that produce the unrefined raw materials out of which finished products are made are involved in primary – or first level – production. They are in the **primary sector** of industry. Examples are: farming, agriculture and fishing, forestry, mining and fuel extraction.

Secondary sector businesses

Secondary sector
the sector of industry that produces finished or part-finished goods

Businesses that use the raw materials produced by primary industries, and change them into finished items, are involved in secondary – or second level – production. They are in the **secondary sector** of industry. Examples are: manufacturing, including refining and processing metals and minerals, chemicals and artificial fibres, engineering and allied trades, food and drink processing, textiles, footwear and clothing, and construction, which includes domestic and industrial building, and civil engineering, such as road and bridge construction.

Businesses in the secondary sector produce both consumer goods, such as books, food and televisions that are bought by individual consumers, and producer goods, such as machinery, commercial vehicles and parts that are bought by other businesses and used in the production of other goods.

Tertiary sector businesses

Businesses that provide services are involved in tertiary – or third level – production. They are in the **tertiary sector** of industry. Examples of tertiary industries are: banking and financial services, insurance, leisure and tourism, transport, retailing and wholesaling, public services, distribution, post and telecommunications, education, and health services.

Tertiary sector
the sector of industry
that provides services

4.3 Activity

1   Investigate primary, secondary and tertiary sector businesses in your country. What are the main businesses or industries in each sector? (>)

2   Find out if there have been any changes in the balance of primary, secondary and tertiary industries in your country over the past twenty years. Consider factors such as production output and levels of employment in each sector - have they risen or fallen? (>>)

3   Suggest reasons for any changes you have identified. (>>>)

Putting the three sectors together: chains of production

Producing and supplying products involves businesses in all three industrial sectors. For example, businesses involved in producing a loaf of bread include the farmer who grows the wheat (primary sector), the miller who turns the wheat into flour (secondary sector), the baker who makes the loaf and the shop that sells it (tertiary sector). Transport (tertiary sector) is needed to get the wheat from the farmer to the miller, the flour from the miller to the baker, and the bread from the baker to the bakery.

Figure 4.4

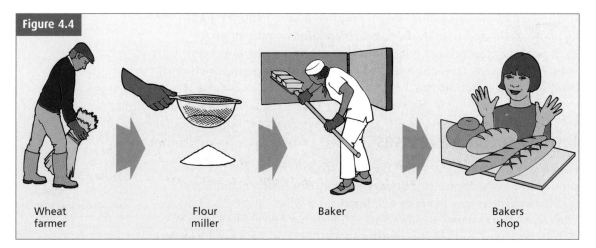

| Wheat farmer | Flour miller | Baker | Bakers shop |

Chain of production of a loaf of bread

Chain of production
a sequence of stages of production

Each business forms part of a **chain of production**, and every business is dependent on other businesses in the chain. At each stage, the business adds value to the raw materials as they are changed into a finished product that satisfies the needs of customers.

4.4 *Activity*

In Activity 4.1, you conducted a survey of businesses in your local area. Select three of the businesses you identified and construct chains of production for their products. (>)

Summary

- Business owned by private individuals or groups are in the private sector.
- Businesses owned by the state are in the public sector.
- Businesses and industries may be taken into state ownership through a process known as nationalisation.
- State-owned businesses may be returned to the private sector through a process known as privatisation.
- Products go through many stages of production.
- The different stages of production of a product are linked in a 'chain of production'.
- Businesses may be in the primary sector, secondary sector or tertiary sector, depending on where they are in the chain of production.

5 Is size important?

In this unit you will learn that the size of a business can be measured in different ways, depending on the reason for measuring. You will also learn that the local, national or international environment in which they operate influences businesses and that the structure and experience of individual firms and industries in different localities vary.

Businesses come in all sizes. Some are small, owned and run by just one person, while at the other end of the scale are giant companies, familiar to us all, which operate all over the world. Businesses grow in different ways, and for different reasons.

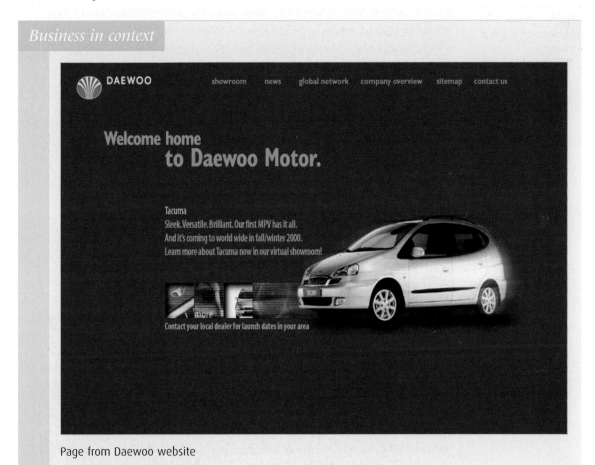

Business in context

Page from Daewoo website

Daewoo International started in 1967 as a small textile exporter based in Korea. The company is now a leading multinational company. Daewoo's products include steel, metals, automotive components, machinery, industrial plant, electronics, textiles and chemicals, international finance and investment, and project management. Daewoo now operates in over 165 countries around the world through a network of over 200 branch offices and subsidiaries.

A major part of Daewoo International is its motor division. Daewoo Motor has been a major force in the development of both Korea's auto industry and national economy for twenty-five years. It has successfully helped to make Daewoo into a truly global company with an extensive international network integrating research and development, production, sales and services. Now Daewoo cars are rolling off the production lines of 12 plants in 11 different countries, in addition to its production facilities in Korea. Daewoo has a worldwide capacity of 2.3 million vehicles per year.

Questions

1 In which country did Daewoo start operating? (>)

2 How many countries does Daewoo operate in now? (>)

3 According to the case study, how many different types of goods and services does Daewoo produce? (>)

4 Most people would consider that Daewoo is a large company, although it had small beginnings. How do you think Daewoo grew to be the size that it is now? (>>)

5 Do you think that Daewoo benefits from operating in many different countries? Explain your answer. (>>>)

The size of firms

Individual businesses vary considerably in size. They can be classified as large or small according to various objective measures and this may be of importance to various stakeholders. Banks and other financial institutions want to know how secure a loan is likely to be; shareholders and investors may base their investment decisions on the size of a business; businesses need to know the size and strength of their competitors; governments need to know the effect of different businesses on employment and the economy.

The main methods of measuring the size of a business are by:

- output of goods and services
- turnover
- profit
- number of employees
- capital employed
- number of outlets.

Units of production could be used to compare the size of firms in the same industry, but care is necessary. Two fast food restaurants each serving 1,000 meals a day might be considered the same size, but two firms each producing 1,000 motor cars cannot be compared on the same basis if one produces luxury limousines while the other produces family saloons.

| 5.1 | Activity |

Investigate businesses in your own country. Construct a table listing the five largest judged against output of goods or services, by turnover, by profit, by number of employees, by capital employed, or by the number of outlets. Would the order change if they were measured against different criteria? (>>)

How do firms grow?

Some industries are dominated by large firms. Most businesses begin small, however, and grow over a long period of time. Growth may be internal or external.

Internal growth

Some businesses grow because their market grows, and they are able to maintain their share of the market. Other businesses try to develop new markets for their products, perhaps internationally.

New products, especially in the field of information technology, can generate increased sales for a business. Thus the development of computers, software and mobile phones has given rise to the growth of major businesses such as IBM, Microsoft and Vodaphone.

But often internal growth is a slow process with markets growing only slowly if at all. New products may involve many years of research, development and testing before they can be marketed. Aggressive companies may want to increase the scope of their activities more quickly. This has led to the expansion of the process of external growth.

External growth

Takeover
one company gaining
control of another

Merger
two companies joining
together by mutual
agreement

External growth involves a merger with another business or a takeover of that business. A **takeover** is where one company gains control of another. A **merger** is where two companies join together by mutual agreement – sometimes establishing a new distinct business, sometimes retaining their separate identities.

- Horizontal mergers occur where the two companies are engaged in the same stage of production of the same good. The merger of two bakers or two motor vehicle assemblers would be examples of horizontal mergers.
- Vertical mergers occur between two companies engaged in different stages of the production of the same good. A producer of dairy products such as milk and cheese might take over a farm in order to safeguard its supply of raw materials.
- Lateral mergers involve two companies producing related goods that do not compete directly with each other. The common link may be at one end of the process only. Supermarkets and hardware stores operate in different markets, but a lateral merger between them might lead to some cost cutting.
- Conglomerate, or diversifying, mergers occur where the products of the companies involved are unrelated. The acquisition of a cosmetics or potato crisp manufacturer by a tobacco company constitutes a diversifying merger. Such mergers may be defensive, in anticipation of a decline in the acquiring company's main market.

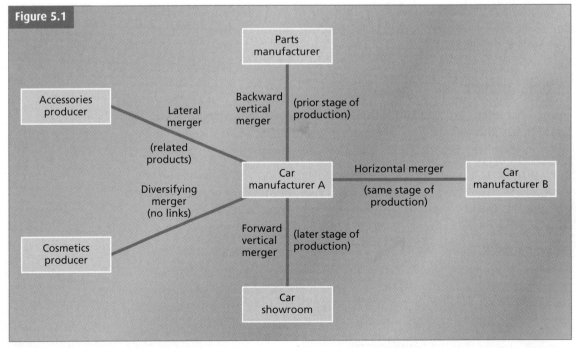

Figure 5.1

Types of merger

Consider the following mergers and identify what type of merger was involved: a national newspaper buying a paper mill in Canada; General Motors buying a motor manufacturer in another country; a furniture manufacturer buying a chain of high street furniture stores; a major food manufacturer taking over a manufacturer of toiletries; a computer software developer taking over an Internet service provider. (>)

Multinational businesses

A **multinational** company is a business with operations in countries other than that in which it is based. We have already met Daewoo; other well-known examples are BP, Microsoft and Nike.

The annual sales of some multinationals are larger than the total output of many individual countries. These companies have considerable influence in the countries in which they operate. In developing countries the establishment of a multinational may well cause more problems than it solves.

Other things being equal, most firms would prefer to expand in their domestic market rather than abroad. Limits to the size of the home market, however, mean extra sales can eventually be achieved only by selling abroad. There are often obstacles, such as trade restrictions and import taxes, placed in the way of exporting goods from one country to another, however, and companies may seek the alternative route of actually producing goods abroad and avoiding the need to export.

Sometimes a business may establish factories overseas for other reasons. The availability of raw materials or cheap labour may attract the multinational. Governments, anxious to attract investment, may offer tax advantages or other incentives.

Some of the main effects of the development of multinationals are: employment will increase in the host country – this may, however, be at the expense of employment or potential employment in the home country; multinationals transfer technology from one country to another, facilitating economic progress; the level of economic activity should increase in the host country.

But not all the consequences of the multinationals are beneficial:

- Multinational businesses will do what is best for the company, not for the country they are operating in, switching production between countries according to need, regardless of the effect on the economy of the country or unemployment.

Multinational
a business operating in more than one country

- Multinationals may take advantage of their situation to minimise their taxation. Multinationals located in developing countries may be able to dictate to governments anxious not to jeopardise investment and employment by the multinational.
- The establishment of a multinational company in a country may harm domestic businesses; some smaller businesses may even fail in the face of strong competition.

As multinationals grow even larger and spread even wider, governments increasingly have to consider their policies in relation to them so that their possible disadvantages do not outweigh their benefits.

How do small firms survive?

We saw earlier that there is no satisfactory single measure of the size of businesses. Different criteria are used in different industries.

The difficulty can be understood if we consider just two areas: oil refining and taxi services. Whatever method is used to measure the size of businesses in these industries – turnover, capital or employees – we can be sure that the smallest firm in the oil refining industry is far bigger than the largest firm in the taxi industry. This is why different measures have to be employed.

Whatever measures are used, however, and despite the fact that the biggest firms continue to increase in size, there is a large and growing small firms sector which is vital to the economy of countries throughout the world. Small firms are especially active in the service sector, where they have the largest share of the market.

There are several reasons why small firms continue to thrive. Many people value independence. They may also make a greater contribution to the economy of a country by running their own businesses than they would if submerged in a larger organisation. A large number of small businesses could expand but do not as their owners want to retain control and do not want the anxiety that a larger organisation would bring.

Markets that are small and geographically dispersed, even throughout the world, are best served by small firms that can concentrate on the needs of the smaller market. Large firms tend not to be interested in producing custom-made goods. A large construction firm that specialises in building motorways or power stations will not waste resources on building an extension to your home, which is the type of job ideally suited to a small builder.

Small firms also frequently provide an important service to large firms by providing them with components. This enables the larger firm to concentrate on its main tasks.

Small firms can be more creative. Managers and owners of small businesses are closer to their customers than the top management of large firms. They may be able to identify the significance of and need for new developments more quickly. Decisions can be taken quickly, without the need for a large bureaucracy. Small businesses are more flexible, and perhaps more responsive to the changing needs of their customers.

In many countries, assistance is available to people considering starting their own business. Various grants, subsidies or tax concessions ensure that activity in the small firms sector is maintained. A government's main reason for providing such support may be the hope of reducing unemployment. Most new jobs are created in small businesses.

Each year a large proportion of small businesses fail. Others succeed and grow, while more are established for the first time. In any event, there seems to be no end to the flow of people prepared to start their own businesses.

5.3 Activity

Select one small and one multinational business to examine. These businesses should operate in your country, and if possible in your area. Write an account of each explaining why it is its present size. In particular you should consider the influence of the local, national or international context in which the business first developed and now operates. Are there any special features of the localities where the businesses operate, such as access to raw materials or the presence of suppliers of parts, or of the structure of their particular industry, such as a preponderance of large international companies or smaller companies serving a local or specialised market? (>>>)

Summary

- The size of a business can be measured in terms of output of goods and services, turnover, profit, number of employees, capital employed, or number of outlets.
- Businesses may grow internally or externally.
- External growth involves mergers or takeovers.
- Multinationals operate in more than one country.
- Many multinationals have significant influence over the governments and economies of the countries in which they operate.
- Despite the trend towards larger businesses and multinationals, many businesses remain small.

Revision questions

1 Explain the terms specialisation, the division of labour, and exchange.

2 Identify three groups of stakeholders.

3 How do the objectives of non-profit-making differ from the objectives of private enterprise?

4 Explain how might the priorities of a business change over time?

5 What are the features of a market economy?

6 Why are most economies mixed economies?

7 Give three examples each of primary and secondary sector business activities.

Past examination questions

1 Yasmin Ltd is described as a small business.
(a) Explain how the size of a business can be measured.
(b) What problems are there in measuring the size of any business?   *(4 marks)*

IGCSE Paper 2, May/June 2000

2 (a) The state-owned railway system in country Y is to be privatised (sold to the private sector).
  (i)   How might the business objectives of the private sector differ from those of the public sector? *(4 marks)*
  (ii) Do you think this change in ownership will benefit the customers of the railway system? Explain your answer.   *(4 marks)*
(b) (i)   What do you understand by tertiary business activities?   *(3 marks)*
    (ii) Give an example of a business activity that would be classified as being tertiary.   *(1 mark)*

IGCSE Paper 1, May/June 2000

3 (a) Explain what is meant by a
    (i) private sector business   *(2 marks)*
    (ii) public sector business   *(2 marks)*
(b) Why might the aims of public sector businesses differ from the aims of private sector businesses? *(4 marks)*

IGCSE Paper 1, November 2000

6   *Sole traders and partnerships*

In this unit you will learn about unincorporated businesses: sole traders and partnerships. You will see that there are two main types of partnership: ordinary (or general) partnerships and limited partnerships.

In Unit 4 we saw that businesses in the private sector are owned by private individuals. There are two forms of private sector businesses:

- unincorporated businesses, which do not exist separately from their owners
- incorporated businesses, which are legally established as separate entities.

The owners of unincorporated businesses mainly have unlimited liability. This means that they are personally responsible for the affairs of the business – including the whole of any debts the business may have. The owners of incorporated businesses are not personally responsible for the affairs of the business, since the business exists as a legal entity in its own right. However, if an incorporated business fails, the owners may lose all the money they put into the business.

In this unit, we will examine unincorporated businesses – sole traders and partnerships. We will look at incorporated businesses, private and public limited companies, in Unit 7.

Business in context

When Sofia Akram was made redundant from her job at a local garage, she decided to use her redundancy money to realise her dream and open a small hotel near the sea.

She found a large house that would suit her needs for sale in a village near the coast, although her redundancy money would only pay the deposit she needed. Still, there was enough accommodation for her to live in the house as well as let four bedrooms. If she sold her own house and took out a mortgage on the new one, she should have enough – with a little left over to help her through the first few months.

'It's exciting', Sofia told her sister Tina. 'It's what I've always wanted to do. I'll be my own boss and rise or fall on my own efforts. All the profits will be mine; they will not go to the head office of a big company. I'll advertise and I think it will be a success.'

Tina was not so sure. 'But you'll be on your own,' she said. 'Think of the long hours you'll have to put in. It's not just cooking breakfasts and making beds. You'll be on call all the time. You'll have to do the books, take stock, place orders and things like that. You've never run a business yourself before. What about the accounts and paperwork? You may not find that as much fun as serving breakfasts and chatting with your guests – but you've got to do it, because there won't be anyone else to do it for you. And what will you do if it all goes wrong? What if you have a poor year and you don't get as many bookings as you hope for? You could lose everything – not just the business, but your home and livelihood as well.'

Questions

1   What are the advantages Sofia has put forward for running her own business? (>)

2   What disadvantages has Tina raised? (>)

3   If you were Sofia, what would you do? Give your reasons. (>>>)

Sole traders

Sole trader or sole proprietor
a business that is owned by one person

Self-employed
a person who works for himself or herself rather than for another employer

A **sole trader** (sole proprietor) is someone who owns his or her own business. There is one owner (the sole trader), who makes all the decisions and is responsible for the day-to-day running of the business. While many sole traders are people working on their own, a sole trader can employ others. People who work in the business, apart from the owner, are actually employed by the owner. The owner is **self-employed**.

Typical sole trader businesses are local independent shops, plumbers and similar trades people, freelance artists and other self-employed people.

Setting up as a sole trader

It is very easy to set up as a sole trader, as there are few legal formalities to go through.

The sole trader must tell the tax authorities that they have set up a business and are self-employed. He or she must declare any profit or loss made during the financial year, as this will be their income for tax purposes. Sole traders may also have to pay other taxes, such as purchase tax or Value Added Tax where these apply. A sole trader must also keep employment records in respect of any employees.

Some businesses, such as hairdressers, employment agencies and businesses dealing with food, must be licensed, and all businesses employing people must comply with employment laws and health and safety regulations.

Where does the money come from?

Partly because they are small businesses, there are few sources of finance available to sole traders, apart from the personal funds of the owner. These include any savings the owner may have, redundancy payments from previous employment or loans from the bank. In addition, grants may be available from local or national government, and private organisations.

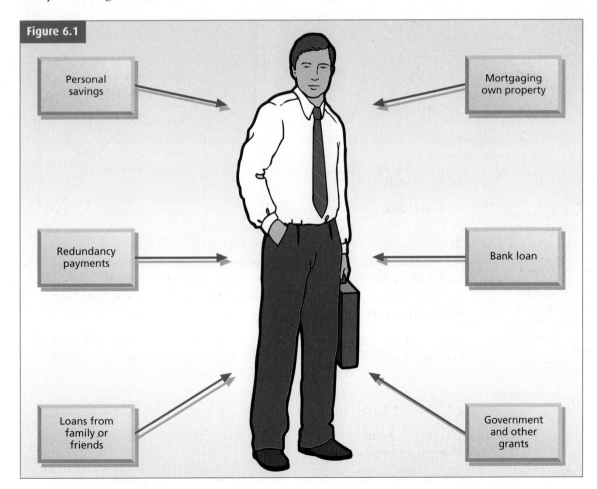

Figure 6.1

Personal savings

Mortgaging own property

Redundancy payments

Bank loan

Loans from family or friends

Government and other grants

The main sources of finance for a sole trader

What happens if things go wrong?

A sole trader is an unincorporated business. This means that the business is not considered to be separate from its owner: the affairs of the business are considered the same as the affairs of the trader.

In the case of a sole trader, therefore, it is the owner himself or herself who employs people, owns the property of the business and borrows the money that the business needs. If things go wrong the owner has unlimited liability for any debts the business has. If the business is unable to pay its debts because it has insufficient funds available, the owner must pay the debts in full, even if he or she has to sell all their personal possessions including their house and car to do so.

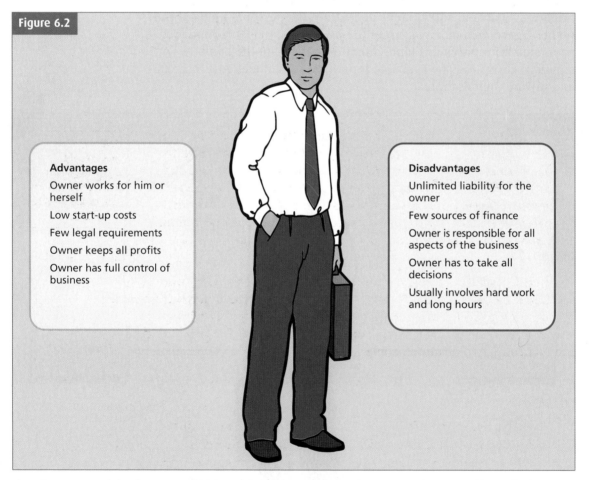

Figure 6.2

Advantages

Owner works for him or herself

Low start-up costs

Few legal requirements

Owner keeps all profits

Owner has full control of business

Disadvantages

Unlimited liability for the owner

Few sources of finance

Owner is responsible for all aspects of the business

Owner has to take all decisions

Usually involves hard work and long hours

The advantages and disadvantages of operating as a sole trader

1   Find out the name of a local sole trader business.
    You can do this by looking in your local paper. (>)
2   What goods or services does your selected business
    provide? (>)
3   Why do you think the business operates as a sole trader? (>>)

Your friend is thinking of starting his or her own business by
buying a small shop. They have asked you for advice. Write a
short letter to your friend giving him or her your advice about
starting out as a sole trader. (>)

Partnerships

A **partnership** is an unincorporated business that is owned by two or
more people (the partners). A partnership can normally have up to
twenty partners. Some major professional firms of accountants, such
as Ernst and Young which has offices in more than 130 countries
throughout the world, and international firms of solicitors such as
Linklaters with operations in Asia (including China), Europe and the
USA, have several hundred partners, reflecting the large scale and
global scope of their operations.

The partners are self-employed. People other than the partners who
work in the business are employed by the partners. Typical partnership
businesses are local professional firms such as accountants, architects,
solicitors and doctors' practices, shops and similar small businesses that
are owned by two or more people.

**Ordinary
partnership**
an unincorporated
business with two or
more owners who have
unlimited liability

Business in context

The Design Partnership is a firm of architects and interior designers
that provides a complete service to business and private clients.
Taleni joined the firm three years ago and became a partner last year.
In order to become a partner, Taleni had to put an amount of capital
into the business.

Before she joined the Design Partnership, Taleni ran her own practice
as an architect. She felt limited on her own, however, and believed
that joining the larger firm would allow her to develop her own career,

while at the same time providing her clients with a wider range of services.

Together with the other partners, she is responsible for making sure that the firm has enough clients and business to pay its expenses – including the salaries of three assistants and a receptionist – and make a profit. The money she and the other partners earn is based on the amount of profit the firm makes.

Business has been harder to get over the last few months and this has caused a drop in the firm's revenue. Taleni wants to produce a new brochure, but Jatura, another partner, thinks a glossy brochure is a waste of time and money. He thinks clients should come through personal recommendation and networking. He wants the partners to spend more time socialising and making contact with prospective clients through local organisations such as the Rotary Club and Chamber of Commerce.

The third partner, Namene, caused a disagreement last week. She bought herself an expensive new company car, without consulting the others. When Taleni and Jatura complained at her actions, Namene pointed out that as senior partner she had overall responsibility for decisions. Namene also told Jatura that since she was the one who would probably spend most time at Rotary Club and Chamber of Commerce meetings and social events getting clients, as Jatura had suggested, she ought to have a decent car to be seen in.

Questions

1 Who are the partners of the Design Partnership? (>)

2 What does the Design Partnership do? (>)

3 Why did Taleni decide to join the partnership? (>>)

4 How will being a partner in the Design Partnership enable Taleni to develop her own career and also provide her clients with a wider range of services? (>>>)

5 How might the partners resolve the difficulties they are experiencing? (>>>)

Setting up a partnership

Although it is not a legal requirement in most countries, many partnerships are established with a **Deed of Partnership**. This sets out the 'rules' of the partnership, including how much money each partner has to put into the business, who is responsible for decision-making, specific responsibilities of partners and how the profits of the business are to be shared or used, the procedure for removing a partner or introducing a new one to the business and arrangements for dissolving the partnership and ending the business. In the absence of a partnership agreement, any dispute between partners will normally be settled on the basis that each partner shares equally in the management and responsibility for decision-making in the partnership, as well as any profits of the business and responsibility for debts of the partnership.

Deed of Partnership
a legal agreement of the terms and conditions of the partnership, signed by all partners

6.3 *Activity*

1 In groups of two or three, discuss a business that you could set up as a partnership. (>)
2 Agree on a name for the partnership, and the terms that should be included in a Deed of Partnership. (>)
3 Draw up a Deed of Partnership including the terms you have agreed so that each partner is happy to sign it. (>>)

What is a limited partnership?

A **limited partnership** is a special type of partnership in which one or more of the partners have limited liability. This means that the limited partner or partners can only be held liable for the affairs and debts of the partnership to the extent of the money they originally put into the partnership.

Limited partnership
an unincorporated business with two or more owners, at least one of whom must have unlimited liability

Limited partnerships are rare, and there are restrictions on their formation: at least one partner must have unlimited liability; partners with limited liability must not take any part in the management of the business. Some countries require limited partnerships to be registered with the authorities.

Where does the money come from?

As with sole trader businesses, there are few sources of finance available to partnerships, other than the partners' own funds, including savings, and redundancy payments from previous employment, and loans or grants from local or national government. Because there are more owners of the business, however, partnerships may often be set up with more capital than sole trader businesses. In addition, each partner may take out a loan individually, so reducing the amount owed by any one partner.

What happens if things go wrong?

As a partnership is an unincorporated business, the partners, other than limited liability partners, have unlimited liability for any debts the business has. Moreover, each partner is liable for the business debts of the other partners. Therefore if one partner defaults, the remaining partners are fully responsible for the whole of the debts of the business.

Figure 6.3

Advantages
Owners are self-employed
Owners have full control over business and profits
Few legal formalities

Disadvantages
Unlimited liability for each of the owners
The partners have full responsibility for all aspects of the business
Disagreements between partners may cause difficulties with the business
The business may not survive the loss of one the partners

The advantages and disadvantages of partnerships

1 Meka Wakama and Delyth Evans are both self-employed business consultants. Meka specialises in financial management, while Delyth advises on marketing. How might forming a partnership help both them and their clients? (>)

2 What disadvantages might there be to the partnership? (>)

3 To develop the partnership, Meka and Delyth need to raise additional finance quickly. How might they do this? (>)

4 After the partnership has been trading for a year, several clients complain to Delyth that Meka has misled them over prices, quoting a low price to get the business, and then charging far more than the quote. How might Delyth deal with this matter? (>>)

Summary

- A sole trader is someone who owns and controls his or her own business.
- A sole trader is the simplest form of business to set up.
- A sole trader makes all the decisions about the business.
- The owner keeps all the profits of the business, but has unlimited liability with regard to any debts the business has.
- Partnerships are unincorporated businesses that have more than one owner.
- The rules of a partnership are set out in a Deed of Partnership.
- Partnerships are shared businesses which enable the owners to share responsibilities, workload and decision-making.

7   Limited companies

In this unit you will learn about the different types of limited companies. You will find out that the owners of limited companies are called shareholders, and have limited liability.

Limited companies are incorporated businesses, or corporations – that is they are set up as legal entities in their own right and exist quite separately from their owners.

The owners of limited companies are called shareholders, because they own a part, or share of the company. As a legal entity a limited company is responsible for its own affairs and debts. The owners or shareholders of the business have limited liability for the debts of the business. A limited company can own property and equipment, employ people and borrow money. It also pays business taxes on its profits.

Business in context

At the end of World War I, Jack Cohen formed a partnership with T. E. Stockwell. Their aim was to supply groceries to the growing after-war market.

For several years they worked as market traders with their own stalls in several local markets. As the years passed, however, and the partnership became increasingly successful, they began to get ambitious. In 1929 they opened their first shop in a nearby town. They named it using the initials of T. E. Stockwell, and the first two letters of Jack Cohen's last name: Tesco.

The shop became an immediate success, and Cohen was ambitious. In 1932, Tesco became Tesco Stores Limited, a private limited company. Cohen wanted to take advantage of the growing population, and knew that he needed more capital than he was able to raise in order to develop the business. By 1934, Tesco had fifty stores in prime locations that were supplied from a state-of-the art central warehouse.

The business had come a long way since the early market stall days. And it had a long way yet to go.

Types of limited companies

There are broadly two types of limited companies: **private limited companies** and **public limited companies**. Private limited companies are normally smaller businesses. The number of shareholders of a private limited company may be restricted; shares cannot be offered for sale to the general public or transferred without the agreement of all the shareholders.

Public limited companies are generally larger than private limited companies. Shares in public limited companies can be offered for sale to the general public and may be freely bought and sold on the **stock market** of the country in which the company has been registered.

While the general principles of private and public limited companies are similar throughout the world, specific legislation concerning the establishment and running of limited companies does vary. In Bermuda, for example, companies are classified as 'local', 'permit', or 'excepted'. At least 60% of the shareholders of local companies must be Bermudian. Permit companies may be incorporated outside Bermuda, but are permitted to trade within the country. Excepted companies are exempt from the 60% rule, but may not normally compete with local companies within Bermuda. In South Africa, a special type of corporation known as a 'closed corporation' exists with up to ten members who 'contribute' to the capital of the corporation, rather than buy shares in it.

Similarly, the titles used in different countries vary. Many countries have adopted the term 'limited', or 'Ltd', after the name of the company, as in JCB Ltd, the British-based company that produces and sells heavy earth-moving machinery throughout the world. To distinguish between private and public limited companies, some English-speaking countries have adopted the initials 'plc' after the company's name to denote a public limited company.

In other countries, such as Australia and South Africa, private limited companies are known as 'proprietary' limited companies, which are abbreviated to 'Pty Ltd' after the company's name. French and Spanish

Private limited company
a limited company whose share cannot be sold to the general public

Public limited company (plc)
a limited company whose shares can be freely bought and sold by members of the public

Stock market
the market for shares in public limited companies

speaking countries, such as Argentina and Brazil, use 'SA' (French: Société Anonyme; Spanish: Sociedad Anomina) to identify public limited companies. Japan has joint stock companies (KK), which are similar to public limited companies in most respects, and limited liability companies (YK).

How do you set up a limited company?

It is more difficult to set up a limited company than a sole trader business or a partnership. The company must be registered with the Registrar of Companies (in some countries the Commercial Registry, Inspectorate of Corporations or other body responsible for registering limited companies and corporations) and have a Memorandum and Articles of Association. These are drawn up by a solicitor.

The Memorandum must give: the name of the company and the address of its registered office; the purpose for which the company has been set up; the amount of share capital to be issued and the number of shares; a statement that the liability of shareholders will be limited; the names and addresses of at least one director and the company secretary.

The Articles of Association cover: who manages the company; shareholders' rights; procedures and frequency of shareholders' meetings; how the profits of the company are to be distributed. The Articles of Association can be altered later as long as they do not conflict with the Memorandum.

A Certificate of Incorporation is issued before the company can commence trading. All companies must lodge their accounts, including balance sheet, note to the accounts, and reports from the directors and auditor, with the Registrar of Companies or other appointed body. These can be inspected by the public.

| 7.1 | *Activity* |

We have seen that the exact form and regulations governing private and public limited companies varies between countries. Research private and public limited companies in your country and answer the following questions.

1 What are the different forms of limited companies in your country? (>)
2 How are the different forms of limited companies identified? (>)
3 Who is responsible for registering limited companies in your country? (>)
4 Why does an incorporated business have a Memorandum and Articles of Association? (>>)

Who owns and runs a limited company?

A limited company is owned by its shareholders. A share is literally a part of the company. Each share represents an equal part of the value of the company, and gives equal voting rights in the running of the company and an equal share in any profit the company makes.

Shareholders normally buy 'blocks' of shares, however, and the more shares a shareholder owns, the more he or she can influence the company. A shareholder with more than half the shares in a company has a controlling interest in the company.

The proportion of profits that is paid to shareholders is called the dividend. This is considered to be part of their income and taxed as such, although the tax is deducted and paid to the tax authorities by the company before the dividend is paid.

Most private limited companies are family businesses, or have developed from smaller unincorporated businesses. The shareholders of private limited companies are therefore usually closely connected with the running of the business. Shares in private limited companies can only be bought and sold with the agreement of other shareholders.

Whilst a limited company is owned by its shareholders, the shareholders appoint directors to run the company on their behalf. There is thus a **divorce (separation) of ownership from control** of the company. The directors are elected at an Annual General Meeting (AGM) of shareholders and directors. Together, the directors form the board of directors, and are responsible to the shareholders for the day-to-day running and long-term planning of the company. A limited company must also appoint a company secretary, who may be a director, to deal with the legal aspects of the business, and arrange shareholders' meetings.

Divorce of ownership from control
the delegation of direct control of a limited company from its owners (shareholders) to directors

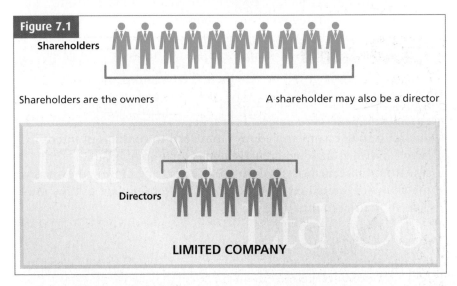

Figure 7.1

Shareholders

Shareholders are the owners

A shareholder may also be a director

Directors

LIMITED COMPANY

How a limited company is owned

Where does the money come from?

Most of the capital of a limited company comes from selling shares. For a private limited company this is restricted to the amount that can be raised by the small number of shareholders.

Besides issuing shares, a limited company can raise money by borrowing from banks and other financial institutions. Any loan is made to the company. Neither the shareholders, nor the directors, nor anyone else connected with the company, therefore, has personal liability for the debts of the company.

What happens if things go wrong?

Creditors
people or organisations
to whom money is owed

If a company gets into debt and cannot pay the money it owes, its **creditors** can sue the company to recover their money. An official receiver may then be appointed to find a way for the company to pay its debts. If a way cannot be found, the company will go into liquidation. The assets of the company will be sold and the proceeds used to pay all or a proportion of the company's debts. The company itself will be closed down. A limited company may also be closed down if it has not complied with its statutory, or legal, duties.

What are the main advantages and disadvantages of private limited companies?

The main advantages of private limited companies are:

- the owners have limited liability;
- the business has access to sources of far greater finance;
- it is easier for a limited company to borrow money;
- the business exists separately from its owners and has continuity of existence regardless of changes in ownership.

The main disadvantages of private limited companies are:

- setting up a limited company involves more legal formalities;
- limited companies are subject to legal constraints;
- divorce of ownership and control may lead to conflicts of interest;
- large companies may require large and complex administrative structures (bureaucracies), which are cumbersome, slow and expensive;
- the affairs of limited companies cannot be kept private as they must publish their accounts.

A friend of yours has recently been made redundant. She worked for a chocolate manufacturer, and thinks she has identified a gap in the market for handmade chocolate novelties. She is thinking of setting up her own business to do this and knows three others who would like to join her. Although she has her redundancy money, she needs to raise finance for premises, equipment, ingredients etc. She will be glad of the help of her friends, who know more about running a business and selling than she does. She also thinks she will need to employ a couple of staff. She is quite excited about the venture, but also a bit worried about the responsibility, and what might happen if things go wrong.

Write a short report to your friend explaining the different types of business. Your report should cover the features of each type of business, the advantages and disadvantages of each, and how each is set up. In your conclusion, say which type of business you think is most suitable for your friend to set up. Give your reasons. (>>>)

What is the difference between a public limited company and a private limited company?

The principal difference between a public limited company and a private limited company is that public limited companies can sell their shares to the general public. In this way, they have access to virtually limitless funds that they can use to develop the business.

Because their shares can be bought by anyone, large public limited companies, such as Shell and General Motors, are amongst the largest businesses in the world with millions of shares owned by several hundred thousand shareholders. In practice, large financial institutions such as insurance companies and pension funds buy the majority of shares in successful public limited companies. The owners of public limited companies usually, therefore, have little involvement with – or interest in – the running of the company they own. As a limited company grows, therefore, the divorce of ownership from control becomes greater.

In order to offer their shares to the general public, companies that intend to become public limited companies must issue a prospectus describing the company and its prospects, and detail the offer of shares. Subsequently, the plc must send a copy of its accounts and chairperson's report to every shareholder each year and lodge its accounts with the Registrar of Companies.

After shares in a public limited company have been sold initially by the company, they can be traded freely on the stock market of the country in which the company is registered, although the company itself will gain no further money from this. The value of the shares on the stock market will reflect how well the company is performing. If the company performs well, its shares are likely to be thought of as a good investment. They will be in demand, and their value will rise. The value of shares is published daily in many newspapers, and also on the Internet. Public limited companies whose shares are available on the stock market are vulnerable to **takeovers**, which may result in the present directors losing control.

7.3 *Activity*

This activity should be carried out over a three-month period.

1 Obtain a copy of a newspaper that has the prices of shares on the stock market. Select five companies whose share prices you will track over a period of three months. (>)

2 Draw up a table, either by hand or using a computer spreadsheet package, on which you can enter the prices of the shares once a week. Enter today's prices of the shares you have selected. (>>)

3 On the same day each week, over a period of three months, enter that day's price for each share in a new column on your table. As you build up your table, construct a graph to show the price movements of each of your shares. If you have access to a computer, you can do this using the graph feature. Each share should be represented by a different line. (>>)

4 Investigate each of the companies you have selected. What is the nominal value of each share? Suggest reasons for the current share price. Can you explain the changes in prices of your shares over the three-month period? (>>>)

Why go public?

Most companies who decide to go public (become public limited companies) do so because this gives them access to an almost limitless source of capital. In reality the amount a business can raise depends on how well it is expected to do. Many businesses are able to fund expensive development and expansion programmes in this way.

The major disadvantage is that control of the business is divorced from those with an interest in the business itself. Most shareholders of public limited companies are mainly interested in the value of their shareholding and the dividend they receive. The senior directors of the business may be voted in or out at the next shareholders' AGM, and must act in accordance with the wishes of the shareholders rather than the business itself.

In addition, companies whose shares are freely available on the stock market are liable to takeover, in which case all decision-making on the running of the business will pass into the hands of another company.

7.4 *Activity*

In Activity 7.2, you advised your friend about setting up in business making handmade chocolate novelties. The business has now had a very successful first five years, and your friend wants to expand the market. To do this she needs to open a much larger factory and employ more staff. Write another report advising her of the possible advantages and disadvantages of going public. (>>)

Summary

- Limited companies are incorporated businesses that exist quite separately from their owners.
- The owners of limited companies are called shareholders and have limited liability.
- Private limited companies are not allowed to sell their shares to the general public.
- Public limited companies are among the largest businesses in the world.
- Public limited companies can sell their shares to the general public, which gives them access to vast sources of capital.
- The owners of public limited companies usually have little involvement in the running of the company.

8 Other types of business organisation

In this unit you will learn about other types of business organisations: franchises, co-operative ownership and joint ventures. You will also learn about the types of business organisations that are owned by local or national government and are in the public sector.

Some types of business organisations are a result of co-operation between businesses, either as a **joint venture** or as one business operating in the name of and providing the products of another. These spread the risks involved between one or more businesses. In a **co-operative**, all members share the risks and the benefits of the business.

Co-operative
a business organisation formed by members for their mutual benefit

Joint venture
an enterprise undertaken by two or more business organisations which pool resources

FRANCHISE OPPORTUNITIES

Energy Efficiency Inc. Provide annual major home appliance tune-ups, plus products and services which improve energy efficiency, home health and safety. First franchise established: 1996. Number of franchises world-wide: 6. Start-up cash required: $12,000 to $25,000.

Kitchen Solutions for Any Budget Ltd. On-site wood and cabinet restoration and repair services, and several lines of custom cabinets. No previous experience necessary. First franchise established: 1988. Number of franchises world-wide: 300. Start-up cash required: $16,500 to $21,500.

One-Stop Home Services Ltd. A home-based service that offers homeowners a one-stop resource for all of their home service, repair and maintenance needs. First franchise established 2001. Number of franchises world-wide: 28. Start-up cash required: $8,400 to $20,600.

Franchise opportunities

Franchises

A **franchise** is an agreement allowing one business to trade under the name of and sell the products or services of another. The business granting the franchise is called the **franchiser**; the business taking out the franchise is called the **franchisee**.

Taking out a franchise is a way of avoiding many of the risks involved with starting up a business. For the business granting the franchise, it is a way of developing the business and expanding without committing the resources of the business. Success of both franchiser and franchisee depends on close co-operation between both businesses.

The business is owned and run by the franchisee. However, the franchiser usually retains some control over the franchisee in matters of product design and brand name, advertising and service. Some franchisers, such as McDonald's, control almost the whole of the franchise operation, supplying equipment, ingredients, staff uniforms, training, and setting menus, prices, portion sizes, cooking times and so on.

Franchise
an agreement allowing one business to trade under the name of and sell the products or services of another

Franchiser
a business granting a franchise

Franchisee
a business taking out a franchise

 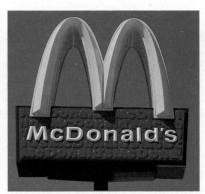 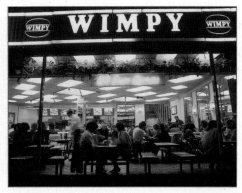

KFC, McDonald's and Wimpy are major international franchise operations

Where does the money come from?

Sole traders, partnerships or limited companies may own and run franchises, and the sources of finance to purchase the franchise are largely the same as for these types of business. The initial cost of a franchise varies according to the product, type of premises and other equipment required, and the company selling the franchise. Sometimes the franchiser may help with finance for the franchisee.

Besides the original purchase price of the franchise, the franchisee has to pay an annual fee, usually based on a percentage of sales. This must be paid even if the franchisee has made a loss. In this case the franchisee must apply to his or her bank for a loan or overdraft.

8.1 Activity

Look again at the advertisements for franchise opportunities in Business in context on page 62.

1 Which type of business organisation (sole trader, partnership or private limited company) do you think would be most appropriate to run each franchise? (>>)

2 How might an applicant for each franchise obtain the necessary finance? (>>)

What happens if things go wrong?

The success of a franchise is the responsibility of the franchisee. If the franchisee is a sole trader or partnership they will have unlimited liability (see Unit 6) which means they could lose everything if the business goes wrong and they are left with large debts.

However, the success and reputation of the franchiser depends on its franchisees succeeding. It is therefore in the interests of the franchiser to help the franchisee as much as possible.

What are the main advantages of a franchise?

By operating under the name and logo of a well-known company, a franchise business has a much greater chance of success. Apart from providing a proven product, the franchiser may well provide national and local advertising and training in business and other important areas.

Although they are small businesses, franchises operate as though they were part of a larger business. This means that they are often able to benefit from bulk purchasing arrangements. Banks, too, are often prepared to make loans to franchisees on the basis that they carry less risk.

There are advantages, too, for the franchiser. By selling franchises, a business is abler to expand without committing its own resources. The risk is spread between businesses, and both benefit from the arrangement in that their success is in part dependent on the other. In addition, by franchising a part of its operation, a business is able to concentrate on its core activity.

What are the main disadvantages of a franchise?

There are also some disadvantages for both franchiser and franchisee. The franchiser is dependent on the franchisee for the success of the business. The franchisee, on the other hand, has less control of their own business than they would if they remained an independent sole trader or partnership. They are tied to the franchiser and their success depends on the success of the franchiser's product. Franchisers have little control over areas such as product development. The franchisee also has to pay a continuing annual fee, regardless of any loss the business may make.

8.2 *Activity*

This activity should be carried out in groups of three or four. Imagine your group is applying to open a KFC franchise fast food restaurant. As a group, either (a) write a report to KFC, or (b) prepare and make a presentation in front of your teacher. You should give details of the business you will set up and your application for a franchise. In particular you must cover:

1 The type of business you will form.
2 Your reasons for applying for a KFC franchise.
3 The intended location of your restaurant and why you think the location is suitable.
4 How you going to raise the finance to pay for the franchise and set up the restaurant. If possible, you should use a computer to produce your report or to prepare visual aids for your presentation. (>>>)

Co-operatives

Co-operatives are business enterprises that are owned jointly by members, who may be private individuals or other business organisations. They exist for the mutual benefit of members, who share equally in the decision-making and management of the co-operative. Finance is raised by the members, who generally receive a share in the profits of the co-operative.

There are four main types of co-operative:

- retail co-operatives, which buy goods in bulk at an advantageous price and re-sell them to members as cheaply as possible;
- trading co-operatives, which are formed to distribute and sell the products or services of their members (members are usually small businesses, which join together as a co-operative in order to gain the benefits normally associated with larger businesses – see Unit 31 where economies of scale are discussed);
- worker co-operatives, which are businesses owned and run by their employees;
- housing co-operatives, which develop, maintain and manage low-cost housing on behalf of their members.

In some countries, where there are a large number of small businesses in an industry, such as farming and agriculture, the formation of co-operatives is encouraged. In India, for example, the government encourages growers in some agricultural industries such as sugar, jute and cotton, to form co-operatives to ensure the sharing of techniques and technology so as to improve efficiency and productivity. For example, a combine harvester can immensely improve productivity in farming. However, they are expensive, and often quite beyond the reach of a small farmer. Several small farmers forming a co-operative, however, may well be able to afford one between them. Each farmer in the co-operative can then share use of the combine harvester.

Joint ventures

Increasingly, large projects are being undertaken as joint ventures. Joint ventures may be between two or more businesses in the private sector, or in the private sector and the public sector. For example, a new hospital or railway may be built as a joint venture between the government and private enterprise. Sometimes a joint venture, such as the development of a new aeroplane, may involve businesses in more than one country. In this way, each business only has to find part of the cost of the project, and the risk is spread between all the businesses in the joint venture.

Public sector organisations

Public sector organisations are owned and run by local or national government. They are mainly large organisations that are either expensive to run and need a considerable amount of capital investment, or are essential services considered too important to be left to private enterprise. In recent years there has been considerable debate over whether the government should be involved with running businesses or whether this is best left in the hands of private individuals.

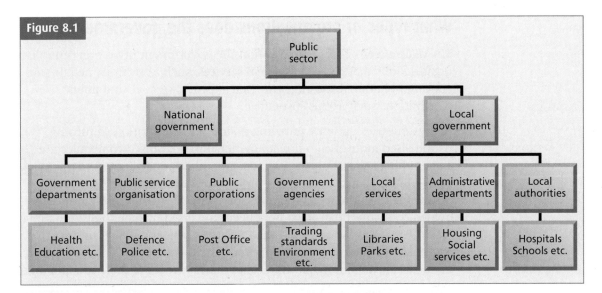

Figure 8.1

Public sector organisations

Many countries have a Post Office that provides a national postal service. The objective of the Post Office is to deliver letters to customers no matter where they live in the country for the same price. Packets and parcels can also be delivered anywhere in the country. Again the price is the same nationwide, although the heavier the item the more expensive it is to send. This postal service is greatly valued as being available to everybody who wants to use it and it is usually at a relatively low cost. Most national Post Offices are owned and operated by the government.

Questions

1. How much does it cost to post a letter in your country? (>)

2. Are there any other ways of sending letters anywhere in the country? (>)

3. What do you think are the benefits of a postal service owned by the government? Can you say why? (>>)

4. What do you think would happen to the postal service if it was taken over by private enterprise? (>>>)

What types of organisations does the government own?

The main types of organisations that the government owns are: centralised organisations that provide essential services, such as security, health and education; nationalised industries, such as steel or coal; and public corporations such as the Post Office.

Many countries are now pursuing policies of privatisation (returning nationalised industries to private ownership). Privatised companies are responsible to shareholders, just like any other public limited company. In Brazil, for example, the government has been pursuing a policy of privatising state-owned companies since the early 1990s. Formerly state-owned companies that have now been privatised include the Companhia Vale do Rio Doce (a mining company), the Companhia Siderurgica Nacional (the national steel mill), Rede Ferroviaria Federal SA (the national railway line), and Mafersa (a manufacturer of railroad equipment).

8.3 Activity

1 Find out which services are currently provided by public sector organisations. (>>)
2 Think carefully about the services on your list and give reasons why they are provided by government-owned organisations rather than private businesses. (>>)
3 Suggest other goods or services that should be provided by government rather than private business. Justify your answer.(>>)

Summary

- Running a franchise operation removes some of the risks involved in a small business.
- A franchise operates under the name of another company, using their business idea and selling their products or services.
- Sole traders, partnerships or limited companies may own and run franchises.
- Co-operatives are owned and run by members for their mutual benefit.
- Joint ventures can enable businesses to pool resources and spread the risk involved in an enterprise.
- Organisations owned by the government on behalf of the general public are in the public sector.
- The government owns different kinds of organisations that are considered to provide essential services, or services that would not be adequately provided if left to private sector businesses.
- There is considerable debate over whether governments should be involved with running businesses.

9 Is there a best type of business?

In this unit you will see how deciding on the best type of business depends on a number of factors.

One of the first decisions a person setting up in business must make is which type of business organisation is most appropriate. Choosing the right type of organisation involves considering several factors about the business and the person setting it up. Later, as the business develops and grows, its needs, and the needs of its owners, are different, so that a different type of ownership may be more suitable.

Business in context

Tandi came home from work one night feeling depressed. She had just been made redundant from her job as a new business clerk at the head office of a large insurance company.

When she told her husband, Sipho, however, he was very supportive. 'Well you've never liked that job, have you? Why don't you do something about that idea you used to have of setting up your own business?'

'But what would I do?' Tandi asked.

'Think about it. You know about bookkeeping and accounts, and you know how to use a computer. There are a lot of small businesses out there that would like to use your skills. And I can probably help with some things.' Sipho was an accountant with a local engineering company.

Over the next few days and weeks, Tandi did think about setting up her own business. First of all she contacted several small local businesses including a garage, three restaurants, a doctor's surgery, a vet's, some shops, and the offices of three local companies. The response was encouraging. Many of the businesses said they would be interested in Tandi's services. Three asked her to start doing their books and other administration straight away. One restaurant asked if she would type up their menu each day. And one company asked if she could prepare their annual accounts. She explained that she was not qualified to do this but would ask her husband.

Sipho groaned when he heard, but said that he would do their accounts as long as he could do them at the weekend, and it didn't happen very often. Working all week and then doing another company's accounts at the weekend wasn't what he had thought of when he suggested that Tandi should start her own business. Tandi wrote to the tax office to say that she was self-employed, used her redundancy money to buy a new computer with a scanner, printer and fax machine, and set to work.

As the months passed, Tandi's workload increased. Sipho often lent a hand, as he found helping Tandi in her business was interesting and he gained satisfaction from it. 'I think I could earn more working in our business than I do now', he said. Tandi smiled. 'Our business', she said humorously.

Questions

1 Why did Tandi need to start her own business? (>)

2 What was Tandi's main source of finance? (>)

3 What type of business is it? (>>)

4 What other types of ownership might be suitable for Tandi's business? (>>)

5 Write a letter to Tandi pointing out the advantages and disadvantages of each type of ownership for her business. (>>>)

Factors influencing the choice of type of business organisation

Ownership

Ownership is perhaps the most obvious factor affecting the type of organisation appropriate for a business. In some cases this will be the factor that dictates the type of organisation chosen.

For example, a small trader who intends to work on his or her own in a business, such as that of a dressmaker or plumber, will almost inevitably set up as a sole trader. A sole trader may, however, decide to take on a partner, perhaps to help them in an area of business where they do not feel they have sufficient skills, such as in finance and administration. Setting up a partnership rather than a sole trader business allows for a division of labour, with each partner specialising in one area of the business. Many professional firms are set up in this way.

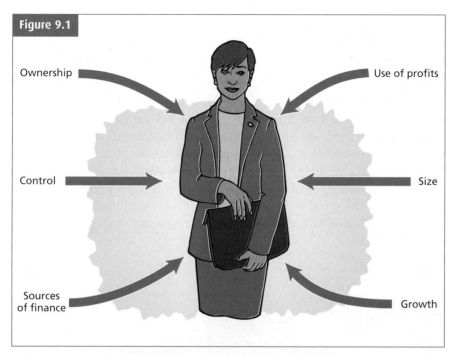

Figure 9.1

Ownership →

Use of profits ←

Control →

Size ←

Sources of finance →

Growth ←

Influences on the choice of the type of business

Where more owners are involved, or where continuity of the business is needed, perhaps in a family business, it may be more appropriate to set up a private limited company. The owners will have a share in the business, which can be increased or transferred if necessary. The death or retirement of one of the shareholders will not affect the existence of the business, and shares can be passed from generation to generation.

Control

The type of organisation appropriate for a business very much depends on the amount of control over the running of the business the owners want to keep for themselves. A sole trader has complete control over all decisions regarding the running of the business. Partners share control as set out in the partnership agreement.

Control of a limited company is shared by the shareholders in proportion to the number of shares they own. In the case of a private limited company, the shareholders are normally closely involved with the day-to-day running of the company, and control is therefore largely kept within the company. Control of a public limited company, on the other hand, passes to the shareholders, who are mainly outside the company itself. It is even possible for a public limited company to be taken over by another company. In this case control would pass to an entirely different company.

Sources of finance

Venture capitalists
people or groups willing
to provide capital for a
business, usually in return
for a share in the business
and any future profits the
business makes

We have seen in previous units that more sources of finance are available to incorporated companies than to unincorporated businesses. This is important if a business needs access to large amounts of finance. While a sole trader may be able to finance the purchase of small premises and limited equipment from his or her own resources, a manufacturing business needing a factory and expensive machinery may need the additional sources of finance available to a limited company, including banks and **venture capitalists** (see Unit 10). Businesses requiring really large amounts of capital may need to consider becoming public limited companies by offering shares to the general public, although this is not suitable for start-up businesses.

Use of profits

Figure 9.2

Tax

For the owners

Dividends

Reinvestment

The use of profit

The owners of unincorporated businesses such as sole traders and partnerships have complete control over the use of any profits of the business. Such profits can be re-invested in the business, perhaps to buy new equipment or fund expansion, or kept by the owners. The owners of unincorporated businesses pay normal income tax on the profits of the business as if those profits were their private income.

The profits of a limited company, however, must be used, firstly to pay business tax to the government (see Unit 12), and secondly to pay a dividend to shareholders as their reward for investing in the company. Only after these items have been paid can a decision be taken on how to use any remaining profits: to re-invest in the company, or perhaps distribute part to employees as a bonus in recognition of their efforts.

Activity

1 In groups, think about and discuss as many ideas for
   businesses that you could set up either individually or as
   a group. (>)
2 Select one of these businesses. (>)
3 Discuss the most appropriate type of business for the idea
   you have selected. (>>)
4 Make a list of the reasons for deciding on that type of
   business. (>>)

Type of business	Control	Main sources of start-up capital	Profit or loss
Sole trader	One owner	Personal funds of the owner, bank loans or mortgages; grants and subsidies from government and private organisations	Owner free to dispose of any profit as he or she wishes, but is liable for any loss.
Partnership	Shared between partners	Personal funds of the partners, bank loans or mortgages, grants and subsidies	Partners share profit and liability for loss.
Private limited company	Delegated to directors by shareholders	Shares sold to shareholders; bank and other loans to the company	A percentage of profit distributed among shareholders as dividend; some must be paid to the government as tax; the remainder retained within the business. Any loss is borne by the company.
Public limited company	Delegated to directors by shareholders	Shares sold to the general public and other organisations including financial institutions; bank and other loans to the company	A percentage of profit distributed among shareholders as dividend; some must be paid to the government as tax; the remainder retained within the business. Any loss is borne by the company.
Franchise	Franchisee, but with restrictions imposed by franchiser	Depends on the type of business that buys the franchise	A percentage of turnover is normally paid to the franchiser regardless of whether the business makes a profit or a loss; any remaining profit is at the disposal of the franchisee. The franchisee is responsible for any loss.
Co-operative	Members	Members' resources	Distributed among the members.

Table 9.1

Size

The size of a business can be measured in several ways: by sales turnover; by number of employees; by number of outlets. One person can run a small business more easily than a large business, since there is less involved. Larger businesses have to employ specialists in various aspects of running the business, such as financial management, administration, personnel and so on.

Generally speaking, therefore, sole traders tend to be the smallest type of businesses, followed by partnerships. Limited companies tend to be larger, with public limited companies the largest of all.

There are some notable exceptions to this, however. JCB is privately owned, although it rivals all but the largest of public limited companies. Similarly, some large firms of accountants, such as Ernst and Young and KPMG, are partnerships although they are as large as many private and public limited companies and operate internationally.

Growth

As a business grows it may have different needs and these will determine which is the most suitable type of organisation. A sole trader may need to take on a partner in order to cope with the additional work. If additional finance is required, perhaps to purchase a larger factory or office, or buy more machinery, the business may consider becoming a private or even a public limited company in order to gain access to more sources of finance.

9.2 Activity

Getting There Limited is a successful company that organises specialist walking holidays for small groups throughout Africa and the Caribbean. The Managing Director, Luisa Calvi, wants to build on the success of the last few years by opening outlets in major cities throughout the world, and purchasing a few select properties to use as bases for the holidays. To do this will require more finance than Getting There is able to raise either from its own resources or at present from the bank. Luisa is therefore considering floating Getting There as a public limited company, and has asked for your advice. Write a memo to Luisa explaining what going public involves, its advantages and disadvantages, and advising her whether or not you think Getting There should become a public limited company.

Summary

- Several factors affect the choice of type of organisation for a business.
- These include: type of ownership; the degree of control the owner requires; the amount of finance needed; how profits are to be used; the size of the business.
- As the business develops, a different type of organisation may be more suitable.

10 *Where does the money come from?*

In this unit you will find out why businesses need finance and the main sources of finance available to businesses.

Finance
the money a business
needs to operate

All businesses need money, or **finance**, in order to operate. They need finance for: start-up items such as premises, equipment and initial advertising; the ongoing running costs of the business, including raw materials, wages and salaries, administrative costs, maintaining and renewing machinery and equipment, and any temporary problems arising from a shortage of cash; expansion, including purchasing additional equipment, larger premises, or even financing the takeover of other businesses.

Business in context

Khanya Hyde had been in business as a sole trader making gold earrings and bracelets for a year. Her sales for the year at $100,000 were even higher than she had expected, and this produced a profit of $20,000. She had just $10,000 worth of goods in stock and owed her suppliers $6,000. In turn Khanya was owed $8,000 by customers.

Looking to the future, Khanya forecast that sales in the next year would increase to $150,000 – an increase of 50%. Her bank manager had told her that she would need additional capital of $6,000 to fund this. In addition, she was worried about one of her customers who owed her $2,000. She was afraid that the customer would be unable to pay, and this would become a 'bad debt'.

**Internal sources
of finance**
sources of finance within
the business or provided
by its present owners

Sources of finance

Finance can be generated either from within the business (**internal sources**), or outside (**external sources**).

**External sources
of finance**
sources of finance from
outside the business or
its present owners

1 How much profit did Khanya make in her first year? (>)

2 How much finance will she need to cover the additional capital required for expansion, and the bad debt? (>)

3 What profit did she make expressed as a percentage of sales? (>>)

4 Assuming it will be the same percentage of sales as last year, how much profit will she make next year? (>>)

5 If $100,000 sales produced $20,000 profit, what is the value of sales that Khanya must make in order to recover the bad debt? (>>)

6 Khanya has drawn the whole of this year's profit and is likely to need at least $26,000 next year to cover her own living expenses. Suggest sources of finance for the additional capital required for expansion and to cover the bad debt. (>>>)

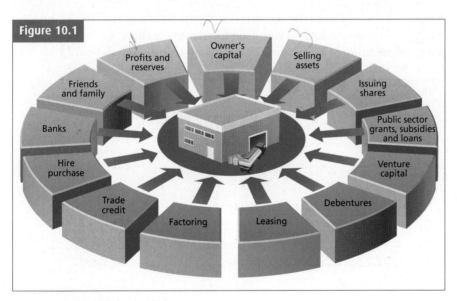

Figure 10.1

How a business may be funded

Internal sources of finance

Profits and reserves

Most businesses retain part of their profits to buy new or replacement machinery and equipment. If the amount retained is not needed immediately, it can be kept as a reserve for future use, either for expansion or in an emergency.

Selling assets

Many businesses have assets such as machinery, vehicles and property that they can sell. If a business needs to raise finance quickly, selling assets may be the best way to do this, especially if the assets are surplus to requirements or under-utilised. Selling an asset to a finance house, and leasing it back can be a way of raising finance while retaining use of the asset.

Owners' capital

Short-term
a period of up to three years

Small businesses are usually set up with finance provided by the owners. The advantage of this is that there are no interest or other charges. The disadvantage is that the owners risk losing the money they put into the business.

Medium-term
a period of between three and ten years

External sources of finance

Short-term, medium-term and long-term finance

Long-term
a period of more than ten years

Short-term finance is finance that is required for up to three years; **medium-term** finance is required for between three and ten years; **long-term** finance is required for more than ten years.

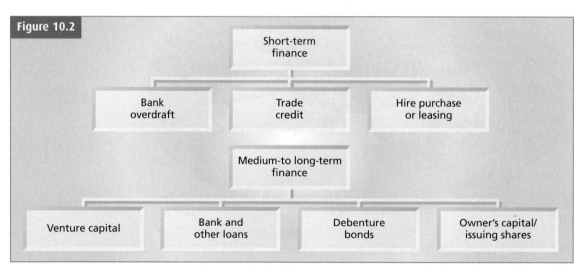

Figure 10.2

Short-term, medium-term and long-term sources of finance

Friends and family

Small business owners may be able to borrow from friends and family. Such loans may well be given without security or charging interest. Normally, however, the amount raised will be small and may only be suitable for short-term finance.

Banks

Banks provide two principal types of finance for business: overdrafts and loans.

An overdraft is an agreement whereby the business can draw on its bank account more than it has deposited. Interest charged on the amount overdrawn is usually higher than on finance from other sources, and overdrafts are only appropriate for short-term finance, for example to cover cash-flow problems.

Banks also provide loans, usually for a set period and purpose. Interest is charged on the amount of the loan. With medium- and long-term loans for larger amounts, security is often required so that if the business is unable to repay the loan the bank will be able to sell the item given as security and recover its money. When considering making a loan to a business, a bank will want to see a business plan including budgets, forecasts and cash-flow forecasts to ensure that the business will be able to repay the loan.

In many Muslim countries, banks are forbidden to charge interest on loans. Instead, Muslim banks may provide finance for business by providing capital in return for a share in the profits of the business.

Hire purchase

Hire purchase is a form of credit arranged through a manufacturer or finance house (like a bank). An item such as a vehicle or large machine is bought and paid for in instalments. Each instalment includes an element of interest on the purchase price. Although the business making the purchase has use of the item throughout, it does not become the property of the business until the final payment is made.

Trade credit

Most business purchases are made on the basis that payment will be made at a later date, usually within thirty days of purchase or by the end of the following month. This is called trade credit. If the customer has sufficient standing with the supplier, it may be possible to extend the period of credit. While this may give the purchasing business some additional finance for a short time, it is only appropriate for very short-term finance.

Factoring

To overcome the cash-flow problems associated with supplying goods and services on credit and not being paid until some time later, some finance houses provide a factoring service. A factoring house will pay the business up to 80% of the value of its invoices each month immediately. The supplying business therefore receives an immediate injection of cash without waiting for customers to pay their invoices. The remaining 20%, less the factoring house's commission, will be received when invoices are paid to the factoring house.

Leasing

An alternative to buying items such as property, machinery and vehicles is for a business to lease them from the supplier or a specialist leasing company. A lease is for a set period of time and while the business leasing the asset (the lessee) has full use of the asset during that time, the asset remains the property of the leasing company (the lessor). Leasing assets avoids paying large sums to purchase assets, enabling the money to be used for other purposes. The length of leases tends to make leasing appropriate as a source of medium- to long-term finance.

Debentures or corporate bonds

Debentures or corporate bonds are long-term fixed-period loans to the business by individuals or financial institutions. They are secured against the business and carry a fixed rate of interest throughout the period of the debenture. The rate of interest is lower than other types of loan.

Venture capital

Capital
the money invested in a business by its owners

Venture capitalists are specialists in providing finance mainly for smaller businesses usually in return for a shareholding in the business. There is thus an element of risk to the person or organisation providing the **capital**. Venture capital is long term, and may be substantial.

Issuing shares

A private or public limited company may raise finance by issuing additional shares, as long as the total number of shares issued is within the company's authorised capital. In the case of a private limited company, additional shares can only be issued to the present shareholders, or new shareholders, with the agreement of the current shareholders. Any person or organisation such as a financial institution can purchase new shares in a public limited company. Public limited companies are able to obtain very large amounts of finance in this way. The principal advantage of raising finance by issuing shares is that the money raised does not have to be paid back.

Public sector sources of finance

Grants and subsidies for business can sometimes be obtained from local and national governments or other public bodies. These normally do not have to be repaid, but are usually only available in particular circumstances, and with conditions attached. For example, a government trying to attract new businesses to locate in an area of high unemployment may offer a grant in respect of every new job created.

10.1 *Activity*

You are the financial director of a small, private limited company. The board has agreed that an objective of the company should be to go for growth over the next five to ten years. Suggest appropriate sources of medium- to long-term internal and external finance. (>)

How do businesses decide?

When seeking finance, businesses consider various criteria to ensure that the source they choose is appropriate to their needs. The main criteria businesses use are:

1 How long is the finance required? A bank overdraft may be suitable for short-term finance, but is very costly in the long term, when a loan may be more suitable.

2 What is the purpose of the finance? A small start-up business may look to finance from its owners in the first place, while an existing company wanting to ensure a regular cash flow could consider factoring.

3 How much is required? A small amount may be covered by an overdraft, while a successful business seeking large sums in order to expand, perhaps by taking over another company, may seek funding from a venture capitalist, or issue shares.

4 What risk is involved? All business activity involves some risk. However, a business taking out a loan or overdraft must pay interest. If the business is unsuccessful, the interest must still be paid and the loan repaid. The higher the risk involved, therefore, the more likely a business is to seek finance from issuing shares, venture capitalists or the owners of the business, since these sources do not bear interest or have to be repaid.

5 Is the gearing too high? The gearing of a business is the ratio of long-term loans to the capital employed. If loans amount to more than about 50% of capital employed, the business is said to be highly geared. This means that the business is relying on borrowed money, and has to pay substantial interest charges. A business that is already highly geared will try to avoid taking out further loans since this will only increase gearing.

This should be carried out in groups of three or four. As a group you are going to buy a franchise to run a fast food restaurant. The initial cost is $150,000, and between you, you are able to raise 50% of this. (a) Decide on the type of business you will set up to run the franchise. (b) Discuss the likely sources of finance available to cover the remainder. (c) Looking to the future, you hope to expand to three restaurants within the next two years. The cost of each restaurant is likely to be similar to the first. Discuss appropriate sources of finance for the expansion. (d) Write a report for the franchise company outlining how you anticipate financing your business. (>>>)

What do providers of finance consider?

Providing finance to business always involves some risk for the provider. In order to reduce the risk, banks, shareholders, other financial institutions and other providers of finance will therefore consider the following questions:

1 Will the business be able to make interest or other payments such as dividends? In deciding this, the provider of finance will consider the past financial record of the business, including the business's accounts, and forecasts of future financial performance.

2 Is the business too highly geared? The higher the gearing, the higher the risk of providing further finance, since a higher proportion of the capital of the business is in the form of loans. If the business fails, it may not be able to repay all the money it owes.

3 Is the business efficiently managed? Providers of finance will look carefully at the experience and skills of the people who direct or manage the business, to ensure that their money will be well used.

Summary

- All businesses need money, or finance.
- Short-term, medium-term or long-term finance can be obtained from internal or external sources.
- Internal sources include: profits and resources; the sale of assets and owners' capital.
- External sources include: loans; hire purchase; trade credit; factoring; leasing; venture capital and share issues.
- Choosing a source of finance that is inappropriate to the needs of the business can be a costly mistake.

11 How much does it cost?

In this unit you will learn that the costs of a business are identified and classified in different ways according to their behaviour and the purpose of the classification.

All resources cost money. In order to pay for the resources it uses, a business must make and sell enough of its goods, or provide enough of its services. It is important, therefore, that when a business is setting up or planning its future activities, it takes all its likely costs into consideration.

Business in context

Zebada runs her own business making and selling decorative mirrors and other glass objects. She rents a small shop with a workshop behind the shop area. Like anyone running his or her own business, she is very conscious of how much it costs just to keep the business going. On most days she is able to keep her eye on the shop while she is working in her workshop. On Saturdays, however, when Zebada is normally very busy, she employs a part-time assistant to help in the shop.

Questions

1   Make a list of the costs you think Zebada has to meet in running her business. (>)

2   How can Zebada get the money to pay her costs? (>)

3   What do you think will happen if Zebada does not pay for the resources she uses in her business? (>)

4   If Zebada decided to work in the shop on Saturdays, instead of making items for sale in the workshop, what might be the result? (>>)

5   Why do you think Zebada is 'very conscious of how much it costs just to keep the business going'? (>>>)

Types of costs
Fixed costs

Fixed costs are those costs a business must pay, regardless of whether it actually produces anything or not. These costs do not change no matter how many of its products the business actually makes or sells. Examples of the typical fixed costs of a business are: premises costs (for example, rent and rates); insurance; interest on loans and overdrafts; salaries and wages of employees involved in running the business.

Fixed costs may change in the long term. For example, the rent of a factory may be increased, or salaries may rise following a pay increase. However, doubling its output will not affect the level of rent or salaries that a business has to pay, unless it also has to increase its capacity and rent larger premises.

Variable costs

Variable costs do change with the amount of its products a business produces. The more goods or services produced, the higher the variable costs that have to be paid. The fewer goods or services produced, the lower the variable costs that have to be paid. Examples of the typical variable costs of a business are: raw materials; parts and components; wages of employees directly involved in making the product.

Is there a relationship between output and costs?
What is output?

The total amount of goods or services produced by a business in a given period is called the **output** of the business. Similarly, the output of an employee, or group of employees, or a machine is the total amount of goods or services produced by that employee, group of employees, or machine in a period of time.

Calculating costs

Businesses need to be able to calculate how much it costs them to produce their output of goods or services. This is called the cost of production, and as you will see when you are studying the accounting and finance units, it is a very important piece of information. Table 11.1 shows the costs of production of a business at different levels of output. The diagram based on the table shows you the relationship between output and costs.

Output (units)	Fixed costs ($)	Variable costs ($)	Total costs ($)
0	10,000	0	10,000
1,000	10,000	750	10,750
2,000	10,000	1,400	11,400
3,000	10,000	2,150	12,150
4,000	10,000	2,900	12,900
5,000	10,000	3,750	13,750

Table 11.1

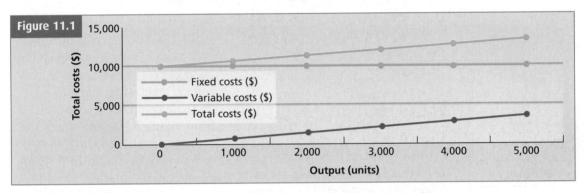

Figure 11.1

How a business may be funded

11.1 Activity

The following are the costs of Zebada's business.

Level of production	Fixed costs	Variable costs	Total costs of production
0 mirrors	$4,500	$0	
50 mirrors	$4,500	$300	
100 mirrors	$4,500	$600	
150 mirrors	$4,500	$900	
200 mirrors	$4,500	$1,300	
250 mirrors	$4,500	$2,000	

1 Complete the table by calculating Zebada's costs of production. (>)
2 Draw a graph showing the relationship between Zebada's output and her costs. (>>)
3 Using your graph, explain the relationship between output and costs in Zebada's business. (>>>)

Average costs and marginal costs

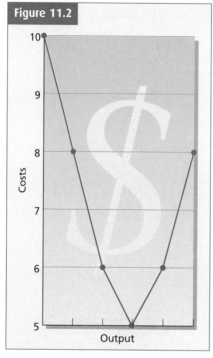

Figure 11.2

The costs of a business over different
levels of output

By calculating the **average costs**, or unit costs, of production, a business can tell how much on average it has cost to produce one unit of its goods or services. The formula for calculating average costs is: average cost per unit = total costs/total output.

Often, when a business produces more, the average cost per unit falls. Sometimes, however, when average costs have reached a certain level, they start to increase again, as you can see from Figure 11.2. The lower the average costs of production, the more efficient the business is at producing its product.

11.2 Activity

The following are the total costs of production of a business.

Level of production	Cost of production	Average cost per unit
5,000 units	$300,000	60
7,500 units	$375,000	50
10,000 units	$450,000	45
12,500 units	$525,000	42
15,000 units	$690,000	46
17,500 units	$840,000	48

1. Complete the table by calculating the average cost per unit at each level of production. (>)
2. Construct a simple graph showing the relationship of output to average cost. (>>)
3. Explain the level of output that the business should aim for, based on your graph. (>>)
4. Give your reasons. (>>>)

It is also often important for a business to know its marginal cost of production. Marginal cost is the amount by which total costs increase with the production of one additional unit. If the marginal cost of an additional unit of production is greater than the additional sales revenue generated, then the business should not produce the additional unit.

Direct costs

The **direct costs** of a business are those costs that are directly incurred in the production process. They include items such as the raw materials and components that are used to produce goods, and the labour (often called direct labour) of the employees who actually make the goods.

Indirect costs

Indirect costs are all the costs of a business that are not directly incurred in the production process. They include items such as the wages and salaries of all other employees (including factory supervisors and managers who oversee the production of goods rather than make them themselves), rent and rates, advertising and marketing, telephone, gas and electricity, postage and other general administrative costs. Indirect costs are sometimes called '**overheads**'.

The break-even point

The **break-even point** is the volume of goods or services that a business must produce and sell in order to cover its costs. To calculate the break-even point of a product a business must identify the fixed and variable costs incurred and calculate the revenue generated from any given level of sales of the product, by multiplying the price per unit of product by its price.

Calculating the break-even point of a product assumes that its price has two parts. The first part covers the variable costs of producing one unit of the product. The second part contributes to the fixed costs of the business. This is called the contribution. Once enough units of the product have been sold so that the contributions from each cover the fixed costs (the break-even point), the contribution from each additional unit sold contributes to the profit of the business.

The break-even point of a product can be calculated mathematically using the **break-even calculation** formula or by using a **break-even chart**.

Calculating the break-even point of a product mathematically

The break-even point of a product is the number of contributions (at one contribution per unit of production) required to cover the fixed costs of the business. To calculate the break-even point mathematically the business must know: the selling price per unit of product; the variable costs per unit; the total fixed costs. The formula for calculating the break-even point is:

Selling price per unit – variable costs per unit = contribution

$$\frac{\text{Total fixed costs}}{\text{contribution}} = \text{break-even point}$$

To find out how much profit a given level of sales will generate, a business can use the formula:

(Contribution × units produced) – fixed costs = profit

To find out how many units must be sold to generate a target profit, the formula is:

$$\frac{(\text{Target profit} + \text{fixed costs})}{\text{contribution per unit}}$$

Any change in the level of fixed costs, variable costs or selling price per unit will result in a new break-even point and levels of profit or loss produced by given levels of production and sales.

Having calculated the break-even point of a product, the business can decide whether it is able to produce and sell this number of units of product in the time period – for example has it enough facilities, such as machinery and employees. If the business can produce and sell more than the break-even level, then it will make a profit. This information will help the business decide whether or not to produce the product.

Calculating the break-even point of a product using a break-even chart

Once the fixed and variable costs of a product and the selling price per unit are known, the break-even point can be plotted graphically on a break-even chart. It is then an easy task to read off the profit or loss that will be produced by any given level of production and sales.

You are planning an end-of-term party to celebrate the successful completion of your IGCSE Business Studies course. The cost of hiring a hall, DJ and equipment, publicity (printing posters to put up around your school or college), and printing the tickets will be $750. These are the fixed costs of the party. You are also planning to have food at a cost of $3 per head, which will be included in the price of the ticket (and will therefore only be provided for the number of tickets sold). This is the variable cost of the party.

You feel that tickets for the party should be priced at $7.50. Using the formula in the text:

1 Calculate the break-even point for the party. (>>)
2 Calculate the new break-even point if, in addition to the cost of the party, you were going to make a donation of $100 to your school or college funds.(>>)
3 The maximum number that the hall will hold is 180. Should you go ahead with your party?

In Figure 11.3, the line DD represents the fixed costs of the business, which remain constant for all volumes of output. Line DC is the total cost line (variable costs plus fixed costs), which rises as output increases. Note that the variable cost line starts at the level of fixed costs, since even when nothing is produced, the business still has to pay its fixed costs. Line AA is the revenue line. This starts at 0, since

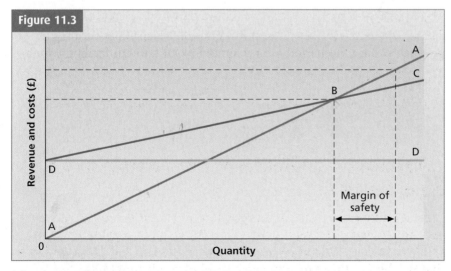

Figure 11.3

A break-even chart

when nothing is sold there is no revenue. The point at which the total cost line and the revenue line intersect (B) is the break-even point.

The difference between the point on AA and the corresponding point on DC for a given level of sales is the profit or loss produced by that level of sales. If the volume of sales is higher than the break-even point, the difference between the actual level of sales and the break-even point is called the margin of safety.

11.4 *Activity*

1 Construct a break-even chart for the end-of-term disco in Activity 11.3 including the donation to your school or college. (>)
2 You have found a larger hall in which to hold the disco. Using your chart, calculate how many tickets you must sell in order to be able to increase your donation to $250. (>>)

Summary

- All businesses incur costs.
- The costs of a business can be identified as fixed or variable costs, or direct or indirect costs.
- The lower the average cost per unit of output, the more efficient the business.
- Costs are used in forecasting and planning.
- The break-even point of a business or product is the point at which revenue from sales just covers the running costs of the business or product.

12 Accounting for success

In this unit you will learn about the purpose of accounts and how they help a business to plan and control its activities. You will also learn about the different accounts that are produced in business.

All businesses must produce accounts at the end of each year to show how much profit or loss they have made. These accounts are known as final accounts.

Different types of business produce their accounts for different purposes. A sole trader with a small business and employing no one may produce simple accounts so that he or she can report their earnings to the tax authorities for income tax purposes. A private or public limited company must produce more complex accounts for both tax purposes and to send to shareholders.

Accounts are used in planning and controlling the activities of a business. They provide a measure of the success of a business in achieving its financial objectives. It is the role of the accounting function to gather financial information about the activities and performance of the business and to prepare, interpret and analyse the accounts. We look in detail at interpreting and analysing accounts in Unit 13.

Trading accounts

The first part of the final accounts is called the **trading account**. This shows the gross profit of the business. **Gross profit** is the amount left out of sales revenue after the direct costs (the costs of actually producing the goods sold: the labour, raw materials and components, called the cost of sales) have been deducted, but before other costs, such as administration and marketing are taken into consideration.

Trading account
the first part of a profit and loss account, showing the gross profit of a business

Gross profit
sales revenue less cost of goods sold

Figure 12.1

Southern African Engineering plc
Trading Account
Year ended 31 March 2001

	$'000	$'000
Sales revenue		7,842
Less cost of sales		
Opening stock	189	
Purchases	4,968	
	5,157	
Less closing stock	53	
	5,104	5,104
Gross profit		**2,738**

Southern Africa Engineering Trading Account

Southern Africa Engineering plc is a medium sized manufacturing company. Their trading account for the year ended 31 March 2001 is shown in Figure 12.1. The top figure in the right hand column is the total sales revenue for the year. The amount of stock the company had at the beginning of the year is shown as the opening stock figure. The purchases figure is the direct costs of producing goods to be sold. This is added to the opening stock figure to give the total cost of all goods available for sale during the year. The closing stock of unsold goods is then deducted to give the actual cost of goods sold during the year. This is subtracted from the sales revenue to give the gross profit (i.e. the profit before other costs of running the business are taken into account).

Questions

1 What was Southern Africa Engineering's sales turnover for the year? (>)

2 How much stock did the company have left at the end of the year? (>)

3 What was the company's total expenditure? (>>)

4 What were the direct costs of the company? (>>)

The profit and loss account

The gross profit is not the final profit of the company. The second part of the final accounts of a business is the **profit and loss account**. This extends the trading account to show the final profit, the **net profit**, of the business, taking into consideration all other items of income and expenditure.

Profit and loss account
a statement of the amount of profit or loss made by a company over a period, taking into consideration all sources of income and expenditure.

Net profit
sales revenue less total costs

Business in context

Figure 12.1 shows that in the year ended 31 March 2001, Southern Africa Engineering made a gross profit of $2,738,000. This, of course, only takes into consideration cost of sales, and there are many other items of expenditure that have to be deducted before arriving at a net profit figure for the company. The full profit and loss account for Southern Africa Engineering is shown in Figure 12.2.

Figure 12.2

Southern African Engineering plc
Profit and Loss Account
Year ended 31 March 2001

	$'000	$'000
Sales revenue		7,842
Less cost of sales		
Opening stock	189	
Purchases	4,968	
	5,157	
Less closing stock	53	
	5,104	5,104
Gross profit		**2,738**
Less overheads and expenses		1,700
Net profit		**1,038**

Southern Africa Engineering Profit and Loss Account

Questions

1. What types of costs have been included in the cost of sales figure for Southern Africa Engineering? (>)
2. What types of costs have not been included in the cost of sales figure? (>)
3. Make a list of the items of cost that you think Southern Africa Engineering has probably incurred but that have not been included in the trading account. (>>)

What goes into the profit and loss account?

While the major part of the income of a business comes from selling goods or services produced, some businesses may receive income from other sources such as: selling assets; dividends or interest from investments; rent from leasing unused land or premises to other businesses.

The expenses that have not been included in the trading account are overheads. These include items such as: salaries and wages (other than for direct labour); office expenses; advertising and marketing; rent and rates; heating and lighting; telephone and postage; insurance; vehicle expenses; depreciation; interest on loans; bank charges; professional fees.

Depreciation is charged to the profit and loss account for large capital items that are not fully written off to profit in the year they are purchased. For example, a car costing $20,000 may be expected to last for four years before the business trades it in and buys a new one. If the full cost of the car is written off against profit in the year it is purchased, this will not give a fair picture of the profit of the business.

Instead, the anticipated trade-in value of the car in four years' time is deducted from the price paid, and the balance divided by four to arrive at an annual depreciation figure. This is called the straight-line method of depreciation, since each year's depreciation is the same. Therefore if the anticipated resale value of the car is $4,000, the annual depreciation is:

$$\frac{(\$20,000 - \$4,000)}{4} = \frac{\$16,000}{4} = \$4,000 \text{ per year}$$

The appropriation account

Appropriation account
the last part of the profit and loss account, which shows how much of a company's profit is paid in tax and dividends

Unfortunately, few businesses get to keep all the profit they make even after all their expenses have been deducted. A part of the net profit of a company has to be paid to the government as business tax. Another part must be paid out to the shareholders in the form of a dividend on the shares they own. Only when these items have been paid out can the business retain the remaining profit. These last calls on the profits of a company are added to the profit and loss account in the form of an **appropriation account**. The appropriation account for Southern Africa Engineering is shown in Figure 12.3. The trading account, profit and loss account, and appropriation account are normally incorporated in a single document called the profit and loss account.

Southern African Engineering plc
Appropriation Account
Year ended 31 March 2001

	$'000
Net profit	1,038
Less	
Tax	225
Dividend paid	391
Retained profit	422

Southern Africa Engineering Appropriation Account

The balance sheet

The last part of the final accounts of a business is the **balance sheet**. This shows the value of the business in financial terms at one moment in time (unlike the profit and loss account which shows the activities of the business over a period of a year). Items included on the balance sheet are:

Balance sheet
a statement of the worth of a company

- assets – everything that the business owns that has a monetary value, including debtors, or money owed to the business
- liabilities – everything the business owes to other businesses or individuals and has a monetary value
- capital – money that is invested in the business.

The balance sheet for Southern Africa Engineering is shown in Figure 12.4. Although there is no set format for a balance sheet (as long as it includes all the appropriate items) the format of Southern Africa Engineeering's balance sheet is fairly standard.

12.1 Activity

1   What kind of fixed assets do you think that Southern Africa Engineering has? (>)
2   Who do you think Southern Africa Engineering's debtors are? (>)
3   Who do you think are Southern Africa Engineering's creditors?(>)
4   Comment on Southern Africa Engineering's figure for stocks. (>>>)

Figure 12.4

Southern African Engineering plc
Balance Sheet
Year ended 31 March 2001

	$'000	$'000
Fixed assets		
Land and buildings	1,556	
Plant and equipment	83	
Furniture and furnishings	23	
		1,662
Current assets		
Stocks	53	
Debtors	2	
Cash	5	
	60	
Creditors falling due within 1 year	6	
Net current assets	54	
Creditors falling due after more than 1 year (Bank loan)	−75	
		−21
		1,641
Capital and reserves		
Called up share capital		
Profit and loss account		1,219
(retained profit)		422
Capital employed		
		1,641

Southern Africa Engineering Balance Sheet

What is the purpose of accounts?

Accounts are produced for several purposes: the business can assess its own performance and compare it with previous years and other companies; the tax authorities can use the accounts for taxation purposes; other companies can compare their own performance with the business; shareholders and lenders can see how well the company is doing and see how secure their investment or loan is.

Summary

- All businesses produce final accounts.
- The first part of the final accounts of a business is the trading account, which shows the gross profit.
- The profit and loss account extends the trading account to show the net profit of a business, taking into consideration all sources of income and expenditure.
- The appropriation account shows how much of the net profit of a business is paid to the government as business tax, to investors as dividends, and retained within the business.
- The balance sheet is a statement of the net worth of the business, taking into consideration assets, liabilities and capital.

13 What do the accounts mean?

In this unit you will learn how accounts are analysed using various accounting ratios.

A full analysis of the final accounts of a business involves the use of several important ratios (**ratio analysis**). These help in judging how well the business has performed, and allow a meaningful comparison to be made with previous years' accounts or with the accounts of other businesses.

Ratio analysis
a method of analysing the final accounts of a business with the aid of financial ratios

Business in context

Siphiwe of Southern Africa Engineering was sitting in the accountant's office.
The final accounts of Southern Africa Engineering had just been published, and Siphiwe had brought a copy round to show Aliena, his accountant, straight away.

'The trouble is', Siphiwe said, 'I'm not exactly sure what the accounts mean.
I'm an engineer, not an accountant like you. I can see that we've made a profit – but I could tell that anyway, by looking at the company's bank balance. I just feel that after all the hard work of preparing the accounts, there must be more use we can make of them.'

Aliena smiled. 'There is', she said. 'Your final accounts can help you in many ways. But you have to look further than just to see whether you have made a profit or not. You have to analyse them.'

'How do I do that?' Siphiwe asked.

'It depends on what you want to know. Let's have a look at your accounts and see what we can find out.'

1   Is Siphiwe right when he says that he could tell that the company has made a profit by looking at its bank balance? (>)

2   Explain the difference between the amount of money in the bank account at the end of the financial year, and the profit the business has made during the year. (>)

3   Obviously, a business needs to know if it has made a profit or a loss, but what other financial information would be useful in helping it judge its performance? (>>)

4   What type of decisions do you think the business will be able to make, based on financial information in the final accounts? (>>>)

5   Who besides Siphiwe and the accountant might be interested in the final accounts of Southern Africa Engineering, and why might Southern Africa Engineering be interested in the final accounts of other companies? (>>>)

Who wants to know?

There are several groups of people and organisations both inside and outside a business that are interested in the final accounts of the business. These groups are known as stakeholders. As mentioned on page 14, a stakeholder is someone who has an interest in the activities and performance of a business.

The main groups of stakeholders who will be interested in the final accounts of a company are:

- shareholders – they will want to know how well their company has performed, how efficiently it is being run, and whether they are getting a good return on their investment;
- managers – they are responsible for running the business efficiently and will use the accounts to help in obtaining further loan capital as an aid to making decisions on future action such as improving cost-effectiveness, marketing strategies, takeovers and mergers;
- employees – they will want to see how well their employer is doing in order to judge their job security;
- trade unions – they may use the accounts to support a wage claim on behalf of their members;
- creditors, including lenders and trade creditors – they will want to know how secure their money is, and whether the company would have trouble repaying them in an emergency;

- suppliers – they will want to know how sound their customer is, especially if they are considering supplying large orders on credit;
- customers – they will want to know that they can count on the business to continue supplying quality goods and services when they are needed;
- the government – it wants to know the profit of a business for tax purposes, and also how well it is performing so that it can plan strategies for possible future training needs, unemployment, regional development and so on.

What are the ratios to use?

There are two main types of accounting ratios that you need to know and understand: ratios that analyse the profitability of the business, and those that analyse liquidity. The main value of using ratios is that they enable you to compare the final accounts of a business with previous years' final accounts, to identify trends in the performance of the business, and with the final accounts of other business, including those of competitors.

How profitable is the business?

The main profitability ratios are: gross profit margin; net profit margin; and return on capital employed (ROCE).

The gross profit margin shows the relationship between gross profit (i.e. before overheads) and turnover. The formula is:

$$\text{Gross profit margin} = \frac{\text{gross profit}}{\text{turnover} \times 100\%}$$

Obviously, the higher the margin the better. However, margins vary between types of business, and this must be taken into account. It is a useful ratio for comparison with other businesses in the same industry. Gross profit margin may be improved by increasing sales or reducing the cost of sales.

Net profit margin measures the relationship between net profit and turnover. The formula is:

$$\text{Net profit margin} = \frac{\text{net profit}}{\text{turnover} \times 100\%}$$

Again, the higher the margin the better. The net profit margin shows how successful a business is in controlling overheads. It can be improved by increasing sales revenue or reducing overhead expenses.

Return on capital employed measures the efficiency with which the business uses its capital to generate profit. The formula is:

$$\text{ROCE} = \frac{\text{operating profit}}{\text{capital employed (from the balance sheet)}} \times 100\%$$

This can be compared with previous years and other companies. It is also useful to compare it with the interest rates offered by other forms of investment, since ROCE shows the percentage return on money invested in the company. There is no ideal level for ROCE, but unless it compares favourably with interest elsewhere the owners of the business may be better off putting their money in a bank or building society! ROCE can be improved by increasing the level of profit generated by the same level of capital employed, or reducing the level of capital employed while maintaining the same profit.

13.1 Activity

1   Calculate the gross profit margin of Southern Africa Engineering. (>)
2   Calculate the net profit margin of Southern Africa Engineering. (>)
3   Calculate Southern Africa Engineering's return on capital employed. (>)
4   In the role of Southern Africa Engineering's accountant, write a letter to Siphiwe explaining what the ratios mean in relation to Southern Africa Engineering's accounts. (>>>)

What is capital?

The ratio ROCE is a measure of operating profit in terms of capital employed. The capital employed in a business is the total capital amount that has been used to purchase the assets of the business. Capital employed consists of the money invested in the business by its owners or shareholders, plus long-term loans and liabilities.

Accountants also identify two other types of capital: capital owned and working capital. Capital owned consists of capital employed less long-term loans and liabilities. Working capital is the amount available for the day-to-day running of the business and to settle short-term debts. Working capital is therefore an important item. It is calculated by the formula:

Working capital = current assets – current liabilities

How liquid is the business?

Liquidity ratios measure the short-term financial health of a business. They are concerned with working capital and how efficiently it is being managed. If the business does not have enough working capital, it may not be able to pay its debts. If it has too much, it may not be making the best use of its resources.

The current ratio measures the relationship between current assets and current liabilities. The formula is:

Current ratio = current assets : current liabilities

Unlike the previous ratios it is expressed as a simple ratio, not as a percentage. For example, if the current assets of a business are $100,000, and its current liabilities are $50,000, the calculation is:

Current ratio = 100,000 : 50,000
= 100 : 50
= 2 : 1

In this case the current ratio shows that the business has twice as many current assets as current liabilities, meaning it has $2 of assets to pay every $1 short-term debt. This is a good figure, although many accountants would recommend a ratio of around 1.5:1. A higher figure suggests that some of the assets should be used more profitably. If the current ratio is too low it may be improved by selling under-used assets or raising more long-term capital, for example by issuing shares or increasing long-term borrowing.

The acid test is sometimes called the quick ratio. It measures liquidity by comparing current assets with current liabilities. Stocks are left out of the current assets, however, as these are the hardest current assets to turn into cash quickly, without a loss in value. The remaining current assets are already in the form of cash, or cash that can be called on quickly (e.g. debtors). The formula is:

Acid test = (current assets − stock) : current liabilities

Like the current ratio it is expressed as a simple ratio. Most accountants consider a ratio of 1:1 to be ideal, since this means that the business has $1 of cash or near-cash for every $1 of short-term debt. A business with an acid test ratio of less than this could have difficulty making short-term payments. Some businesses, however, such as supermarkets, which have a high turnover of cash and stock, may be able to operate well on a low acid test ratio.

Judging the success of a business

While various stakeholders use ratios such as gross and net profit margin and ROCE to judge the success of a business in achieving its financial aims, they are not the only measures of business success.

In Unit 2 we saw that businesses have various objectives besides making a profit, such as increasing sales and enlarging their market share. When judging the success of a business, therefore, its performance must also be compared with these objectives and questions asked such as:

- Has the business enlarged its market share in the last year?
- Has the quality of the business's products improved?
- Has the business met its environmental objectives?
- How good are employer–employee relations?

Answers to questions such as these, together with measures of financial success, give an overall indication of the success of a business.

13.2 Activity

1 Calculate the current ratio of Southern Africa Engineering. (>)
2 Calculate the acid test of Southern Africa Engineering. (>)
3 In the role of Southern Africa Engineering's accountant write a letter to Siphiwe explaining what the ratios mean in relation to Southern Africa Engineering's accounts. (>>>)
4 Obtain the latest final accounts of two well-known plcs in the same industry. For example you might obtain the annual reports of two supermarket chains, car manufacturers or telecommunications companies. (>)
5 Do a full ratio analysis of the accounts of each company and compare the results of each. What do they show? (>>>)

Summary

- The stakeholders of a business are interested in its final accounts for different reasons.
- The final accounts of a business can be fully analysed by using ratio analysis.

14 How do forecasts help decision-making?

In this unit you will see how financial forecasting can help the process of decision-making in business.

Businesses produce plans for several reasons: to ensure they make a profit; to help them obtain loans and grants; to check their performance; to enable owners and managers to set targets. A good **business plan** will show how the business can achieve its objectives.

Forecasting is an important part of business planning. A forecast looks to the future and tries to predict how significant changes throughout the period of the plan might affect the performance of the business.

Business plan
an outline of the business and its objectives, normally including a budget and cash-flow forecast

Business in context

Daniela had always been interested in fashion. When she was twenty-two, she realised her dream and opened her own fashion shop.

She rented premises in the town centre and had them fitted out to look stylish and attractive. Then she bought the stock she would need initially from fashion houses in the capital. She knew this was going to be expensive, but she had saved some money of her own and was able to borrow some from her parents. She also obtained a bank loan. The bank manager was very encouraging, but insisted that she prepared a full business plan, giving details of the business and her anticipated costs, sales and profits in the first year before he would consider her application for a loan.

Once she had paid her start-up costs, she had very little of her original finance left. She knew that it was important to sell her stock quickly to get the cash to pay her ongoing costs, such as heating and lighting, telephone, postage, insurance, and the weekly advertisement she placed in the local newspaper. She also needed to pay for new stock, which she bought every week, and also to draw some for her own expenses. This meant hard work attracting customers and anticipating trends so that the shop always had the clothes that customers wanted to buy.

Daniela found out the hard way that she needed to keep track of her costs, when a large bill came in unexpectedly. She had just bought and paid for a lot of new stock, and had no cash left to pay the bill. Luckily her bank agreed a temporary overdraft, but warned her that she must plan her spending more carefully. Daniela realised that if the bank had not agreed to the overdraft, she would not have been able to pay the unexpected bill, and her business could have failed, even though on paper it was making a good profit.

Questions

1 List Daniela's start-up costs. (>)

2 What sources of finance did Daniela use to pay her start-up costs? (>)

3 Why do you think the bank manager insisted on a business plan before he would consider her application for a loan? (>>)

4 What sources of finance does Daniela use to pay her running costs? (>)

5 How might Daniela plan her future spending? (>>>)

Figure 14.1

Preparing a business plan

What is a business plan?

A business plan is a scheme showing the aims of the business and how it will achieve them. The main elements in a business plan are:

- details of the business (name and address, type of business, owner and any staff)
- aims and objectives
- information about the product or service, including the results of market research showing the likely strength of demand; pricing policy and break-even point (see Unit 11)
- financial matters including details of start-up costs (if appropriate), a **budget** showing anticipated profit and a **cash-flow forecast**.

Cash-flow forecast
a forecast of cash inflows and outflows over a given period

Budget
a forecast of the profit a business expects to generate in a given period

Your business plan

Name of business

Address

Post code

Telephone number

Sole trader   Partnership   Franchise   Limited Company

Start-up target or date business began trading

Type of business

Planning ahead

My ultimate goal is _____

_____

I expect to achieve the following over the next few years

Year 1 _____

Year 2 _____

Year 3 _____

Knowing your market

My market may be described as (eg. type, size, location) _____

_____

_____

_____

_____

_____

My customers may be described as _____

_____

_____

_____

_____

_____

	my product/service	**Competitor A**	**Competitor B**
Price			
Quality			
Availability			
Customers			
Staff skills			

Reputation			
Advertising			
Delivery			
Location			
Special offers			
After sales service			

Product/service comparison table

My product/service is special because

_____

_____

_____

_____

The main advantages of my product/service over my competitors' are

Competitor A _____

_____

_____

Competitor B _____

_____

_____

Promotion and selling

My competitors promote and advertise as follows

Competitor A _____

_____

Competitor B _____

_____

My promotion and advertising intentions are

Method _____ Approximate cost _____

_____ _____

_____ _____

_____   _____
_____   _____

I believe these methods are appropriate for my market because

_____
_____
_____
_____

Staying in control

My sales projections are based on the following assumptions

_____
_____
_____
_____
_____

The firm orders I already have are

Date	Order	Details	Delivery date
1			
2			
3			
4			
5			

My current business assets are (eg. equipment, machinery, vehicles)

Item	Value	Life expectancy

I will need the following assets to start-up and then throughout my first year

Start up

Item	Value
Item	Value

Year 1

Item	Value
Item	Value

The way I intend to pay for these are

	Value	Date
Grants		
Own resources		
Loans		
Creditors		

I can obtain the following credit from my suppliers

Supplier	Estimate value of monthly order	Number of days credit

Premises

My business will be located at

because _____

_____

_____

_____

Details of my lease/licence/rent/rates/next rent review (delete as appropiate) are _____

_____

_____

Details of key staff (if any)

Name _____   Name _____

Position _____   Position _____

Address _____   Address _____

_____   _____

_____   _____

Age _____   Age _____

Qualifications _____   Qualifications _____

_____   _____

Relevant work experience _____   Relevant work experience _____

_____   _____

Present income _____   Present income _____

I will need to buy in the following skills during the first two years _____

_____

_____

_____

I estimate the cost of employing people or buying any services I may need in the first two years as

Number of people	Job function	Monthly cost	Annual cost
_____	_____	_____	_____
_____	_____	_____	_____
_____	_____	_____	_____

My personal details

Name _____

Address _____

_____

_____

_____

                                Post code _____

Telephone (home) _____   Telephone (work) _____

Qualifications _____

_____

                                Date of birth _____

Relevant work experience _____

_____

_____

Business experience _____

_____

_____

_____

Courses attented _____

_____

_____

_____

Source: adapted from Barclays bank business plan.

All the major high-street banks are keen to help new businesses that want to open accounts with them, and perhaps use them as a source of finance. They do this in the hope that the business will be a success, so benefiting both the business and the bank.

One thing that banks require before they will become too involved in a new business is a sound business plan. A business plan will enable the bank to see just how sound the new business idea is, and will also provide the new business with a means of monitoring its progress.

Business plan template – Barclays

Constructing a full business plan is especially important for a business that is just starting up, but all businesses should produce budgets and cash-flow forecasts annually.

14.1 *Activity*

1 Decide on an idea for a new business you would like to set up. (>)
2 Find out the information about your business idea that is required to complete the business plan shown above. (>>>)
3 When you have all the information, construct a business plan for your idea, using the business plan above as a basis. You should keep your business plan for further activities in this unit. (>>>)

What is a budget?

A budget is a forecast of the profit a business expects to generate in a given period, usually a year. It sets targets for income and expenditure during the period. Estimates are made of the anticipated income that the business will receive from selling its product, and its expenditure on items such as raw materials, personnel costs, advertising, power, transport and administration.

Since the budget forecasts events up to a year ahead, the estimates are really only guesses. However, the more accurate the guesses the more accurate the forecast – and the more useful it will be. While the budget normally covers a full year, it is divided into shorter periods of perhaps a month, so that the actual income and expenditure of the business can be compared with the forecast figures on a regular basis. In this way, if there is any variance so that it looks as though the business may not achieve its anticipated profit it can decide on the appropriate action.

This may involve increasing sales to generate more revenue, or reducing expenditure. The more detailed the budget is, the easier it is to identify what action the business needs to take.

When preparing the budget, each department in the business will forecast its own costs for the period. This is done on the basis of past experience (for example how much things cost last year) and knowledge or expectation of future trends. In a similar way, the sales department will forecast sales for the period. From this information, each department will produce its own budget. Most departments' budgets other than the budget of the sales department will consist only of expenditure. When all the budgets have been prepared, they are combined into a master budget which shows anticipated expenditure, income and profit for the whole business. The business can then decide whether the anticipated profit is as required, or whether action must be taken to increase sales or control expenditure in order to generate further profit.

14.2 *Activity*

For Activity 14.1 you completed a business plan for your business idea.
1 Identify all the costs that would be incurred by that business in the first year of trading. (>>)
2 Estimate the value of sales that you will achieve in the first year. (>>)
3 Construct a budget for the first year of trading. (>>>)

What is a cash-flow forecast?

It is important to distinguish between the profit a business makes and the amount of cash it has. Profit is the amount by which sales revenue exceeds expenditure in a period. However, during any given period sales may have been made, and therefore included in the profit and loss account, but not yet paid for by the customer. For example, goods may have been sold on credit.

Similarly, a business may have purchased goods and services on credit, so that the expenditure on those items is included in the profit and loss calculation although the goods and services have not yet been paid for. A business can only spend the cash it has in the bank, not the profit shown on the profit and loss account. A cash-flow forecast estimates the flow of cash into and out of the business and shows how much money a business has available at a given time to pay any expenses that are due.

Money coming into the business is called inflows, money going out of the business is called outflows. The major sources of inflows are: revenue from sales; injections of capital such as bank loans and finance provided by the owners; government grants and subsidies. The main sources of outflows are: payments to suppliers, rent and rates, employees' wages and salaries, telephone, electricity and water, advertising, payments to the government for items such as tax, national insurance and VAT.

Inflows and outflows are shown on the cash-flow forecast in the month in which the money is actually received or spent. Income for goods sold on thirty days' credit is shown in the month the business expects to receive it not when the goods were sold. In this way, a cash-flow forecast shows how much cash a business expects to have at the end of each month, rather than the profit it expects to make.

A business can foresee any shortfall of cash, and make appropriate plans. For example, the cash-flow forecast of a business may show that in one month it will not have enough cash in the bank to pay the wages of its employees. This may be because payment for a large order will not be received until the following month. By identifying this, the business can tell its bank that it will need an overdraft or loan to cover the shortfall well before the shortfall actually occurs. Since the business has planned its cash needs in advance, the bank will be more prepared to allow the overdraft.

14.3 *Activity*

1 Construct a cash-flow forecast for the first year of trading for your business idea. (>>>)
2 Identify any periods when the business will require additional finance. (>>)
3 Suggest sources of finance to cover these. (>>>)

Summary

- Businesses produce plans to ensure they make a profit, help them obtain loans and grants, monitor their performance, and enable managers to set targets.
- Forecasting is an important part of business planning.
- A budget is a plan showing how a business is going to achieve its financial targets in a given period.
- A cash-flow forecast shows the cash inflows and outflows for the business.

15 Structuring for growth

In this unit you will learn about the internal organisation and structure of business organisations.

As a business grows it develops a structure that reflects the interrelationship of the different parts of the organisation. The structure may show a steep or flat **hierarchy** and be centralised or decentralised according to the factors that shaped the organisation.

Hierarchy
the levels of management in an organisation

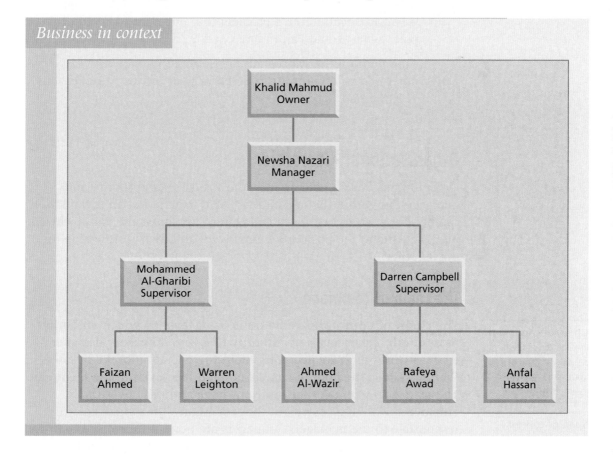

Business in context

Organisational hierarchies

Organisations develop hierarchies: the structure of authority and management within the organisation. The structure of an organisation can be shown in an organisational chart. This shows the various levels of management, the position of employees and their relationship to one another.

The chain of command

Chain of command
the line through which decisions are passed from senior managers to employees

Span of control
the number of employees over whom a manager has authority

The **chain of command** is the framework through which authority passes from higher levels of authority to lower. Managers at higher levels of authority take decisions about the operation of the business that must be carried out by employees at lower levels in the hierarchy. The managers who take the decisions have authority over the employees who must carry out those decisions; the employees are responsible to the managers. Managers are nevertheless responsible for ensuring that their decisions are carried out correctly, and for the outcomes of those decisions. The number of employees over whom a manager has authority is called their **span of control**.

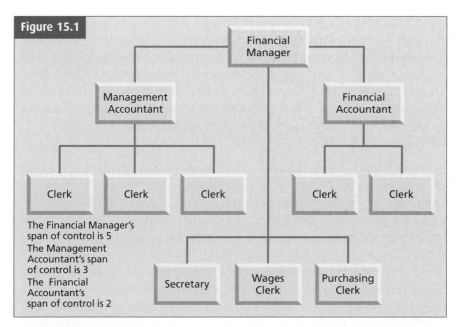

Figure 15.1

The Financial Manager's span of control is 5

The Management Accountant's span of control is 3

The Financial Accountant's span of control is 2

Spans of control

15.1 *Activity*

1   Is there a best size for one person's span of control? (>>)
2   What factors would influence how many people one person could effectively manage? (>>>)

Organisational structures

The two main types of **organisational structures** are: hierarchical (tall or flat) and decentralised.

A hierarchical organisation is one that consists of a number of levels of authority. Decision-making for the whole organisation is centralised at the top of the hierarchy. A tall hierarchy is one with many levels of authority – in other words an organisation with a long chain of command. A flat hierarchy is one with only a few levels of authority.

In a tall hierarchy, where there are many levels, managers and supervisors have fewer employees reporting to them than in a flat organisation. This means they have a smaller span of control. The length of the chain of command and the spans of control of the managers and supervisors in a given organisation are interdependent: the fewer managers and supervisors in an organisation, the wider their spans of control because each will have authority over relatively more employees.

There are advantages and disadvantages to both broad and narrow spans. A narrow span of control can provide more opportunities for

Organisational structure
the shape of an organisation based on levels and centralisation of management and spans of control

promotion and a clearer long-term career path for employees rising through the hierarchy. Managers who have few subordinates are able to maintain a closer working relationship with each of them and may see more of them. Both these aspects of narrow spans of control can increase the motivation of employees, and their commitment to the organisation. However, communications within the organisation tend to be poor when they have to pass through several levels both upwards and downwards.

Delegation
the process of giving authority for decision-making to subordinates

A broader span of control, with fewer levels of management, may offer employees less in the way of promotion prospects, but this is often countered by increased **delegation** to subordinates of authority to make decisions. Such delegation of authority helps to boost morale and increase motivation as employees feel they are playing a more significant part in the organisation. Communications are quicker and more efficient when there are fewer levels to pass through, speeding up the decision-making process and helping senior management to keep in close touch with what is happening in the organisation. There are, of course, limits to the number of employees one person can effectively supervise and therefore to the size of a workable span of control.

An organisation consisting of a central administration unit (such as a head office) and several operating units may develop a satellite structure. Here each unit has its own hierarchy and procedures for decision-making. The various units are responsible to the central administration unit, which exerts some control over them, and the organisation still has a centralised structure. Because they are small, however, the separate units tend to have a flatter hierarchy with more authority delegated to unit managers. This structure is most appropriate when conditions require a significant amount of local decision-making by units.

Function
a specific area of business activity, such as production or marketing

Decentralised structures may occur if an organisation has several distinct areas of operation, which require different methods of management and control. In a decentralised structure, each operational area has responsibility for its own activities. Large organisations may be decentralised on the basis of: **function**, product, market or systems. Decentralisation can benefit a business where the various parts require specialist skills or knowledge.

> **15.2** *Activity*
>
> 1 Draw an organisational chart for your school or college. (>>)
> 2 Does your school or college have a tall or flat organisational hierarchy? (>>)
> 3 What are the advantages and disadvantages of its particular structure for your school? You may like to ask some teachers and other staff for their views on this. (>>>)

The functions of businesses

Most large business organisations are made up of smaller **departments**.
Each department carries out a specific function, or activity, that is
essential to the success and smooth running of the organisation. By
having departments carrying out functions, the people who work in
different departments are able to specialise in their particular area of
activity. In this way the organisation benefits from employees who are
able to develop skills and knowledge of their own area.

> **Department**
> a section of a business
> whose role is to carry
> out a specific function

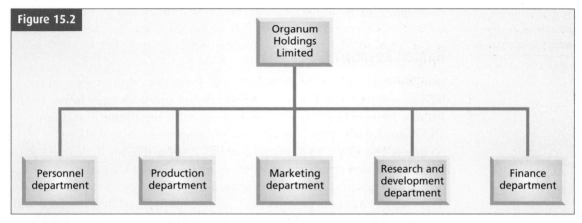

Departmental organisation of a large business

Production

The Production Department is responsible for organising the
production of the goods or services of the business. It must also
monitor things like wastage, the usage and cost of raw materials and
bought-in parts, and the quality of goods produced. It may design
special tools and equipment to help make the product more efficiently
and cost effectively. An essential aspect of the work of the Production
Department is ensuring that the rate of production is sufficient for
customers' orders to be met on time.

Research and Development

The purpose of the Research and Development Department is to make
sure that the organisation's products are suited to the needs of the
market place today. The Research and Development Department must
continually develop and improve the organisation's products not only
so that they fulfil customers' requirements and expectations, but also
anticipate what those requirements and expectations will be in the
future. The Research and Development Department must also make
sure that the organisation's products are better, more cost effective and
more up to date than the products of competitors.

Marketing

The work of the Marketing Department starts with carrying out market research to find out exactly what customers want and how much they are willing to pay. The Marketing Department then works in close conjunction with both the Research and Development Department and the Production Department to plan and produce a product that will fulfil customers' requirements. Product planning includes developing the packaging for the product, promoting it through advertising and sales promotions, and arranging appropriate distribution of the product.

Human Resources

Human Resources involves planning to meet the requirements of the business in terms of employee numbers and the skills they have. The Human Resources Department carries out the recruitment, training and dismissal of employees, looks after matters such as welfare, contracts and other legal matters, and is responsible for developing disciplinary and grievance procedures and ensuring they are carried out. It also advises the senior management of the organisation on pay, terms and conditions of work and other employee-related matters, and in negotiations with trade unions. The Human Resources Department must keep records of employees, including pension contributions and sick pay. A major area of this department's work is concerned with ensuring the organisation complies with employment law in such areas as equal opportunities and discrimination.

Finance

The Finance, or Accounts, Department deals with the financial side of the business, and pays the wages and salaries of employees. This department manages the financial resources and monitors the performance of the organisation in money terms. It is the responsibility of the Accounts Department to prepare financial forecasts and co-ordinate the plans of other departments to ensure that these can be achieved. The department produces invoices and keeps records of all financial transactions. Information in the form of cash-flow analyses, accounts and reports is produced for the senior management of the organisation. In this way senior management can see whether the financial targets of the organisation are being met – and take appropriate action if they are not! The Accounts Department also produces financial information for government departments.

Other departments

Most business organisations also have other departments to help in the running of the business. The Administration Department is responsible for legal and other matters such as insurance, buying office equipment, maintenance of the offices, making planning applications and so on. The Administration Department also provides a service for other departments in the organisation in areas such as designing and printing forms, photocopying, telephone and fax services, word processing, organising meetings and business travel, and so on. An efficient Administration Department is essential to the smooth running of the organisation.

The Purchasing Department orders and buys the raw materials and parts needed by the Production Department to produce the organisation's goods. It must obtain these in the right quantities and of the right quality to ensure that the needs of production and the requirements of customers are met at a price that provides the maximum profit for the organisation. The Purchasing Department must work closely with the Production and Marketing Departments.

The Distribution Department delivers the goods produced by the organisation to customers or retail outlets, if the goods are to be resold. It must make sure that the goods are delivered on time (that is when the customer wants them) and undamaged. Goods may be distributed on the organisation's own vehicles, on the vehicles of private haulage companies or a combination of these methods. Lightweight goods may also be delivered by post. If the organisation runs its own vehicles, the Distribution Department must keep records of drivers and journeys, keep the vehicles maintained, and ensure that licences and insurance are up to date. The Distribution Department must also monitor the cost of fuel and maintenance, and arrange for goods to be delivered by the most cost-effective route.

15.3 Activity

1   Explain in your own words the functions of the main departments normally found in large organisations. (>)
2   Using examples, show how the departments of an organisation are interdependent. (>>>)
3   What are the advantages and disadvantages of working in departments? (>>>)
4   How do departments make specialisation easier? (>>>)
5   What other departments, besides those described in this Unit, might you expect to find in (a) a newspaper; (b) a hospital; (c) a bank? (>>>)

What are the responsibilities of different types of employee?

Job description
a document outlining the tasks, duties and responsibilities of a job holder

While the actual tasks of different jobs vary from organisation to organisation, there are two indicators of what is involved in a particular job. These are the job title and the **job description** (areas of responsibility of the job). The job title gives an indication of the job holder's position in the organisation, the department in which he or she works and the nature of the job. The job description shows the types of tasks the job holder will undertake (see Unit 21).

Summary

- Organisations develop structures based on their hierarchies.
- An organisation with many levels of management and a narrow span of control has a tall structure.
- An organisation with few levels of management and a wide span of control has a flat structure.
- The chain of command in an organisation passes through the different levels of management.
- Managers may delegate authority for decision-making to subordinates.
- Most large business organisations are made up of smaller departments.
- Each department carries out a specific function, or activity.
- Working in departments enables employees to specialise and develop their skills in a particular area.

16 *Is it worth the risk?*

> *In this unit you will learn about the roles of entrepreneurs and managers. You will also see how judgement can be used to reduce the risks involved in business decision-making.*

All business activity involves an element of risk: things can go wrong and the business might fail. This risk is greatest for start-up businesses, where the venture is new and untried. The person setting up the business must accept and try to minimise the risk, as well as gather all the resources needed to start the business.

Business in context

The Body Shop and Virgin are two of the most successful businesses in the UK today.

The Body Shop makes body, skin and hair care products, using natural products from all over the world. Anita Roddick founded the business in 1976. She started with one shop selling around 25 products. Now the business manufactures more than 400 products and sells them throughout the world.

Richard Branson started the Virgin Group in the early 1970s. His first business ventures were a student magazine and selling records by mail order. Now Virgin includes air and rail travel, music, mobile phones, energy, wines, financial services and a lot more. Like The Body Shop, Virgin is a British-based group of businesses that operates throughout the world.

Questions

1. Make a list of all the types of resources that you think are used by both The Body Shop and Virgin. To get you started, one example is buildings: The Body Shop has a factory and offices; Virgin operates in offices and shop premises. (>)

2. How important do you think Anita Roddick and Richard Branson have been to the success of their businesses? (>>)

3. Give reasons for your answer to question 2. (>>)

What is an entrepreneur?

Anita Roddick and Richard Branson are **entrepreneurs**. An entrepreneur is somebody who has the ability, enthusiasm, vision and skills to come up with a business idea and gather together the resources to enable production to take place.

Being an entrepreneur involves an element of risk. The entrepreneur has to invest his or her own time and money in getting their business idea up and running. If the business fails, they will lose everything they invested in the business – and perhaps a lot more.

Besides entrepreneurship, there are three other types of resources needed for production to take place: land, labour and capital. These four types of resources are called the **factors of production**.

Figure 16.1

Factors of production

Land

Land consists of all the natural and unrefined resources that are found in nature and used to produce goods and services. It includes farm and agricultural land, forestry land, quarries and mines, rivers, the sea and the atmosphere, and everything that lives and grows in or on them.

Labour

Labour is the work that is performed by people. It includes not only physical work like building or operating a machine in a factory, but also work requiring more mental effort, like computer programming – or even teaching!

Capital

Capital includes those items used by businesses that do not occur naturally: buildings such as offices, factories and hospitals, machinery and other equipment, materials and parts.

16.1 *Activity*

1 Identify the factors of production used by your school or college. (>)
2 Is there an entrepreneur at your school or college? Who is it? (>)
3 Explain your conclusion to question 2. (>>>)

Why do businesses need managers?

As a business grows, it becomes more complex, with more employees carrying out different functions and in different departments. The larger and more complex the business becomes, the more difficult it is for one person – the entrepreneur – to control.

Managers with specialist skills perform various functions in businesses: planning; problem-solving; making decisions; and co-ordinating the efforts of the staff for whom the manager is responsible.

Manager
person responsible for the day-to-day operation of a department or function

What do managers do?

We have seen that most large organisations consist of several departments. Each department is normally responsible to a director (the Marketing Department is responsible to the Marketing Director). The day-to-day running of the department is the responsibility of a manager (called a departmental manager).

Managers have general areas of responsibility. These include:

- carrying out the instructions of the directors
- allocating work to the other members of their department
- taking action to ensure that the department's targets are met
- solving the day-to-day problems that arise within their department
- managing people – getting the most out of the members of their department
- managing finance – keeping watch over the money their department spends.

In addition, managers have specific responsibilities relating to the department they manage. This is reflected in their full job title. Some typical job titles of managers, and their specific areas of responsibility are:

- Marketing Manager – responsible for running the Marketing Department and the organisation's marketing activities
- Accounts Manager – responsible for running the Accounts Department, and for the financial reporting and management of the organisation
- Production Manager – responsible for running the Production Department of a manufacturing organisation, for ensuring the right goods of the right quality are produced at the right time to meet customers' requirements
- Human Resources Manager – often called the Personnel Manager, is responsible for running the Human Resources Department and ensuring that the organisation has the employees it needs to operate. This involves working closely with other departments. The Human Resources Manager must be aware of developments in employment law and training
- Sales Manager – responsible for the Sales Department or Sales Team of the organisation, and for ensuring that sales targets set by the directors are met, so that the organisation has the income it needs to cover its costs and make a profit.

16.2 Activity

The following is a typical day for Antjie Krog, Production Manager of Webb Furniture:

08.30 Arrive at the factory. Collect the latest batch of customers' orders from the Sales Department. Go through production schedules with the foreman and allocate individual jobs to production workers and machines.

09.10 Meeting with six production workers who are operating the new woodworking machines. They are unhappy that they are expected to learn to use the new technology, which calls for new skills. They feel that they should be paid a higher rate. Antjie manages to avoid a dispute by promising to take the matter up with the Human Resources Department.

11.00 Antjie attends a meeting with other departmental managers on the development of a new range of furniture to be launched later in the year. After the meeting, she speaks to the Sales Manager about the likely level of sales of the new furniture and the levels of production that will be required. Antjie decides to tell her production workers about the new range, as it will involve additional overtime working in the initial stages, and she feels they should be prepared for this. It may mean that she will have to negotiate a bonus payment for those involved on the new furniture.

13.00 After lunch, Antjie spends some time on the factory floor, talking individually to her staff. She checks production levels to ensure that production scheduled for the day will be completed. One production worker complains that some of the equipment is old and keeps breaking down. They do not seem to get a sufficient allocation of time from the Maintenance Department. Antjie promises to raise the problem for them at the next weekly management meeting.

16.00 Two production workers who are working on a special one-off order come to Antjie to ask for her help. They are having difficulty with one of the joints and, knowing Antjie has been making furniture for a long time, want her advice. Antjie readily agrees to show them. She is aware that the other workers respect her for being able to do any job she asks them to.

17.00 The day's production has now been completed. Anjie has some returns to complete for the Finance Department, before getting things ready for tomorrow. She makes sure to say 'good night' to as many of her staff as she can as they leave. She is normally the last one in the department to go home.

In the above context, identify the roles of a manager that Antjie has fulfilled during her day. (>>)

Figure 16.2

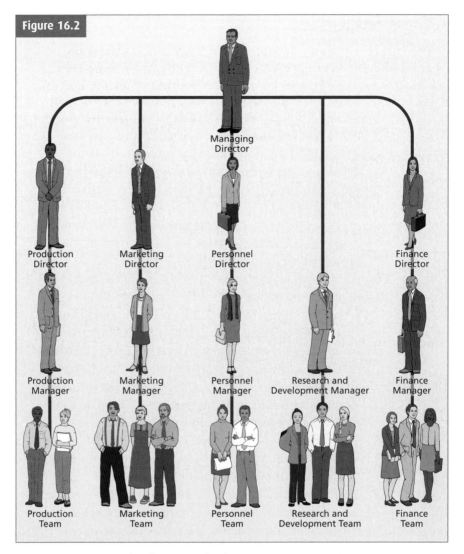

Management structure in a large organisation

Is it worth the risk?

All business activity involves taking decisions. Initially the entrepreneur will take decisions such as what goods or services to produce, how to produce them and how much to charge. Managers also take decisions such as how to achieve the targets set for their department; how many people are needed; how should the work of the department be allocated to individual employees, and so on.

Types of decisions

Three types of decision can be identified: strategic, tactical, and operational. **Strategic decisions** are decisions on the long-term future activities and performance of the business. They are normally taken at the highest level in a business, and include matters such as developing new products, increasing productive capacity by investing in a new factory, or taking over another business.

Tactical decisions are short-term decisions. They are taken on matters such as what course of action should be taken to achieve set targets, how many staff are needed, and how much stock is required. Tactical decisions are taken at a lower level than strategic decisions, normally at departmental management level.

Operational decisions are taken on matters concerning the day-to-day running of the business. They may be taken by departmental managers, or lower-level managers who have responsibility for decision-making in certain areas. For example, a decision to purchase additional raw materials to produce a special order for goods may be taken by a stock controller rather than the manager of the production department.

Decisions involve risks

All decisions in business involve some risk.

An entrepreneur who opens a fast food restaurant will lose the restaurant and everything he or she has put into it if the prices charged are too high so that consumers will not eat there.

A strategic decision by the directors of a mobile telephone company to increase production and open an expensive new factory with the latest technology will be a costly mistake if demand for mobile phones does not grow as expected.

A production manager who employs additional staff and increases the stock of raw materials in anticipation of a new contract will be left with the additional staffing and raw material costs if the contract is cancelled.

When taking decisions in business, therefore, it is important that the risks involved are identified, and as far as possible limited. The decision-making process should follow these stages:

1 Identify the problem – be clear about why the decision is necessary. The problem for the mobile phone company mentioned above, for example, is lack of capacity to produce sufficient mobile phones to meet anticipated future demand.

2 Decide what you want to achieve – establish the objectives and hoped-for outcomes of the decision. For the mobile phone company this is increased production capacity to meet the anticipated future demand.

Strategic decisions
long-term decisions about the future of a business

Tactical decisions
short-term to medium-term decisions about how to achieve the objectives of the business

Operational decisions
short-term decisions about the day-to-day operation of a business

3 Consider all possible alternatives – do not make the decision based on consideration of only one possible course of action. The mobile phone company could increase productivity by: opening a new factory; employing additional staff, perhaps on a temporary basis, who may work shifts in order to increase production at the existing factory, or by subcontracting production to other firms. The last two alternatives provide more flexibility. If the anticipated future demand does not happen, the additional staff can be laid off, or subcontracted work cancelled.

4 Take action – when all alternatives have been considered, decide which is the most appropriate. This should be based on factors such as: which alternative carries the least risk or greatest chance of success, flexibility, costs involved, time-scale and so on. If the mobile phone company decided to subcontract production to another firm, this would reduce the risk involved, while increasing flexibility. Such a course of action, however, would be more expensive in terms of the costs of production of each phone, at least in the long term, and should therefore only be considered as a short-term measure.

5 Monitor effectiveness – once the decision has been taken, regular checks should be made to ensure that the course of action is achieving its objectives. If it has been decided to subcontract production, the mobile phone company needs to ensure that levels of production and quality are being achieved, and that the phones are being produced on time.

6 If necessary, make changes – if the objectives are not being achieved, or circumstances alter, be prepared to respond by changing the decision. A wrong decision that is not put right can be very costly indeed. If the mobile phone company subcontracted production and the anticipated demand did not materialise, the company would be left with an additional stock of mobile phones. If it had bought a new factory and equipped it with the latest technology and employed staff to operate it, the company would be left with the additional stock of phones and also the costs of the factory, equipment and staff to pay.

You are a manager in Sun Chinese Foods Limited. Over the last year, there has been a significant decline in demand for Sun's current range of products. Research indicates that while there will always be a market for the foods produced by Sun, tastes in Chinese foods has changed. Your Finance Director has told you that the company must take some action now, as it cannot continue to support its production facilities and number of employees with current levels of sales. He said that there were three real alternatives: to reduce production facilities and staffing levels; to spend $1m on advertising in order to increase demand; or to spend $1m developing new products to replace those for which demand was declining.

1   Using the decision-making process described in the text, outline the steps you would go through in order to decide what action Sun Chinese Foods Limited should take. (>>)
2   Are there any other courses of action that Sun Chinese Foods Limited should consider? (>>)
3   What action do you think Sun Chinese Foods Limited should take? Justify your answer. (>>>)

Summary

- An entrepreneur brings together a business idea and the resources necessary to begin production.

- As a business grows it needs managers to control the day-to-day operations of specific functions and departments.

- Three types of decisions have to be taken in business: strategic decisions about the long-term future of the business, tactical decisions about achieving the targets of the business, and operational decisions about the day-to-day running of the business.

- All business decisions have an element of risk, which can be limited by identifying the problem, setting objectives, considering alternatives, monitoring outcomes, and taking further action if necessary.

17 *Letting people know*

In this unit you will learn about the different types of communication used in business.

Effective communications are essential to business. Without them employees would not know what to do, the owners and managers of the business would not know whether the business was achieving its targets or what goods and services its customers wanted, the business would not be able to obtain supplies, and the customers themselves would not know about or be able to purchase the goods and services that the business provides. Communications are used to pass on information, give instructions, check and receive feedback on activities, and to discuss matters of interest or concern.

Business in context

The following is a typical day for Mitesh Mistry, Director of Argon Department Store

08.30: Arrives at the store. Checks orders for new stock from department managers and discusses them with purchasing assistant.
09.10: Works on report concerning the introduction of new technology. Downloads some information from the Internet.
11.00: Meeting with other departmental managers about introducing a new range of ladies' fashions. After the meeting, Mitesh speaks to the manager of the Ladies' Wear Department on the telephone about the likely level of sales of the new range. 13.00: After lunch, Mitesh spends some time on the shop floor, talking individually to the staff. Returns to his office to write two letters: one to a customer, the other to a supplier regarding a batch of faulty refrigerators.
16.00: Two display assistants ask for help with setting up a display of new computers. He shows them how to create an attractive display. 17.30: Mitesh has some forms to complete for the Finance Department showing the cost of goods ordered from suppliers during the day. He says 'good night' to as many staff as possible before going home.

Are you receiving me?

We all communicate with others in everyday life. You must communicate with your teachers in order to get through your course successfully. And you will certainly need to communicate with the examiner at the end of the course, if you are going to pass! You also communicate regularly with your friends and classmates, those at home, shopkeepers, librarians, doctors and so on.

Communications as a system

People communicate with each other in many ways, for example by talking face to face or over the telephone, or by sending e-mails and letters. Yet all methods of communication consist of a sender, the message itself and a receiver. To be effective, the sender must choose a method of sending the message that the receiver will understand and act upon appropriately. There should also be some feedback from the receiver to the sender, so that the sender can check that the message has been received and understood.

Figure 17.1

Sender — Message — Receiver — Feedback

A model of communications

1   In groups, arrange to interview a manager in a local
    business about how they communicate at work. Find out:
    (a) who they communicate with and why;
    (b) what method of communication they use most often;
    (c) what method of communication they think is most
    effective, and why. (>>)
2   As a class, compare the ideas that you have obtained and
    evaluate the different methods of communication. (>>>)

Barriers to communication

Communications are only effective if the receiver actually receives and
understands the message the sender intends. Barriers to effective
communications can arise for several reasons. The most common
barriers are:

- Language – language can affect communications in several ways.
  Most obviously, if the person sending and the person receiving the
  communication are not both fluent in the language used for the
  communication, whether written or oral, misinterpretations of the
  communication may occur.
- Similar misinterpretations and lack of understanding can occur if
  the language used by the person sending the communication is too
  technical or academic for the person receiving it. Many businesses
  and functions within businesses have their own jargon, which is
  used fluently by those in the business or function, but not by those
  outside. Indeed, such jargon often uses words that have other
  meanings in everyday language.
- Atmosphere – the atmosphere in which a communication is made
  can affect its effectiveness. For example, if the atmosphere is
  strained, and the person receiving the communication is nervous,
  perhaps afraid for their job, they are likely to look for hidden
  meanings in a communication – and will often find one that is not
  intended.
- Physical barriers – physical barriers to effective communications
  come in many forms. Some affect the ability of a person to
  communicate normally, but physical barriers also include factors in
  the environment that may interfere with the communication.
  Physical barriers include noise in a factory where a meeting or
  conversation is taking place, interference on a telephone line and so
  on.

- Timing – the timing of a communication is frequently important to its effectiveness. Notification of a meeting or other event, for example, should be given in sufficient time for people to arrange to be present and to prepare for the event. If an organisation must make a decision about action to be taken on Friday, a report containing the results of research which the organisation needs to enable it to make that decision is of little use if it is not completed until the following Monday.

Internal and external communications

People in business have to communicate with others in the same business organisation and with people outside. Communications with people in the same business organisation are called **internal communications**; those with people outside the organisation are called **external communications**.

Internal communications
communications between people in the same organisation

External communications
communications with people outside the organisation

Figure 17.2

Language

Physical

Atmosphere

Timing

The main barriers to communication

Figure 17.3

| Internal communications |
| People within the business, such as: |
| colleagues |
| managers |
| subordinates |
| other employees |

| External communications |
| People outside the business, such as: |
| suppliers |
| customers |
| government bodies |
| other organisations |

Communications in business

How do people communicate?

Oral communications

Oral communications communications using speech

Whenever you speak to somebody, or somebody speaks to you, you are communicating orally. Oral means spoken, and speech is the most common method of communication. Most **oral communications** take place either face to face or over the telephone.

Although we talk to people every day, being able to communicate orally is a skill that must be learned and practised. Using the telephone is more difficult than speaking face to face, and many people are uncomfortable about making telephone calls, although this is becoming less so through the widespread use of mobile telephones.

One of the main problems with telephone communications is that when you talk to someone on the telephone, you cannot see their response or facial expressions. It is especially important, therefore, to listen carefully to what the other person is saying and the way they say it – their tone of voice and the words they use. However, technological developments such as videophones are overcoming this problem.

Oral communications are quick and direct between the person communicating the message and the person receiving it. They also offer an opportunity for discussion and for instant feedback to check that the content of the communication has been understood. The main problem with oral communications is that there is no permanent record.

While most oral communications are between individuals on a one-to-one basis, either face to face or at a distance (e.g. by telephone), there are times when it is appropriate for several people to communicate with each other at a meeting. Modern telephone conferencing facilities also mean that that it is possible for several people who may be at different locations to discuss matters over the telephone.

Written communications

The most common types of **written communications** are letters, written for external communications, and memos (short for memoranda), used for internal communications. Business letters and memos are more formal than the letters you write to your friends, although they serve the same basic purpose – to communicate a message.

Written
communications
communications in
writing

An advantage of written communications is that they are permanent records of the communication. They can be referred to later if required, and read at leisure, which means that they can contain information that may take longer to digest and understand, such as figures and technical data. Pictures, tables, graphs and diagrams can also be included in written communications.

Other forms of written communications are used in business for various purposes. These include: reports, financial documents, advertisements, notices, customer and product information. Written communications should be:

- accurate – everything should be checked, including all facts, spelling and grammar
- clear – the person writing the message must know what they want to say before they begin to write it down, and the person reading the document should be able to understand its content immediately
- simple – short words and sentences are more effective and have more impact than long ones
- complete – a document which leaves a message unfinished or leaves out a vital piece of information will fail in its purpose.

17.2 *Activity*

You work for Direct Communication Systems Ltd. Write a short report to a client, Alpha Management Services, explaining how business communications can be improved by the introduction of modern information technology. Address your report to Anfal Al-Gharibi, the Managing Director of Alpha. If you have access to a computer, you should word process your report using an appropriate computer package. (>>>)

Communications and information technology

Advances in information technology over recent years have led to radical new forms of communication. These include:

- fax machines – which transmit written text, graphics, charts and photographs quickly anywhere in the world
- mobile telephones – which can be carried by people at all times so that they can keep in touch with their place of work
- personal computers with modems and software for sending e-mail, which may consist of text, graphics and even sounds, depending on the capabilities of the sender's and receiver's computers.

Businesses with several computer terminals can link these to a network or intranet, so that each computer can exchange information with the others and even access information held on their hard drives. Employees' home computers may be networked to their employer's intranet so that they can communicate with, and access information stored on, computers at their workplace, using a modem and telephone line.

The Internet is a worldwide network of high-speed computers permanently linked to provide and exchange information. Anyone with a personal computer and a modem connected to a telephone line can connect to the Internet via an Internet Service Provider. The number of computers connected to the Internet is vast, and growing daily, as is the amount and variety of information that can be obtained. The Internet is an invaluable tool for businesses, which can use it for communications, marketing their products, providing customer and technical support, inviting customer feedback and so on.

Summary

- People in business communicate with each other (internal communications), and with people outside the business (external communications).
- Communications may be oral or written.
- Using information technology can improve the effectiveness of oral and written communications.

Revision questions

1 Explain the difference between an incorporated and an unincorporated business.

2 Compare a sole trader business with a partnership.

3 What are the advantages and disadvantages of a limited company going public?

4 What is meant by a joint venture, and what are the advantages to the businesses involved?

5 Explain what is meant by (a) fixed costs; (b) variable costs; (c) direct costs; (d) indirect costs.

Past examination questions

1 (a) In some countries governments give financial aid to help new businesses start up. Why might they do this? *(4 marks)*
  (b) Suggest reasons why new businesses often fail. *(4 marks)*

IGCSE Paper 1, May/June 2000

2 A business must keep financial records of its activities.
  (a) Identify the main items that would be found in the Balance Sheet of a business. *(4 marks)*
  (b) Explain the difference between a cash-flow forecast and a profit and loss account. *(4 marks)*

ICGSE Paper 1, May/June 2000

3 The table shows selective data for company Z. Use it to help you answer the questions that follow.

	1998	1999
Sales ($000s)	100	125
Profit ($000s)	20	30
Capital employed ($000s)	150	150

Table 11.1

  (a) Calculate two accounting ratios which would help you assess the performance of the business over the two years *(4 marks)*
  (b) Using your ratios from a), comment on the performance of company Z. *(4 marks)*

Adapted from IGCSE Paper 1, May/June 2000

Past examination questions (continued)

4   In some large organisations internal communication is not always effective.

    (a) What is meant by effective communication? *(2 marks)*

    (b) Why might communication problems occur? *(4 marks)*

    (c) Explain how any two problems of internal communication could be overcome. *(4 marks)*

IGCSE Paper 1, May/June 2000

5   What functions does the management of a business perform? *(4 marks)*

IGCSE Paper 1, November 2000

18 Why do people work?

In this unit you will find out about the different reasons people have for going to work.

Few people work just because they enjoy it. The majority work because they need to earn money to buy the things they need to live. However, as their basic needs for things that can be bought with money are met, people increasingly look for other factors to motivate them.

Business in context

Carmela Remigio is a computer operator at CTO Food Group plc, a major manufacturer of foodstuffs which are sold to the catering trade. Karen works at the head office, in the Accounts Department, where she is responsible for the recording of payments from customers and credit control.

'Yes, I do enjoy my work', she says. 'Of course, it gets a bit monotonous at times, just inputting customers' payments onto the computer and writing letters when accounts are overdue, but I get a chance to speak to some of the customers if I have a query, and I have a lot of contact with others in this company – especially depot managers. I get on quite well with them: they treat me as an equal. The money isn't wonderful, but it's average for this type of job and I don't think I could get better anywhere else. The people I work with are nice – we have some fun sometimes, but we don't let it interfere with our work. I think what I do is important. My boss says a sale is only a sale when you've got the money in, so no matter how much the company sells, if I don't make sure our customers pay up we won't make a profit. That makes me feel good, and I don't mind putting a bit extra in occasionally. After all, it's better to work for a boss who knows who you are and thinks you're doing a valuable job than one who thinks you're just a number on the payroll.'

Mohammed Al-Wazir is an electrician at a small, privately owned garage.

'I came to work here because I am interested in cars and I like working with them. It's not really what I expected, though. We're a small garage, and Mr Ahsan, the owner, does a lot of the work himself.

He says that it's his responsibility to make sure the customers are happy, or we'd all be out of a job. I suppose he's right really, but it means that I and the others – there are four of us – get the more boring jobs to do. It's as though he doesn't really trust us to do a good job, although I am a qualified motor engineer. There's no real chance of promotion here, it's too small a garage and the owner is the boss. The money's good, though, and I like working with the other lads. We do what the owner tells us, but that's all. I'm looking for another job where I have a chance of getting on.'

Questions

1 What types of work do Carmela and Mohammed do? (>)

2 What do you think Carmela's and Mohammed's job titles are? (>)

3 What do Camela and Mohammed like about their work? (>>)

4 What do they dislike about their work? (>>)

5 Suggest ways in which Carmela's and Mohammed's comments might help their employers to improve their employees' work. (>>>)

What do people get out of work?

People go to work for various reasons. Every individual has his or her own specific reasons for working, but the main reasons are:

- money – people need money in order to buy the things that they need and want
- security – having a job that is likely to last, perhaps with good prospects of promotion or career progression, regular increases in pay, and a pension at the end, gives people a feeling of security in that they can plan for the future
- job satisfaction – people get job satisfaction when they enjoy the work that they do, and feel that it is worthwhile or valuable to society

- a sense of self-importance – some people work because they get a sense of self-importance; this is often coupled with status symbols, like expensive cars and houses – the more expensive the car or house, the more important the person feels
- a sense of belonging – people tend to form groups with which they can identify: a workgroup gives a sense of belonging to an identifiable group, encouraging loyalty to the group and increasing an employee's motivation.

Maslow's hierarchy of needs

In 1935 Abraham Maslow identified five categories of human needs:

- physiological needs – needs for things we cannot survive without, such as food and water, shelter and warmth
- needs for things that give us safety and security
- social needs, such as belonging to a family or group
- needs for recognition and esteem
- needs for self-realisation or achieving personal goals.

Maslow believed that these needs provide the motivation that prompts people to act.

The five categories build upon each other so that a person will only strive to fulfil the higher level needs when those at the lower level have been met. Maslow showed this as a pyramid, or hierarchy of needs, as in Figure 18.1. For example a person who is dying of hunger will be motivated to obtain food before he worries about whether he has the respect of others.

18.1 Activity

Identify which of Maslow's needs the following help to satisfy: money; job satisfaction; challenge; promotion; training; social contact with colleagues; opportunities for career development. (>>)

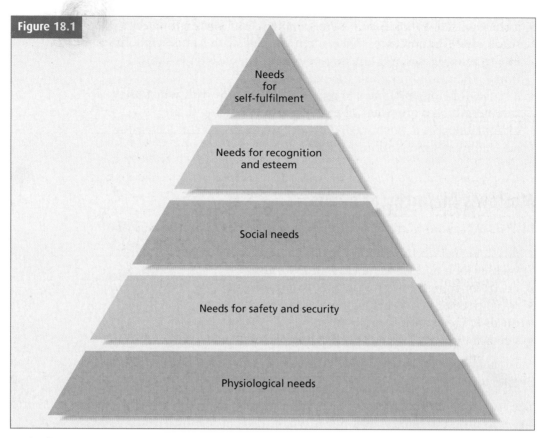

Figure 18.1

Maslow's hierarchy of needs

McGregor's Theory X and Theory Y

Douglas McGregor was a social scientist. In 1960, he put forward a
theory of motivation at work based on assumptions about how
employees felt they were treated. McGregor believed that most
organisations assume employees dislike work and avoid it if they can.
They must be persuaded to work with high wages, controlled with
strict supervision, and threatened with punishment to ensure they put
in the maximum amount of effort. He called this approach to
employees Theory X.

McGregor thought this was wrong. He suggested that people actually
enjoy working and will strive to meet targets and objectives to which
they are committed. Their commitment to work is increased when
they feel 'ownership' of their job or task through increased
responsibility and participation in decision-making. He called this
approach Theory Y.

Some of the ways Theory Y can be implemented are:

• delegating responsibility to employees

- consulting employees about their work and any problems or concerns they may have
- participation in decision-making.

Herzberg's hygiene motivator theory

In 1966, Frederick Herzberg put forward a theory based on research he had carried out by asking employees what really motivated them at work. He believed that basic rewards, such as pay, satisfactory working conditions, helpful organisational policies and administration, management and supervision, do not actually motivate employees. Obviously they are important – not many people would go to work if they did not get paid! If these basic rewards are inadequate employees will fight for them to be improved. Herzberg called these hygiene factors: necessary for people to work, but they do not actually motivate people to work harder.

Motivating factors are connected with the job itself. For example, people are motivated according to how interesting the job is and what opportunities it provides for achievement, recognition, promotion and added responsibility. According to Herzberg, businesses can improve employees' motivation by trying to improve the nature and content of the actual job.

Motivation in practice

Motivation is a complex issue. People are individuals, and the things that motivate them vary from individual to individual. While theories such as those of Maslow, McGregor and Herzberg can give general guidance on what motivates people, businesses must tailor their own motivation strategies to their workforce. To be effective, any motivation package must, however, include both financial and non-financial incentives.

Financial incentives

Financial incentives include:

Time work

Wages are normally paid weekly, and are based on a fixed hourly rate paid for the number of hours worked in a week. Salaries are paid monthly, and are calculated according to fixed annual rates, regardless of the number of hours actually worked.

Financial incentives motivating factors that include an element of money, or which have a monetary value

Productivity agreements

Employees normally expect to receive annual increases in their wage rates or salaries. Such increases are intended to cover increases in the cost of living, or inflation. However, some businesses may agree to increase wage and salary levels in return for an increase in the productivity of employees. These agreements are called productivity agreements. Productivity agreements are often negotiated between employers and trade unions acting on behalf of the employees affected.

Piece work

Employees are sometimes paid according to how many pieces, or units, of work they produce. This is only appropriate for workers who produce identifiable and uniform units. Piece work can encourage employees to work harder and produce more, but it can also lead to poorer quality work, if quality is sacrificed for speed.

Bonuses and commissions

In addition to a basic wage or salary, some employees are paid a bonus or commission. A bonus is an extra payment in recognition of an employee's contribution to the success of the business. Bonuses are usually paid weekly, monthly or annually, and may be linked to individual achievement or the overall profit of the business. Commissions are normally paid to sales executives and similar employees who have a responsibility for selling the company's product. The commission is calculated as a percentage of the value of sales made. The higher the level of sales an employee makes, the more commission he or she will receive.

Profit sharing

Some businesses operate profit-sharing schemes under which employees receive an additional six-monthly or annual payment based on the level of profits the business has made. If employees expect to share in the profits of the business, they will strive to increase those profits, and therefore the share they will receive.

Share-ownership

Similarly, an increasing number of companies are operating share-ownership schemes under which employees are able to purchase shares in the company at a preferential rate. Employees who purchase shares in the company they work for will be motivated by the knowledge that they are working for a business of which they are part owners.

Fringe benefits

Fringe benefits that businesses offer employees include company cars, health insurance, pension schemes, holidays and so on.

Non-financial incentives

Non-financial incentives include:

Job enrichment

Job enrichment is where an employee is given a wider range of tasks and encouraged to take part in the decision-making and consultation process. This may be accompanied by a reduction in supervision and greater involvement in setting targets. The employee gains a greater feeling of responsibility and of being valued by their employer.

Job rotation

Job rotation is where employees are able to do other jobs at different times. This gives them greater variety and interest in their work. Through job rotation employees may also gain new skills and opportunities for career development.

Job enlargement

Job enlargement is where employees are given a greater variety of tasks to perform in order to make the job more interesting and satisfying. For example, an employee who is able to see a process through to completion, rather than simply concentrating on one operation in the process, will gain a greater sense of achievement from their work.

Appraisal schemes

Staff appraisal schemes and interviews are important ways for businesses to find out the needs of their employees. A well-conducted appraisal interview can make an employee feel valued and motivated. There is a danger, however, that poor appraisal interviews can make employees feel threatened and demotivated.

Fringe benefits
additional incentives that an employer may offer to employees

---

Non-financial incentives
motivating factors that do not have a money value but are connected with the job or the well-being of the employee

---

Staff appraisal
a method of assessing the performance and achievements of individual employees through discussion and other means to encourage the employee to set and achieve performance and development targets over a period, normally of one year

---

An appraisal interview

18.2 *Activity*

1 Look at the job advertisements in a newspaper. (>)
2 Select two advertisements for senior positions with large companies. (>)
3 Make a list of the financial and non-financial incentives mentioned for each job. (>>)
4 Write notes explaining how the financial and non-financial incentives you have identified correspond to Maslow's hierarchy of needs, McGregor's Theory Y, or Herzberg's hygiene-motivator theory. (>>>)

Summary

- Employees work because they are motivated to do so.
- People are motivated by financial and non-financial factors.
- Businesses wanting to improve the output of their employees must consider a range of motivating factors.

19 Workgroups and managers

In this unit you will learn about groups in the workplace and the influence of leadership. You will also discover that individuals have different amounts of responsibility in different business organisations.

People are not solitary beings. They tend to come together in groups. This is as true in the workplace as it is in personal life. At work groups may be formally established by the organisation, or develop informally.

Business in context

Nangolo is a trainee electrician at Coldstore Appliances International, a major manufacturer of refrigerators and freezers for the commercial and domestic market throughout the world. He works at the domestic refrigerator factory. He has identified an informal group to which he belongs.

There are four other trainee electricians, although, as each works in a different department, they do not come into contact during the course of their work. They do, however, see each other once a week at college, where they study on one day in the week, and sometimes in the canteen at work. When they are together they talk about their jobs, the company and the world in general. Occasionally, if one of them has a problem, either connected with work or private life, the five of them will talk it through. Sometimes, too, one of them has heard something of interest and shares it with the others. Nangolo thinks that being part of the informal group helps him to have an identity in a large – and to him impersonal – organisation. 'If it wasn't for the others,' he says, 'I'd feel as if I was just a number – and not a very high number at that.'

Why form groups?

People form groups for a number of reasons. Being a member of a group often provides a person with an identity. Groups help to establish relationships and may satisfy a person's need for love and belonging (think of the family group). A group is also able to exert more influence than an individual. Individual members can use a group to further their own personal objectives.

While groups obviously help people to fulfil their needs, they are also an important part of the structure of organisations. Organisations need groups to undertake tasks and procedures that cannot be successfully undertaken by one person alone. Groups are made up of several people, each of whom has different skills and knowledge they can bring to the task. People in groups tend to feel a commitment to their group, so that everybody in the group pulls together to achieve the goals of the group. This increases commitment and motivation. It can also make groups easier to control and manage than a number of individuals each working on his or her own.

Why do people join groups?	
Security	The members of a group are likely to have a wider range of experience, skills and knowledge than one person and this means that a group is more likely to be able to overcome problems. There is safety in numbers.
Recognition	A member of an identifiable group gains recognition from inside and outside the group. He or she may also gain status from being in the group, as well as being able to rise to a position of importance within the group.
Friendship	Being a member of a group will bring the friendship and support of other group members.
Reinforcement	People tend to join groups with which they have a shared interest. Because members of the group are likely to share similar attitudes, this will reinforce the individual attitudes of group members.
Increased knowledge	Groups generally develop their own communications systems. This facilitates the spread of knowledge within the group and can provide a source of ideas and solution to problems.

Table 19.1

Formal and informal groups

Groups can be informal or formal. **Informal groups** often form naturally because of a shared interest or situation. They may be social in nature and meet more or less regularly or on a short-term one-off basis. A group leader usually arises spontaneously, perhaps because he or she is willing to organise the group's activities or act as a contact point for other group members, and so channel information. Examples of informal groups in the workplace are groups of workers who come together to follow a common interest, such as playing football, or even groups of people who meet in the works canteen for lunch and a chat.

Informal group
a group that develops spontaneously with objectives linked to the interests and objectives of the group's members

Formal workgroups are normally established by the business. They are more structured and 'official'. The leader of a formal workgroup is appointed by the business. Often the leader of a workgroup is a member of the management hierarchy and is part of the organisational structure. Examples of formal workgroups are functional departments and teams brought together to achieve a particular objective.

Formal workgroup
a workgroup that is established by the organisation with set objectives and a leader appointed by the organisation

The objectives of groups

Groups have two types of objectives: the objectives of the group, and the personal objectives of individual members.

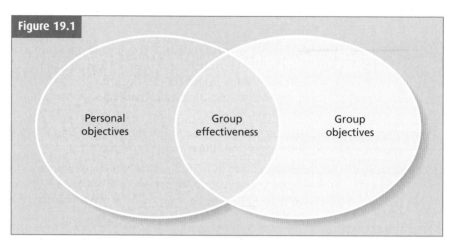

Personal and group objectives and group effectiveness

The objectives of the group are usually connected with the group's task. In a formal workgroup this is the purpose for which the group has been established, whether that task is preparing the company's accounts or designing and manufacturing a new fuel system for the space shuttle. The objectives of the group will include:

- ensuring effective communication to all group members of the task, how it is to be achieved, and their role or function in the group

- completing the task as quickly, efficiently and cost effectively as possible, to the required level of quality or accuracy.

The objectives of an informal group include:

- ensuring group members are informed about matters affecting them and their work

- supporting group members in their work.

The personal objectives of group members are objectives that members themselves want to achieve by being a member of the group. Personal objectives are often referred to as 'personal agendas'. Examples of personal objectives are:

- increased power by achieving a role of influence within the group

- being noticed by senior management by playing an active role within the group

- using the group to achieve career goals, such as promotion

- finding out what is happening in the wider organisation.

Sometimes these personal agendas may conflict with the objectives of the group or of the wider organisation of which the group is a part. When this happens, it is the role of the group leader to resolve the conflict and ensure that the overall group goals are met. In doing this he or she must also try to meet the needs of individual group members.

19.1 *Activity*

Fatima represents her department on the works committee. This is a group consisting of representatives of the workforce and senior management of the company. The purpose of the committee is to discuss the concerns of both workforce and management, to improve motivation and to find solutions to problems on either side. Indeed, the purpose behind having representatives of workforce and management on the same committee is to show that there are no sides, but that everybody works for the same company, and all contribute to its success.

Fatima, however, is ambitious for promotion. She sees being on the works committee as a way of mixing with and getting noticed by senior management. One thing Fatima doesn't want to do is to undermine her chances by seeming to be a troublemaker and making it sound as though her department has a lot of complaints. So she rarely raises her department's interests at meetings, preferring to support the views and suggestions of management.

1 What is the group Fatima is a member of? (>)
2 Is the group a formal or informal one? Explain your answer. (>)
3 What are the objectives of the group? (>>)
4 What are Fatima's objectives within the group? (>>)
5 Using Fatima as an example, show how personal and group objectives can conflict. (>>>)

How managers meet the needs of workers

Managers are leaders of formal groups. To get the best out of the people for whose work he or she is responsible, a manager must listen to their views, opinions and complaints, and be aware of the needs of those people no matter what the work demands of the organisation. Above all, in dealing with people a manager must be an effective leader, someone whom others are willing to follow, who will look after their interests and who can get them to work to the best of their ability for the good of the organisation.

Juan is the Production Manager of Handy Woollen Mills Limited. At 8.00 on Monday morning he is told that a new customer wants a special order completed by Wednesday. Juan will have to fit this in with other orders that are being worked on, but it is important for the company that this order is completed. At 8.30, three production workers telephone in to say they are sick and will not return to work until next week. Juan is under pressure from senior management to complete the order on time. He now has to obtain considerably increased production from the remaining workers in order to meet all orders.

1   How important is it for Juan in this situation to consider the motivation, morale and welfare of his workers? (>)
2   If you were Juan, what might you do in order to get the order completed on time? (>>>)

Managers as motivators

We saw in Unit 18 that motivating people is a complex matter. It depends not only on rewards such as pay and welfare, but on the job itself, the attitude of management and the way employees feel they are perceived and treated at work.

Motivators such as money and other rewards are not sufficient. Obviously an employee must be paid a fair wage for the work he or she does, and looks to the employer for other benefits, such as pensions, sick pay and other welfare schemes. But employees also look for other motivators, such as job interest, training and opportunities for career development.

Job enrichment, job enhancement and job rotation can all help to motivate employees by increasing interest and variety, widening the range of skills an employee has and therefore providing opportunities for improvement, and increasing the employee's involvement in decision-making and target setting.

Managers can also improve employee motivation and attitudes towards work by delegating responsibility, encouraging shared ownership of the results of good performance and allowing employees a larger degree of autonomy. Praise is also a powerful, yet often overlooked, motivator. Employees will feel valued both for the contribution they make to the success of the organisation, and as employees in their own right.

Meeting the needs of employees in these ways will strengthen their commitment. This will result in improved attitudes to work, including greater reliability, loyalty, good will and an eagerness to perform well and meet targets and objectives. The organisation will benefit from better quality and quantity of work, improved relationships between employees and between employees and management.

Managers as leaders

Managers are leaders of the groups they manage. The **leadership style** that a manager adopts (whether intentionally or not) affects the performance of the group and its members.

Theories of management and leadership have usually contrasted three styles:

- autocratic
- democratic
- laissez-faire

In an autocratic management style, the manager exercises power and authority without reference to others within the team or department. The autocratic manager plans and controls the activities of the group, dictating what is to be done and how. Autocratic management tends to be task-centred and more concerned with the satisfactory completion of the task than with the welfare or motivation of employees.

In a democratic management style, while power and authority still lie with the manager, the group as a whole makes decisions on future plans and activities. A democratic manager may even delegate some power and authority for making decisions and taking action to others in the group. Democratic management tends to be employee-centred, as it is based on the theory that employees are more motivated and work better when their views are listened to and considered, and they are involved in decision-making.

A manager who adopts a laissez-faire management style allows members of the team to carry out their functions and tasks without interference. Such a manager will remain in the background, co-ordinating and supporting the work of the team members, and representing them outside the team (for example at management meetings).

Leadership style
the management style adopted by the leader or manager of the group towards its members

Style	Advantages	Disadvantages
Autocratic	The leader feels in control of the situation; with an autocratic leader people know what to do and what to expect; enables fast decision-making.	People can feel oppressed and frustrated; too much dependence on leader; fear of punishments can lead to poor performance; allows no scope for individual contributions from team members.
Democratic	Develops a greater feeling of loyalty and commitment to the team from members who play a part in decision-making; leader feels more supported by team members; contributions are encouraged from team members with a wider range of skills and experience; participation can increase motivation.	Decision-making can be slow; leader may not agree with decision taken, but feel obliged to accept them; team members may not have sufficient knowledge or experience to make decisions; may give rise to conflict within the team.
Laissez-faire	Encourages loyalty and commitment to the team by giving members responsibility for their own actions; allows members to use their own skills to the full.	No real direction; poor co-ordination of team could lead to duplication of effort or working at cross-purposes; may give rise to conflict within the team.

Table 19.2 Advantages and disadvantages of different management styles

Modern theories of management and leadership suggest that there is no one 'right' style of management. The most effective style depends on the situation. In deciding which style of management to adopt in a given set of circumstances managers should consider:

- their own characteristics – are they naturally autocratic or democratic?
- the characteristics of the group members – do they respond better to being given clear instructions, or do they want to decide themselves how to approach a task?
- the characteristics of the task and its objectives – are they straightforward, or complex?
- the wider organisational environment – what part does the group's task play in the organisation.

A manager should try to adopt a style of management that takes into account these factors. In most situations it is necessary to adopt the style that is the 'best fit'. A manager must change factors that can be changed and respond to those that cannot.

Zuriada was recently appointed Credit Control Team Leader at APQ Enterprises. She is responsible for a team of three Assistant Credit Controllers. Zuriada's own inclination is towards a democratic style of leadership, whereby she consults with the other team members about problems and courses of action.

Soon after she was appointed, the Financial Director spoke to Zuriada, and explained that the Company was experiencing cash-flow problems – too many large customers were delaying payment of their accounts. This meant that the company was receiving too little cash, and unless the situation improved would have difficulty in paying its own bills. Zuriada and her team must find a way of reducing the amount of outstanding money that was due to the company.

Zuriada's first reaction was to discuss with the other members of her team how they could do this. As she considered, however, she realised that this course of action would not produce the good, innovative ideas she wanted. None of the other three in the team had been in Credit Control for more than three months. They did not have the experience – or wish – to come up with new ways of reducing the outstanding debt to the company.

So Zuriada took some statistics home that evening and sat working out a new Credit Control strategy. She abandoned the democratic style of management she preferred and the next morning called a team meeting, during which she detailed the new strategy and told team members exactly what he or she had to achieve and what was expected of them. It was easier to do than Zuriada had expected. The team members supported her fully, and were obviously happy to be told what to do.

1   How did Zuriada adapt her style of management to suit the situation? (>)
2   Do you think she was right to do this? (>>)
3   Were there any other courses that were open to her? (>>)
4   Explain how Zuriada's approach will affect the attitudes and work of other group members. (>>>)

Summary

- Groups form in the workplace to help in achieving the objectives of the organisation and the individual group members.
- Groups may be formal or informal.
- Managers influence the performance of groups through their style of leadership and approach to motivation.

20 *Working together*

In this unit you will learn about the importance of co-operation and negotiation in the workplace. You will also find out about the roles of organisations such as trades unions and employers' associations.

Disagreements between employers and employees can arise even where there is otherwise a good level of co-operation between them. Usually, such disputes can be resolved quickly through **negotiation**.

Occasionally, however, disagreements will become industrial disputes, affecting large numbers of employees in a business or an industry. Industrial disputes can lead to non-cooperation, which affects the performance and success of the business. This not only harms employers in the industry, but also customers, suppliers and the employees themselves. Most industrial disputes are resolved through **collective bargaining** between **trade unions**, representing the employees, and employers.

Negotiation
trying to resolve a dispute through discussion of the issues involved

Collective bargaining
where a trade union tries to negotiate with an employer on behalf of its members

Trade union
an association formed for the protection of the rights of employees in a particular trade or industry

Business in context

For several months now, there has been a growing problem because staff in the Administration Department of Office Paper Supplies Limited have become slow to return to their desks after the permitted ten-minute breaks during the mornings and afternoons. The management of Office Paper Supplies has pointed out that this is affecting the productivity and profits of the business.

Management has also pointed out to the staff that the breaks are only a concession. Unless staff keep within the permitted ten minutes, the breaks will be withdrawn and a drinks vending machine placed in the corridor, so that staff can get a drink to take back to their desks while they continue working.

Juanita Cortes, the trade union representative, has accused the company of being mean-minded. She says that as the breaks are obviously not long enough they should be extended rather than withdrawn.

At the moment, each side of the dispute is unwilling to give way to the other. Co-operation between employees and the company is poor. Profits for the year are likely to be low, which means that employees may not get a pay increase next year.

It's good to talk

If the disagreement is between a single employee or a small group of employees and their employer, perhaps because they feel they have been treated unfairly, the first step is to try to resolve the disagreement by direct negotiation between the employee or employees and the employer. This means talking to each other face to face in an atmosphere of mutual respect.

Most businesses have an established grievance procedure for employees to follow in the event of a disagreement. This procedure will identify the person employees should talk to in the first instance, and where the matter should then be taken if it is not resolved. For example, if an employee or group of employees are unhappy about something at work, they should in the first instance discuss it with their immediate supervisor or manager. If the matter cannot be sorted out in this way, then the employees should seek a discussion with management at a higher level.

Where do trade unions come in?

There are times, however, when a dispute or disagreement cannot be resolved through negotiation between employees and their employer. When this happens, if the employees are members of a trade union, they may ask their union to represent them.

A trade union, or labour union, is an organisation that has been established to represent the interests of its members. The members of a trade union are employees in different trades and industries who apply for membership and pay the membership fee. There are many different trade unions of varying sizes. Some are relatively small and represent employees in one particular trade. Other unions are large and cover many different trades. Trade unions provide four main services for their members.

The first service is negotiation with employers. Union representatives find out the views of members working in an organisation and discuss these views with the employer. In some cases such negotiations may involve employees of several employers in an industry. The purpose of negotiation is to resolve any differences of opinion between an employer and union members. This is also known as collective bargaining.

At plant level, shop stewards, who are elected by the employees themselves, represent the workforce. A convenor will arrange a meeting between representatives of the trade union and the employer. The representatives of the trade union will usually be expert negotiators from the head office of the union as well as shop stewards representing the employees. The Personnel or Human Resources Director, or other senior members of the personnel department, will carry out negotiations on behalf of the employer. Joint committees may be set up on particular issues, such as training. Collective bargaining is normally carried out at the highest level and involves members of the Board of Directors, including worker directors if appropriate.

Most negotiation involving trade unions is over pay, working hours, holidays, changes to working practices and protecting the rights of employees. In most countries where trade unions are permitted, employees are legally entitled to belong to a trade union without fear of discrimination from their employer. Some employers have formal agreements with trade unions to consult over matters of pay and conditions of work. An employer may sign an agreement with a single union or with several.

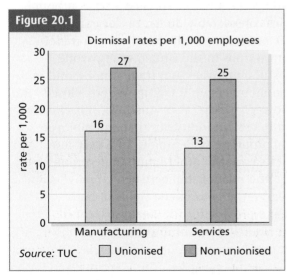

Figure 20.1

Dismissal rates per 1,000 employees

Source: TUC — Unionised — Non-unionised

Unions protect jobs

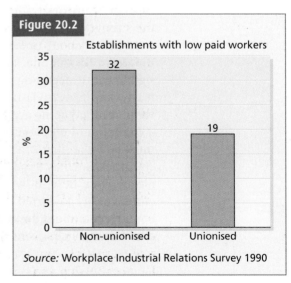

Figure 20.2

Establishments with low paid workers

Source: Workplace Industrial Relations Survey 1990

Unions fight low pay

Besides negotiation or collective bargaining on behalf of their members, trade unions also represent, or act on behalf of, a single employee who feels that he or she is being unfairly treated at work. The union will first try to resolve the matter by negotiation, but if this fails the matter may go to an industrial tribunal (see below). Unions will also represent their members in any court action, for example to get financial compensation for work-related injuries.

Thirdly, trade unions provide information for employees on issues such as maternity and paternity leave, holiday entitlement and training.

In addition, most unions provide other member services, such as running training courses on employment matters; legal assistance with personal matters; obtaining discounts on goods and services; and welfare benefits.

Industrial action
action taken by employees, normally at the suggestion of a trade union, that is intended to put pressure on an employer

Most disputes and disagreements are resolved by trade unions negotiating with employers, but where an agreement cannot be reached in this way, other courses of action are open to both parties to the disagreement. Sometimes a union may suggest **industrial action** intended to put pressure on the employer. Industrial action can consist of working to rule (only doing the basic work required by the contract of employment), overtime bans and even strike action – when employees refuse to do any work for their employer. A strike may be official, in other words approved and organised by the union, or unofficial, being arranged by the employees of an individual employer or even factory. Such industrial action can be very damaging to an employer, and also cause real hardship to the employees, who may only receive reduced wages or, in the case of strike action, no wages at all.

In some countries trade unions are powerful organisations, although the strength of unions varies considerably. In Brazil, for example, the strength of labour unions is increasing, while the power of trade unions in Britain and labour unions in the United states, while significant, is declining. Not all employees join trade unions, and in many countries trade union membership is falling. Where 'closed shop' arrangements are allowed to exist, as in Australia, it is effectively a condition of employment in certain industries that an employee must be a member of the appropriate trade union. In a very few countries, such as Saudi Arabia, on the other hand, trade unions are illegal. Even here, however, the relationship between employers and employees is governed by laws that address the rights of both employers and employees and provide for the establishment of alternative mechanisms for resolving labour disputes.

This should be carried out in small groups.

1   Select a trade union for your group to investigate. (>)
2   Find out all you can about the services and the benefits provided by your selected union to members. You may be able to obtain this information by visiting a local branch office (you will find the address in your local telephone directory), or by writing to the head office of the union. (>)
3   If trade unions are not permitted in your country, find out if there are any alternative organisations that exist to protect the interests of employees in the event of an industrial dispute. (>)
4   When you have obtained all the information, prepare a group presentation. Your presentation should cover the purpose of your selected union, the services it provides for its members, and any campaigns or action it is currently involved in. (>>>)
5   Make your presentation in front of your class as a whole and your teacher. (>>>)

Who represents the employers?

There are many **employer associations** that exist to advise and support employers in employment and other matters. Most industries and trades have their own associations to advise member businesses in their own industry or trade. These range from small associations representing businesses in a limited area, such as the Aberdeen Fish Curers and Merchants Association, to larger associations such as the Food and Drink Federation. Some employers associations, such as the Advertising Association and the Freight Transport Association, represent businesses in different industries.

Employer association
an association formed to represent the views of employers

The major employers' association in the UK is the Confederation of British Industry (CBI). Like other employer associations, the CBI provides advice to its members and negotiates with unions and the government over matters affecting its members. Similar organisations exist in many other countries. Chambers of commerce and industry, such as the Australian Chamber of Commerce and Industry, also provide an effective voice for employers.

What happens next?

In the UK, the Advisory, Conciliatory and Advisory Service (ACAS) has been established by the government to provide a wide range of services to employers and employees. In an industrial dispute, where negotiations have failed to result in an acceptable solution, either side can ask ACAS to arbitrate and help to reach an agreement. ACAS will look objectively at each side of the disagreement and suggest solutions, which might be acceptable to both. They may also suggest a 'cooling-off' period during which each side can stand back and reconsider its position. Many other countries have similar government-sponsored organisations. In Russia, where there are more than fifteen employees in a workforce, they elect a commission on labour disputes, which acts as an intermediary in settling conflicts between a worker or a union and the company. In other countries governments encourage bargaining councils, while in Saudi Arabia bodies to hear labour disputes must be established by law.

Where no solution that is acceptable to both sides of the dispute can be found, other courses of action can be taken. In most cases this involves taking action through civil or special labour or industrial courts.

20.2 *Activity*

1   Find out how industrial disputes are settled in your country. (>)
2   Arrange a visit to an industrial tribunal, or its equivalent in your own country. This can be arranged as a class visit or in smaller groups. You may need to arrange this through your teacher. (>>)
3   When you are at the industrial tribunal or its equivalent, watch the proceedings carefully. What is the tribunal about? Who is doing what? What is the outcome? (>>)
4   Discuss the tribunal, either as a class or in your group. How was it conducted? Did it seem fair? Were all parties satisfied with the outcome? Did you think the outcome was the right one? (>>>)
5   Write notes on your discussion. (>)

Summary

- Disputes between employees and employers are best settled through negotiation.
- In countries where trades or labour unions are permitted employees may be represented by their union in any dispute.
- In countries where trades or labour unions are not permitted the mechanism for settling industrial disputes is usually established by law.
- Employers' associations of businesses in the same or allied trade support and advise any of their members involved in disputes with their employees.
- governments are increasingly becoming involved in the area of industrial relations, providing services such as arbitration.

21 How do businesses find the right employees?

In this unit you will learn how businesses identify, attract and select suitable employees, and the different types and purposes of training offered by employers.

Nearly all businesses need to recruit staff at some time. New employees may be required to fill a vacancy caused by somebody leaving the business, or by the business expanding and needing to take on additional employees. Finding the right employees is a lengthy and often costly process. But the costs of getting it wrong are even greater.

Business in context

Trainee Recruitment Administrator

We are a successful and growing recruitment agency. You are hard working and honest, with excellent keyboard skills and a good knowledge of word processing. 'Usual' duties include answering phones, organising and confirming interviews, keeping records and filing, reading incoming CVs and applications.

If you feel you're right for the job, want to share in our success and have a lot to offer then phone 352-647-43229 soon. I await your call so I can tell you more!

Job descriptions

As mentioned on page 22, a job description is a written account of what a job involves and should be constructed before commencing the recruitment process. This will help in advertising for suitable applicants for the job, and help ensure that only those with the appropriate qualifications or skills will apply. A clear job description tells applicants about the job and helps them decide if it is the kind of job they should apply for. Job descriptions are normally prepared by the Human Resource Department in consultation with the manager of the department that has the vacancy.

A job description should include:

- the job title (for example Accounts Clerk; Computer Programmer)
- the duties involved (for example filing; word processing)
- responsibilities: staff the job holder will be in charge of
- accountability: the person who will be in charge of the job holder.

Most job descriptions also state the department in which the job holder will work, and give a description of the overall purpose or function of the job.

Person specifications

Person specification
an account of the type of person required to do the job

A **person specification** analyses the type of person required to do the job. Person specifications are not given to applicants, but are used by the business recruiting as a checklist of qualities to look for in applicants. Like job descriptions, person specifications are usually drawn up by the Human Resource Department in consultation with the manager of the department that has the vacancy.

A person specification includes the physical or mental abilities and personal skills required to do the job. For example, a person specification for a customer adviser in a building society may state that applicants should have a smart appearance, an aptitude for working with figures, an outgoing personality, and five IGCSEs.

Advertising the vacancy

Job advertisements should be based on the job description and person specification. Suitable applicants for a job may be found internally (within the business) or externally (outside the business). Some businesses have a policy of advertising all job vacancies internally, and this may be done in newsletters or notices distributed to all staff or placed on notice boards where all staff can read them.

Wherever the job is advertised, the style must attract the attention of suitable candidates, giving sufficient information about the job, the rewards and the employer. A job advertisement must also tell candidates how and where to apply – for example, whether to write a letter of application, or to phone or write for an application form. It should also give the closing or final date for making applications.

There are other methods of recruitment, besides advertising. There are many recruitment agencies that obtain candidates on behalf of the employer. Specialist agencies may look for suitable people for very senior positions. The agencies use their own knowledge of successful people, who are normally already employed but might consider moving. It is often useful for someone who is looking for a job to send their details to likely businesses. Such an approach can lead to contacts that may result in the offer of a position before it is advertised.

21.2 *Activity*

Design an advertisement for the job for which you wrote a job description in Activity 21.1. (>>)

Sending out details and application forms

If the vacancy has been effectively advertised, it should result in suitable applications and enquiries. Normally, the business will send out further details of the job to interested people. These will include details of the business and more information about the job, perhaps including the job description.

Some businesses require applications for employment to be made on their own standardised application forms. These ensure that all applicants give certain essential information about themselves, which can be compared with other applicants. The type of information asked for includes name, address, age, education and qualifications, and past employment history and experience. An alternative to an application form is to ask candidates to write a letter of application and send it with a curriculum vitae (CV). A CV should contain similar information to an application form, but a person may put more detailed information, for example about their achievements at school or in employment and any special qualities or skills they have.

Figure 21.1

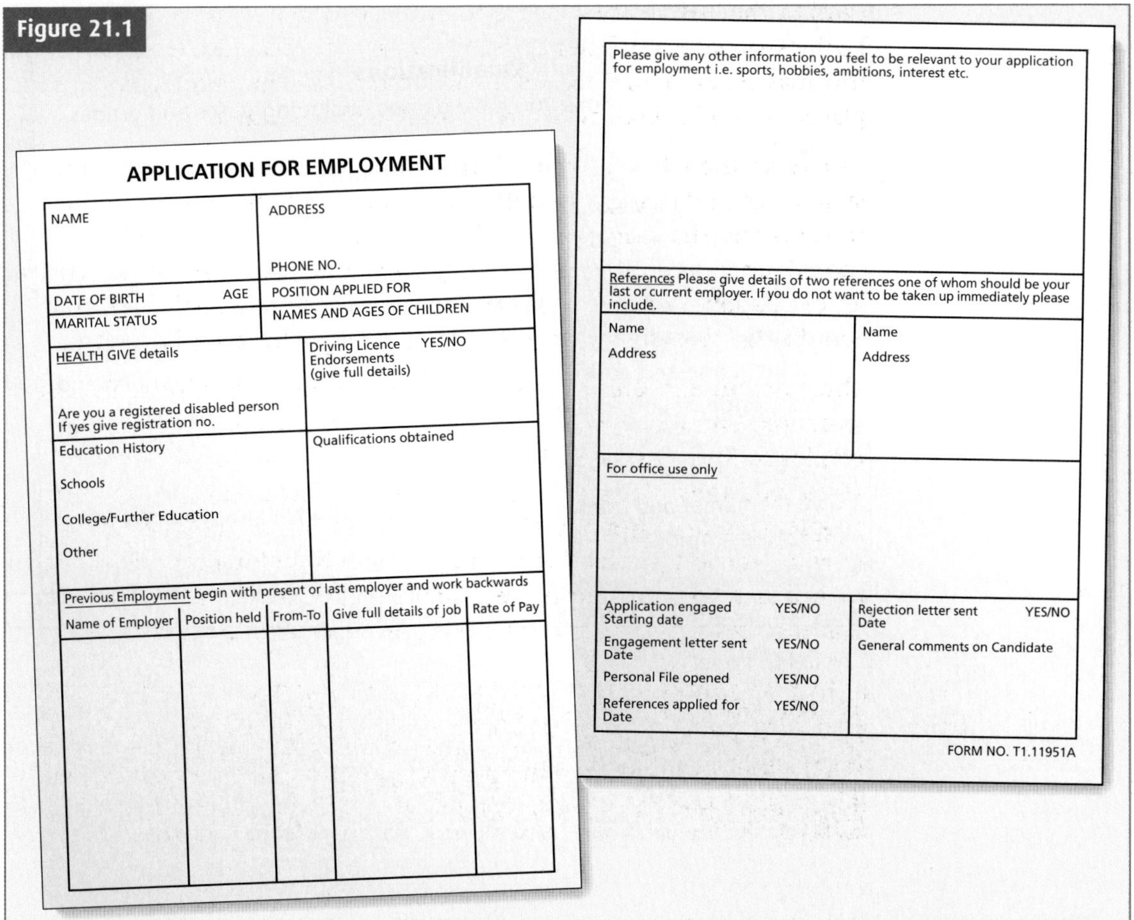

APPLICATION FOR EMPLOYMENT

NAME | ADDRESS | PHONE NO.
DATE OF BIRTH | AGE | POSITION APPLIED FOR
MARITAL STATUS | NAMES AND AGES OF CHILDREN
HEALTH GIVE details | Are you a registered disabled person If yes give registration no.
Driving Licence YES/NO Endorsements (give full details)
Education History | Schools | College/Further Education | Other
Qualifications obtained

Previous Employment begin with present or last employer and work backwards

Name of Employer	Position held	From-To	Give full details of job	Rate of Pay

Please give any other information you feel to be relevant to your application for employment i.e. sports, hobbies, ambitions, interest etc.

References Please give details of two references one of whom should be your last or current employer. If you do not want to be taken up immediately please include.

Name	Name
Address	Address

For office use only

Application engaged Starting date	YES/NO	Rejection letter sent Date	YES/NO
Engagement letter sent Date	YES/NO	General comments on Candidate	
Personal File opened	YES/NO		
References applied for Date	YES/NO		

FORM NO. T1.11951A

Job application form

Figure 21.2

<h2 style="text-align:center">Curriculum Vitae of</h2>

Full Name

<h2 style="text-align:center">Personal Details</h2>

Address
Telephone Number
Date of Birth
Marital Status
Number of Children } **may not be relevant!**

<h2 style="text-align:center">Education</h2>

Secondary School Attended: Dates   Subject Studied
Name
Address

College attended (if appropriate)
Name
Address

<h2 style="text-align:center">Qualifications</h2>

List here all qualifications you have gained, including dates and grades.

<h2 style="text-align:center">Other Achievements</h2>

Give full details here of all other achievements – both in school and outside. Include any positions of responsibility.

<h2 style="text-align:center">Work Experience</h2>

Give details here of any work experience you have had – paid or unpaid. Give the name and address of the employer, the dates you attended and a description of your duties.

<h2 style="text-align:center">References</h2>

Give the names and addresses of two people who will give you references for future employers.

A typical CV layout

Receiving applications

Applications will be received by the business up until the closing date. Then all applications will be sorted. Unsuitable applications will be rejected immediately, perhaps because the application form has been incorrectly filled in, or the application is untidy with poor spelling and grammar, or because the person applying does not have suitable experience or qualifications.

Once all unsuitable applications have been rejected, a **short list** of the best of the remaining candidates will be made. These will be called for interview in order that each short-listed candidate can be considered personally.

Short list
the result of selecting suitable candidates for interview out of all candidates applying for a job

Interviews

Interviews of short-listed candidates may be on a one-to-one basis, or candidates may be interviewed by a panel. Planning is an important part of interviewing. The interviewer must be clear about what the interview is intended to find out about the candidate. Questions designed to find out this information should be developed before the interview. Some interviews involve tests of the candidate's ability in specific areas. For example, an applicant for a job that involves using a computer may be set a simple task to perform on a computer during the interview. This enables the interviewer to assess the candidate's ability. Some businesses also use psychometric and other tests that measure mental ability.

Selecting the right candidate

Once all interviews have been carried out, those involved in the recruitment process will select the most appropriate candidate. This may be at a selection meeting where applicants are matched to the job description and job specification, having regard to their application and performance at interview and any test results. An offer of employment will then be made to the most suitable candidate. This will detail the rate of pay and any specific terms, including the date that the employment will commence. If the offer is accepted, the employer must issue the new employee with a written statement of terms of employment within a set period (usually 13 weeks) of the commencement of the employment.

Equal opportunities

All recruitment and selection procedures must be carried out in accordance with current equal opportunities legislation and good practice. In particular women performing comparable tasks to men should be treated equally, including receiving the same rates of pay; there should be no discrimination in any form on the basis of sex, marital status, race, religion or ethnic origin.

21.3 Activity

1 Obtain an advertisement for a job vacancy that might be suitable for you when you leave school or college. You may find appropriate advertisements in local newspapers, job centres or employment agencies. (>)
2 Give your views on how appropriate and useful the details in the advertisement are. (>>)
3 Create a job description for the vacancy. (>>)
4 Create a person description for the vacancy. (>>)
5 Produce a letter of application for the vacancy, together with a CV. (>>)
6 This role-play activity must be completed in pairs. Each member of the pair is to interview the other member for the job they have selected and written an application letter for. Prepare the interview well beforehand. In preparing for the interview, you should make use of the job advertisement, job specification and person specification. (>>>)
7 After the interviews, evaluate your performance as an interviewer and an interviewee. What went well? What could you improve on? Did you obtain sufficient information to enable you to decide whether to select the person you interviewed for the job? (>>>)

People need training

Training is an increasingly important aspect of human resources. Employees need to know how to do their jobs efficiently and how to adapt to changing circumstances, such as the introduction of new technology.

Employees who receive quality training feel valued and are able to contribute more to their employer. This benefits both employer and employee. Businesses that have an efficient, well-trained workforce are also more successful and competitive, both nationally and internationally.

Types of training

Induction training

Most new employees are given some form of **induction training** when they start with an employer. The purpose of induction training is to introduce new employees to the business and the staff and familiarise them with the procedures and practices of the organisation. The intention is to make new employees feel comfortable with their new employer and to give them confidence and competence in their working environment that will help them carry out their jobs. Induction training often includes background information, such as a tour of the premises to familiarise the employee with the layout and location of facilities (e.g. toilets and the canteen), and information on health and safety policies and procedures.

> **Induction training**
> training aimed at introducing new employees to the business and its procedures

21.4 *Activity*

Design an induction programme for new students at your school or college. Your programme should include: what should be covered; how the training should be carried out; who should carry out each part of the programme. Produce a leaflet that can be given to new students outlining the induction training programme. (>>)

On-the-job training

On-the-job training involves learning job-specific skills at the place of work. It is usually individual training for the employee designed to enable them to successfully carry out their duties, or perform specific tasks. Often an experienced worker works alongside the employee receiving the on-the-job training, showing him or her how the job is done.

> **On-the-job training**
> job-specific training undertaken while working

The main benefit of on-the-job training is that there is an immediate gain in productivity for the company. The trainee is able to carry out their job while they are developing the skills they need. However, the quality of on-the-job training depends on the abilities of the trainer. An experienced worker may have the skills to carry out the work, but may not have skills required for training others effectively.

A man undergoing on-the-job training

Off-the-job training

Off-the job training is training away from the actual place of work. For example, off-the-job training may take place in a college or outside training centre. Some large companies have their own training centres that they use for the off-the-job training of their own employees. Other training centres may be run by independent training organisations.

Off-the-job training is often used to develop more general skills and knowledge in a variety of situations, rather than the job-specific skills taught through on-the-job training. Specialist instructors can be used, increasing the effectiveness of off-the-job training. It is also easier for the company to identify and estimate the cost of off-the-job training, and to monitor the progress of trainees.

A group of people undergoing off-the-job training

21.5 *Activity*

You work for a local company that designs and installs computer systems, including software, for small and large businesses. Your Managing Director has asked you to advise him on training. Write a memo to him explaining the different types of training that might be undertaken and analysing their costs and benefits. (>>>)

Summary

- Most businesses follow a set process when recruiting new employees, involving a job description, person specification, advertising, short-listing candidates, interviewing and selecting.
- Recruitment must be carried out in accordance with equal opportunities and discrimination legislation.
- Many businesses develop training programmes including induction, on-the-job, and off-the-job training.

Revision questions

1 How can work satisfy people's needs?

2 Explain the difference between an informal and a formal group.

3 What benefits do businesses get from forming formal groups in the workplace?

4 How does being a member of a group benefit an employee?

5 State three types of training a business might undertake.

Past examination questions

1 State two benefits that an employee might get from joining a trade union. *(2 marks)*

IGCSE Paper 1, November 2000

2 (a) Explain the difference between paying employees a fixed weekly wage and a performance-related weekly wage *(4 marks)*

(b) Which of the two methods above would you recommend to the manager of a shop who wants to ensure that her sales staff are well motivated? Explain your answer. *(4 marks)*

(c) Why might the shop manager also offer non-financial rewards? *(2 marks)*

IGCSE Paper 1, May/June 2000

3 Identify and explain two payment systems for employees other than time basis. *(6 marks)*

IGCSE Paper 1, November 2000

4 (a) What do you understand by 'motivated employees'? *(4 marks)*

(b) How might a business improve the motivation of its employees other than by increasing pay levels? *(6 marks)*

IGCSE Paper 1, November 2000

5 What functions does the management of a business perform? *(4 marks)*

IGCSE Paper 1, November 2000

22 *What is marketing?*

> *In this unit you will learn about the market for products, and how businesses divide their market into segments. You will also find out about the function of marketing and marketing behaviour.*

People are the most important element in any business. Without people as customers, to buy their products, no business would survive for long. Businesses exist because they can make a profit by supplying the goods and services that people want – that is goods and services that are in demand. People who want to buy a particular product are said to be 'in the market' for that product. But what exactly do we mean when we talk about a market? A market consists of people who want goods and services, and businesses that supply them.

Business in context

What is a market?

Market
a system for bringing together sellers and purchasers of a product

A **market** consists of all the customers and potential customers for a product. It is usually expressed in terms of the total volume, or value of sales of the product by all suppliers in that market. Markets can be identified in various ways:

- markets for individual goods and services, such as the market for bicycles;
- consumer markets for goods and services bought by individual consumers, such as the markets for hairdressing or books;
- commercial markets for goods and services bought by businesses, such as the markets for tractors or business services;
- mass markets consisting of a large number of customers for a standard product;
- niche market consisting of a smaller number of customers for a more specialised product.

Sometimes a niche market is part of a larger mass market. For example, a car manufacturer that produces family saloons operates in a mass market where there is a vast number of customers worldwide. The manufacturer is therefore able to benefit from economies of scale (see Unit 30) by producing a standard car in large quantities. A car manufacturer specialising in armour-plated high security limousines, however, operates in a niche market consisting of a much smaller number of mainly business and government customers. This manufacturer will produce a smaller number of specialised vehicles that may have to be adapted to an individual customer's needs.

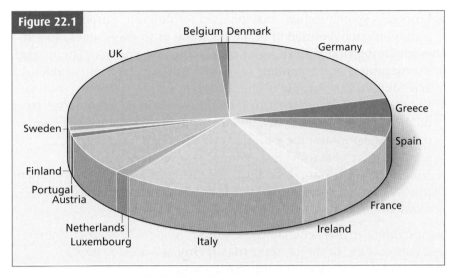

Figure 22.1

Belgium Denmark
Germany
UK
Greece
Sweden
Spain
Finland
Portugal
Austria
France
Netherlands
Luxembourg
Italy
Ireland

Regional market segments for hotels in the European Union 1998

Market segments

While the market for a particular good or service is the total number of customers and potential customers for that good or service, some businesses need to identify a particular section of a market – known as a **market segment** – that has specific product needs. Markets are frequently segmented according to different customer characteristics such as gender, age or income.

For example, the market for magazines is the total number of people who buy all magazines. The publisher of a magazine aimed at the teenagers, however, will want to know the size of that segment of the magazine market likely to buy their magazine – i.e. buyers of magazines for teenagers.

Other ways businesses divide their market into segments are by:

- Product – for example a bank's market consists of people who put their money into current accounts, investors and borrowers, but when considering launching a new investment account the bank will want to know the size of the segment of its market for that type of product.
- Region – different regions within countries and worldwide have different needs, cultures and preferences, which a business must take into consideration when trying to sell its products in that region. A manufacturer of fertilisers is likely to sell more to customers in rural areas than in cities.

> **Market segment**
> an identifiable section of a market that consists of customers with similar characteristics and specific product needs

- Purpose – some products may be used for different purposes: computers may be used at home for study or to play games, and at work for desktop publishing or accounting, for example. The market for computers and computer software can be divided into segments according to the purpose of the customer.
- Price – goods and services are sometimes sold at different prices to different types of customers: children often pay a reduced rate on public transport and for entrance into some leisure attractions; many hairdressers provide a reduced rate service for old age pensioners on certain days; business customers often pay more than private customers for services such as telephone, electricity and waste disposal.

Marketing
the procedures for ensuring that the products of a business meet the requirements of the market, and that the market is aware of them and wants to buy them

Segmenting the market enables businesses to identify their customers and concentrate, or target, their **marketing** activities at them. Businesses can also identify any market segments that are not fully exploited and may offer opportunities for increasing sales.

22.1 Activity

1 Identify the market segments that could be considered by (a) a holiday company; (b) a clothes manufacturer. (>)
2 Suggest ways in which a supermarket could make use of market segmentation. (>>>)

What is marketing?

Marketing is at the interface between customers and suppliers, enabling suppliers to find out about the present and future needs of their customers, produce a product that meets those needs, and tell customers about the product.

Business in context

Elizabeth Luboya and Thismanya Meinert have an instant printing business in Windhoek, Namibia. In addition to offering a full range of printing services to business and private customers, they sell a range of other goods, including computer software and business stationery. They hold their customers' records on their computer system and use the information to compile a sales and marketing database. This enables them to send regular mailings to customers. They can make special offers inform customers about new services they offer. They also use it to prompt customers who had purchased stationery goods to think about re-ordering when their supplies might be getting low.

Questions

1 What kind of business do Elizabeth and Thismanya run? (>)

2 How do they keep their customer records? (>)

3 What do they use their customer records for? (>)

4 Why do Elizabeth and Thismanya want to send regular mailings to their customers? (>>)

5 What are the disadvantages of relying on this method of marketing for Elizabeth and Thismanya? (>>)

Market orientation

Most businesses today have to take account of the needs of the market for their goods or services. They do this by carrying out market research (see Unit 23) to find out exactly what customers want, and then designing their product to meet this. This approach is called market orientation, and businesses that take this approach are called market oriented, or market led.

Product orientation

Businesses that take a product orientation approach are called product oriented, or product led. This approach was common throughout the 1960s and 1970s, when competition between businesses was far less than it is today. Because there was a smaller variety of products available, and the requirements of the market were less, businesses were able to produce a product in the more certain knowledge that they would find customers for it through careful marketing (see Unit 23).

22.2 Activity

It is sometimes said that customers buy benefits rather than products. By this it is meant that when a customer buys a product, he or she is interested in the benefit that he or she will get from the product rather than the product itself.

1 Is this true of all products? Think about mobile phones, trainers and computer software. (>>>)

2 Explain the implications of customers buying benefits rather than products for product-led and market-led companies. (>>>)

What is marketing behaviour?

Marketing is the process of finding out what customers want, developing a product that meets that want at a price that customers are willing to pay, telling prospective customers about the product, and ensuring the product is available for customers to buy when and where they expect.

There are several activities involved in marketing a product or service:
- market research, to find out what customers want
- research and development, to develop a product that meets the wants of customers
- pricing the product at a level that customers are willing to pay
- promotion, including advertising, to let customers know about the product and persuade them to buy
- distribution, so that the product is available to customers where and when they want it.

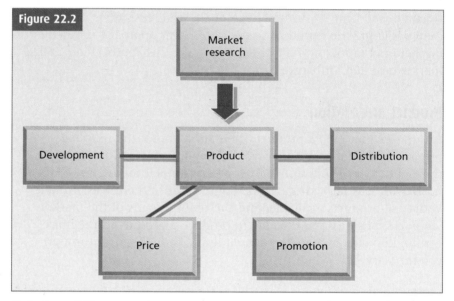

Figure 22.2

Marketing activities

Before a firm can begin the marketing process, however, it must identify its market.

Finding the market

In order to market its products effectively, a business must know its market, and what characteristics customers in that market have. This will enable the business to concentrate its marketing activities specifically on its own market.

Every person is different and has his or her own individual set of characteristics. This means that every customer of a business is different, too. Fortunately there are certain types of characteristic that are shared by all customers. Some of the main types of customer characteristic are age and age groups, gender, income levels, lifestyle and geographical location. A business may use these general characteristics to identify its own customers and potential customers.

In identifying the characteristics of their customers, some businesses find that their products are aimed at a large, or mass, market with a wide variety of customers, while other businesses find that their products are particularly suited to a small, or niche, market with very specific needs that are not met by the products of other businesses.

22.3 *Activity*

1   Select an advertisement from a magazine, newspaper or that you see on TV to analyse. (>)
2   Identify the product being advertised. (>)
3   Write a customer profile for the product. To do this you should analyse the type of customer that the advertisement is trying to attract in terms of characteristics such as age, gender, income and lifestyle. Include any other characteristics that you think may be significant. (>>>)

Bringing buyers and sellers together

The first stage in the process of marketing is identifying the market and what consumers want. Businesses planning to supply products to a market also, of course, need to predict future wants, as it is no use developing a product to meet current wants if they change by the time the product is ready to be sold! A business can find out about the needs and wants of the market by carrying out market research (see Unit 23).

Once the requirements of the market are known and understood, the second stage of marketing involves what is known as the **marketing mix**. This is explained in more detail in Unit 25. The marketing mix involves:

- developing a product to meet the needs of the market
- setting a price at which customers will buy the product
- promoting the product in such a way that customers are made aware of the product and want to buy it
- distributing it to ensure that it is available where customers expect to find it at the time they want to buy it.

Marketing mix
the particular combination of a product, its price, the way it is promoted, and how and where it is made available to customers

Summary

- A market is a system for bringing buyers and sellers together.
- Markets can be split into segments with different customer characteristics and product needs.
- Based upon knowledge of their market, businesses can identify the appropriate marketing mix, including what product to supply, the price to charge, how to promote the product and the most appropriate method of distributing it to customers.

23 *What do customers want?*

In this unit you will investigate market research and learn about its methods.

Market research provides a business with information concerning the needs and wants of its customers, the suitability of its existing or proposed products, and the strength of competition that the business faces. Armed with this information, the business can proceed with marketing its existing products, or developing new products, in the knowledge that those products will meet the requirements of customers and put the business in a strong competitive position.

Market research research undertaken by businesses to establish the needs of customers and ensure the products of the business meet those needs.

Business in context

Lucy Sibanda opened her own hairdressing salon. Soon afterwards she started offering beauty treatments, too. Six months into the business, she decided to analyse her list of customers and how much they had spent since she opened.

She learned that 80% of her sales came from just 20% of her customers. Further analysis showed that much of her profit came from the beauty treatments. These were enjoyed mainly by her more regular customers.

As part of her investigation Lucy asked her customers to complete a questionnaire about the kinds of services they would like. A significant number said they would be interested in massage treatments. This was not something she had thought about before. Encouraged by the response to her questionnaire she did some research on other salons in her neighbourhood and found that none of them offered massage treatments.

Since she was getting to know her customers better, she was able to revise her plans, focusing her attention on the customers who visited the salon most frequently, and on increasing the space and staff she devoted to massage treatments.

What do you want to know?

Most businesses operate in changing and competitive markets. Customers' needs and tastes change, affecting the demand for products and services, and the types of products and services that customers want. Market research to identify customers' changing needs is therefore essential. By maintaining up-to-date and accurate knowledge and awareness of trends in the market, businesses can take decisions responding to changes and staying competitive.

Businesses carry out market research in order to collect information from and about the market for their products - in other words about the needs and buying habits of their customers and potential customers. Based on the information obtained, decisions will be made on action to be taken in response to the findings of the market research. It is vitally important, therefore, that useful information is obtained from the right sources. The kinds of information businesses want to collect include:

- Who are their customers?
- What price are they prepared to pay for the product?
- How can the product be developed to be better suited to customers' needs?
- How does the product compare with that of competitors?
- What types of advertising are most effective?

How will you find out?

Secondary research research using information already available in the organisations existing records, or in published form

Deciding how you will get your information, selecting the sources and the way it is collected are as important as deciding what information is required. Some information may already be available within the business or else in the form of published reports and statistics. Other information will have to be collected.

Researching existing sources of information is called **secondary research**, because the information was originally gathered for another purpose. It is also called **desk research**, because much of it can be done at the researcher's desk. Research that a business carries out to collect totally new information is called **primary research**.

Desk research
research using secondary sources of information

Primary research
research conducted by the researcher to obtain original information

Secondary research

Secondary or desk research involves researching sources of information that is already available. This is often the cheapest, easiest and quickest type of market research.

Since the information was probably originally obtained for other purposes, it may not be as relevant or accurate as the researcher would like. If this is the case, the secondary research may have to be supported by primary research.

Sources for secondary research may be internal (within the business itself) or external (outside the business). Internal sources include: sales records and reports; accounts; customer records. External sources include: articles and reports in journals; research carried out and made available by trade associations; reports and statistics published by government departments; information published by other organisations such as the World Bank, Eurostat and the United Nations.

23.1 *Activity*

Read the section on desk research carefully and visit a library that has a reference section. Investigate the resources that are available, and make a list of sources of information that would be useful if you were conducting secondary research into:
(a) the market for computers in your country
(b) exporting washing machines to the United States and Japan. (>)

Primary research

Primary research is where new information is collected. An advantage of primary research is that the researcher knows where the information came from, the circumstances under which it was gathered, and any limitations or inadequacies in the research. Methods of primary research include: interviews; questionnaires; observation; experiments; consumer panels.

Interviews

Interviews may be conducted face to face or by telephone. The interviewer (the person conducting the interview) can ask the interviewee (the person being interviewed) a wide range of questions, and interviews are particularly useful for obtaining people's views and ideas.

One problem with interviews is that they are subject to bias from the interviewer who may misinterpret or misunderstand the interviewee's responses. A way of avoiding bias is to use a standard questionnaire for each interview.

Market researcher in the street

Questionnaires

Questionnaires are lists of questions designed to obtain the information required in a way that is not open to misinterpretation and can easily be analysed. They can be used with interviews conducted face to face or by telephone, or sent by post.

When designing a questionnaire, the following points should be clarified in advance:

- Who is the questionnaire aimed at (the target population - see random sampling, below)?
- What is the main information required?
- How is the information to be used?

The next step is to draft the key questions. Open questions are difficult to analyse because the range of responses may be so large. An example of an open question is 'How did you get to school today?' However, such questions may provide useful background information. Closed questions are questions that allow for only a limited number of responses. The above question may be rephrased as 'Did you go to school today?' A third type of question is the multiple-choice question, where respondents are asked to select an answer from a limited number of choices.

23.2 *Activity*

You are employed in the marketing department of The Mobile Phone Network, a retail chain selling mobile phones. The company wants to find out about its customers. Specifically, the company wants to know about the age groups of mobile phone users, who actually buys them, whether they are mainly for business or personal use and which model and price is most popular.

1 Design a questionnaire that will obtain the information you require. (>)
2 Interview or ask ten people to complete your questionnaire. (>>)

Random sampling

The information obtained will not be much use if the wrong people are interviewed or sent the questionnaire. Choosing the sample of people to interview or send the questionnaire to is therefore important. The most important requirement is that the sample should be representative of the whole. In other words, if you want to know how many people prefer the taste of Pepsi to Coke, while you obviously cannot ask everybody who ever drinks cola (the target population), the views of the people you do ask must be representative of the target population. The only way to ensure that a sample is representative is by ensuring that the people selected for interview or sending the questionnaire to are selected at random from the target population. This is called a random sample.

Observation

Sometimes it may be more appropriate to obtain information by observation rather than interview or questionnaire. A market researcher who wants to know whether customers for a product in a supermarket are more attracted by blue packaging than red may arrange for the product to be displayed on the supermarket shelf in both blue and red packaging. The researcher can then watch people's behaviour as they choose between the blue and red packaging.

Experiments

Sometimes, especially with new products, the best way to judge consumer reaction to the product is to test market the product. A limited number of units of the product are produced and put on the market in a specific area or areas. In this way the likely success of the product can be seen before incurring the expense of full production and marketing. Foodstuffs and confectionery such as breakfast cereals and chocolate bars are often market tested in this way.

Consumer panels

Occasionally businesses establish permanent panels of their customers to advise them on their products. Supermarkets often work with consumer panels that meet regularly to discuss the products, prices and service offered. Television companies establish panels of viewers to comment on the quality and content of programmes. Such panels are also used to estimate viewing figures.

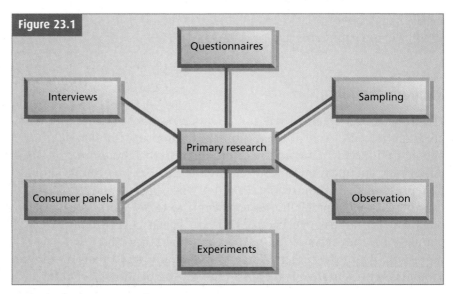

Methods of primary research

Within your class, form consumer panels in groups of four or five. Visit a local supermarket and in the role of consumers, consider the range and prices of goods, on offer. In your panels, discuss what you have seen. Does the supermarket sell a wide range of goods? Are there any other products you think that the supermarket should sell? Are the prices competitive? Do you feel that the supermarket is welcoming and the staff helpful? What do you feel is good about the supermarket? Is there anything that you think could be improved?

When you have completed your discussion, make notes on your conclusions and comments. Compare your findings with those of other groups in your class. (>>)

Research method	Advantages	Disadvantages
Interviews	May be conducted face to face or over the telephone. Interviewer can ask follow-up questions. Useful for obtaining in-depth or qualitative information.	May be expensive. Open to researcher bias. Unless standard questions are asked it is difficult to analyse or compare responses.
Questionnaires	Can be used in conjunction with interviews or sent through the post. Standard questions are easier to analyse and compare. Can avoid questioner bias. CHEAP	Postal questionnaires are cheap but may get low response.
Random sampling	A random sample is the best way of obtaining a sample representative of the population being surveyed.	Needs a sampling frame, which may be difficult to obtain. If the sample is too small, the survey may not be statistically representative.
Observation	Suitable for surveying people's behaviour.	Can be expensive. Open to bias if the observation is carried out at an unrepresentative time.
Experiments	Suitable for testing public opinion or trying out a new product.	Expensive. Experiment must be carried out on a sample representative of the target population.
Consumer panels	Can be used for obtaining valuable feedback on a business's products and customer service. Usually inexpensive. CHEAP	Panel may not be representative of all target consumers.

Handwritten note beside Questionnaires row: NO MISINTERPRETATION

Table 23.1 Table of advantages/disadvantages of different research methods

How will you present the information?

Much of the information obtained from market research will be in the form of numbers. On their own, lists of numbers are confusing and difficult to understand. The results of market research must be analysed carefully and presented clearly. Quantitative data (that is information that is in a numerical form) is easier to analyse than qualitative information. This should be borne in mind when designing questions for interviews or questionnaires. Quantitative data is usually easier to understand and has more impact if it is presented in the form of a graph or chart. We look at simple quantitative statistics and how to present them in the next unit.

Summary

- Businesses use market research to identify customers' needs, and maintain up-to-date and accurate knowledge about market trends.
- Market research involves researching the market, the product and the competition.
- Market researchers can carry out their own research to obtain new information appropriate to their own needs (primary research), or use information that is already available (secondary research).

24 *Handling information*

*In this unit you will learn how to analyse and present
information about markets and marketing behaviour.*

The information that a business obtains from market research is in the
form of raw data – usually numbers. These data are statistics that have
little meaning until they have been analysed, interpreted and
presented in a form in which they can be easily understood.

Business in context

A company sells its product to a number of different countries. The
Chief Executive asks for a report so that he can compare the value of
sales to each country last year. The Assistant Sales Manager reviews
last year's sales figures and writes the report. The following is an
extract from the report:

'During last year, we sold $2m of our product to Japan; $3m to
Germany; $5m to the USA; $1m to Namibia; $2m to Egypt; $4m to
Saudi Arabia and $1m to Brazil.'

Before sending the report to the Chief Executive, the Assistant Sales
Manager shows the report to the Sales Manager for her comments.
The following day she receives a memo with the report saying:

'Good report, but it might be better to give the sales figure in one of
the following ways':

Country	Sales
Japan	2
Germany	3
USA	5
Namibia	1
Egypt	2
Saudi Arabia	4
Brazil	1

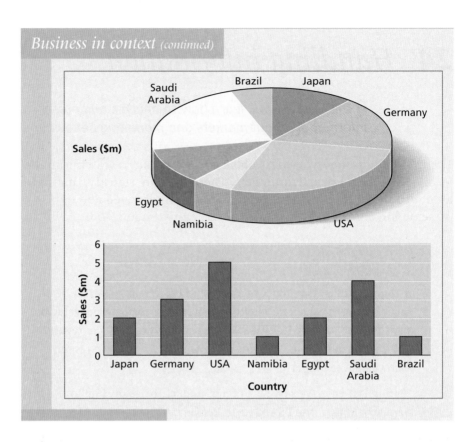

Questions

1 Why do you think the Sales Manager suggested presenting the figures in a different way? (>)

2 Which method of presenting the figures is easiest to read and understand? Why? (>>)

3 Which method has the most impact? (>>)

4 Which method would you use if the purpose is to be able to compare the level of sales to each country? Justify your answer. (>>)

5 What other ways of presenting the sales figures can you think of? (>>)

How do you go about analysing data?

Frequency distributions

When a survey is carried out, the researcher is faced with a large amount of data. This needs to be sorted out and analysed before it can be understood. Often, the first step in analysing statistics is to construct a **frequency distribution**. This is nothing more than a list showing the number of times each item occurs.

For example, Table 24.1 shows the results of a survey of customers telephoning the Customer Service Department of a manufacturer. Table 24.2 shows a frequency distribution constructed from Table 24.1.

Frequency distribution
a list of values giving the frequency of each value

1	3	4	6	4
5	3	6	4	5
1	4	5	7	3
4	3	7	5	7
5	4	3	6	6
4	5	5	3	8
3	7	4	5	3
5	6	3	4	6
5	2	4	5	4
2	3	5	6	5

Table 24.1 Number of customers telephoning the Customer Service Department over a period of fifty days

Number of customers	Frequency
1	2
2	2
3	10
4	11
5	13
6	7
7	4
8	1

Table 24.2

There are some points that can be drawn from the statistics in Table 24.2:

- the number of customers telephoning on any day varies between 1 and 8
- on most days between 3 and 6 people telephone the Customer Services Department
- there are no days on which nobody telephones.

Averages

Averages can be used to give some overall impression of all items in a set of statistics. There are two common types of average that can be used.

The arithmetic mean

The **arithmetic mean** is the most common average used. In fact most people use the term average when they mean the arithmetic mean.

Arithmetic mean
the sum of observations divided by the number of observations

The arithmetic mean is calculated by dividing the total of the data by the number of observations:

$$\text{Arithmetic mean} = \frac{\text{sum of data}}{\text{number of observations}}$$

The arithmetic mean of customers calling the Customer Service Department is therefore: total number of customers/number of days = 223/50 = 4.46. This is, of course, only a representation of the number of customers on each of the 50 days. It may be of use, for example, to the management of the company wanting to reduce the number of calls received per month.

The mode

Mode
the most frequently occurring value

Obviously, the Customer Service Department cannot have 4.46 customers telephoning them on any day. In this case it would be of more value to know the number of customers telephoning on most days. The **mode** is an average that measures the most frequently occurring value. It is easy to pick out the mode from a frequency distribution. It is simply the number with the greatest frequency. In Table 24.2 this can be seen to be 5. This means that on most days five customers telephone the Customer Service Department.

The mode is useful when the statistics being analysed concern units that cannot be divided. For example, a shoe shop wanting to know the most popular size might analyse its sales figures using the mode of sizes bought rather than the arithmetic mean.

Range

Range
the difference between the smallest value and the largest value

The **range** is the difference between the smallest value and the largest value in a distribution. When considering the statistics in the frequency distribution in Table 24.2, we saw that between 1 and 8 people telephoned the Customer Service Department on any particular day. The range is therefore 8 − 1 = 7.

24.1 Activity

The following statistics show the number of units of a product sold over a 25-day period.

7	9	9	11	8
10	8	8	9	9
9	9	10	7	10
8	11	8	9	5
12	9	9	9	6

1   Construct a frequency distribution from the statistics. (>)
2   Calculate the arithmetic mean of units sold. (>)
3   Calculate the mode of units sold. (>)
4   Explain what you think these figures mean. (>>>)

Presenting information

Many people are put off by a lot of numbers in a text and will skip them or not appreciate their full meaning when they are reading. It is usually better, therefore, to separate statistical information and display it as a **table** or a **chart**.

When constructing a table or a chart you should make it as attractive and user-friendly as possible, and include:

- a title
- the source of the data (if known)
- clear headings or a key

Tables

A table is probably the simplest way of presenting statistics. A table is a matrix of data in rows and columns. Rows and columns must have titles.

A table shows the relationship between two variables, such as changes in a company's profit over time, or changes in sales compared with spending on advertising. Table 24.3 shows the sales of cars by a garage between 1992 and 2001.

1992	1,000
1993	2,000
1994	3,000
1995	2,000
1996	2,000
1997	3,000
1998	4,000
1999	4,500
2000	4,000
2001	4,500

Table 24.3 Sales of cars by a garage 1991–2001

Instead of simply presenting numbers in a table, it is often preferable to give a visual representation of statistics in the form of a chart. By using a chart the statistics can be presented in a way that gives more impact to the significance of the statistics, making any trends or other important features stand out. Charts are also more attractive and easily understood than tables. The main types of charts you might use are line graphs, bar charts, pie charts and pictograms.

Line graphs

A graph shows the relationship between two variables in the form of a line. The dependent variable is the variable whose value depends on the value of the independent variable.

For example, in Table 24.3, the volume of sales is the dependent variable since its value depends on the year (time is always the independent variable).

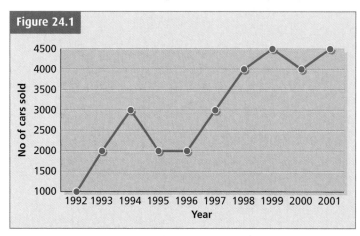

Figure 24.1

Sales of cars 1992–2001

A graph has an x-axis, or horizontal axis, which shows the independent variable, and a y-axis, or vertical axis, which shows the dependent variable. Each axis should be clearly marked with a scale of the variable. To draw a graph line, you should extend the value of each pair of variables from their axes and mark the point at which they intersect (meet). The graph line then connects each of these points. Figure 24.1 shows a graph constructed from the data in Table 24.3.

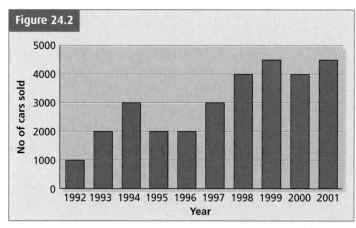

Figure 24.2

Sales of cars 1992–2001

Bar charts

In bar charts, the data are shown as bars or columns. The same axes are used as in line graphs. The length of the bar represents the value of the dependent variable. It is important to label each axis clearly and show the scale for the data. Bar charts clearly show the size of each item, and enable comparisons to be made by comparing the length of each bar on the chart. Figure 24.2 shows a bar chart constructed from Table 24.3.

Bars may be drawn vertically (as in Figure 24.2) or horizontally.

In January, the Pitt Banking Corporation introduced a new type of investment account. In the first year of operation, the following new investment accounts were opened.

Month	Number of new accounts
January	4,000
February	6,500
March	8,000
April	11,000
May	9,000
June	8,000
July	8,000
August	8,500
September	9,000
October	11,000
November	12,000
December	13,500

1   Construct a graph showing the number of accounts opened each month. (>)
2   Construct a bar chart showing the number of accounts opened each month. (>)
3   Compare your two charts with the table as methods of presenting statistics. (>>)

Pie charts

A pie chart shows the relative size of different parts of a whole. For example, a pie chart may be used to show the relative numbers of men and women in the population, or the proportion of different types of costs in a company's total expenditure. It is called a pie chart because it is circular (like a round pie) and each part is represented by a 'slice' of the pie.

To construct a pie chart accurately by hand, you need a protractor, but many computer spreadsheet programmes will construct a pie chart from a table for you. Working out the sizes of the parts, or sectors, yourself involves converting parts of the total into the equivalent degrees of a circle. For example, Table 24.4 shows the costs of a factory.

	$000s
Direct materials	140
Direct labour	60
Production overheads	180
Office costs	20
Total	400

Table 24.4 Factory costs

To convert the different parts into degrees of a circle:

1 Divide the number of degrees in a circle (360) by the total: this gives the number of degrees to each unit.

2 Multiply the number of units in each part by this figure.

3 Mark these on the circumference of the circle

4 Connect each point on the circumference with the centre of the circle.

For Table 24.4 the calculation is:

1 $\dfrac{360}{400} = 0.9$

2 (a) $0.9 \times 140 = 126$

  (b) $0.9 \times 60 = 54$

  (c) $0.9 \times 180 = 162$

  (d) $0.9 \times 20 = 18$

Figure 24.3 shows the completed pie chart.

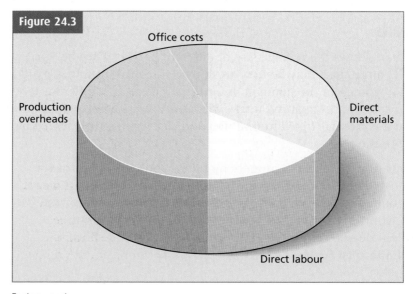

Figure 24.3

Factory costs

A fast food restaurant produces four different types of burger: cheese, vegetarian, chicken and fish. Last year they sold 18,000 cheese burgers, 6,000 vegetarian burgers, 27,000 chicken burgers, and 4,000 fish burgers. Construct a pie chart to illustrate the relative sales volumes of the different burgers. (>)

Pictograms

A pictogram is a statistical chart in which quantities or values are represented by pictures or symbols of the item. Thus a pictogram showing the volume of sales of cars would use images of cars to represent a specific volume of sales. The more images of cars used, therefore, the greater the total sales volume. For example, Figure 24.4 shows a pictogram constructed from the table of sales volumes in Table 24.3.

In Figure 24.4, each picture represents 1,000 car sales. Four cars therefore represent sales of 4,000 cars in a particular year. To represent a smaller quantity, a picture of part of the item can be drawn.

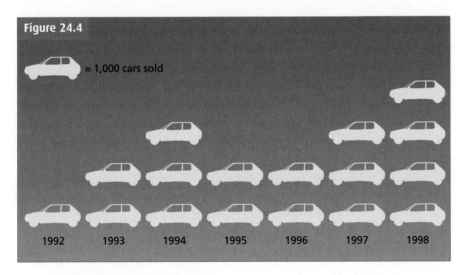

Figure 24.4

= 1,000 cars sold

1992   1993   1994   1995   1996   1997   1998

Car sales represented using a pictogram

When using pictures in a pictogram, the pictures should be clear and easily identifiable. The quantity that each picture represents must be given in a key to the chart (see Figure 24.4). Pictograms can be attractive and give impact to statistics. However, it is difficult to represent exact quantities using pictures (how would you represent 375 cars?).

Summary

- The raw data obtained from a market research or other survey has little meaning until it is analysed.
- Data may be analysed with the aid of a frequency distribution, an average or range.
- Displaying data and statistics in the form of a table, chart or graph gives them greater impact and makes them easier to understand.

25 What product?

In this unit you will investigate the first element of the marketing mix: product and its importance.

The product of a business is one of its most important features. Aspects of its product that a business must consider are the design of the product, including the effects and the rate of change of technology, how the product is packaged, and the stage of the product in its life cycle.

Business in context

SA Fruit Farms Ltd is a consortium of fruit farms established in 1990 to produce and market juices made from fruit grown on the farms. By the early 1990s the SA range of fruit drinks had become well established and sales were as high as $50 million per year. In fact, the company had to buy fruit from other farms in order to produce enough juice to meet demand.

In 1998, however, it became apparent that SA Fruit Farms was unable to maintain its success. Over the next two years, sales dropped to under $30 million. In view of the major investment that had gone into the company since 1990, the directors of SA Fruit Farms asked a marketing consultant to carry out an immediate review of the situation.

In her report, the marketing consultant found that (a) there was strong competition from other brands of fruit drinks; (b) growth in the market for fruit juices was for fruit drinks that were considered good for health and contributed towards a healthier lifestyle; (c) there was a trend towards buying fruit juices in 500 ml single serving plastic bottles, rather than the larger 1 or 1.5 litre bottles used by SA Fruit Farms.

SA Fruit Farms decided to try to revive sales by breaking into the health drink market. The company reduced the sugar content of their fruit juices and marketed them as health drinks that would also help replace lost energy during an exercise session or activity such as cycling or walking. To emphasise this, the new drinks were sold in 500 ml bottles fitted with valve caps that allow consumers to drink without removing the cap.

What product?

Deciding what product to supply is one of the most important decisions a business will make. Before a business begins to produce its goods or services it must check, through careful market research, that there is a market for them and that customers will be willing to buy them in sufficient quantities for the business to make a profit. In particular, the product that the business is planning to supply must:

- satisfy the wants or needs of customers – that is it must be a product that will give customers satisfaction so that they actually want to buy it
- be of an appropriate design – so that it both fulfils its function, and is appealing to customers, and is up to date in terms of design, materials and technology.

How is a product designed?

During the development stage, the design of the product will be decided upon, taking into consideration the requirements of consumers identified by market research. Some products are designed for a mass market, where a standard product is sold to a large number of customers. Other products are designed for a niche market, to meet the needs of a smaller number of customers with specific needs. The product's design includes objective features (those that are an essential part of the product, including specification and quality) and subjective features (those that fulfil the personal wants of consumers, such as taste and appearance). At this stage, consideration must also be given to the level of after-sales service that customers will require, including warranties and guarantees.

Product design is largely the responsibility of the Research and Development Department. In making decisions on the design of the product and methods of production, the Research and Development Department will take into consideration factors such as new technology and the rate of change in technology. New technology can enable a business to improve productivity and the quality of the product while lowering costs by, for example, reducing wastage.

The pictures above show two products.
1 Identify the objective features of each. (>>)
2 Identify their subjective features. (>>)
3 Using the pair of trainers and the pen as examples, explain in your own words the importance of products being given subjective as well as objective features. (>>>)

In **computer-aided manufacturing** (CAM) computers are used to control the machinery and equipment that makes the product. Computer-controlled machinery and equipment is extremely accurate and can automatically correct any faults, resetting machines if necessary to produce goods of a consistently high quality. In **computer-integrated manufacturing** (CIM) computers control an entire production line or even factory. Sometimes this involves the use of robots, as in modern car production lines.

Computers are also used in designing and testing products. Using **computer-aided design** (CAD), a product can be designed and displayed in three dimensions on a computer screen. The design can then be tested using computer programmes that will, for example, calculate the strength of the product made in alternative materials, showing how it will react to different stresses or in different situations. This is important when designing products such as aircraft, motorway bridges and buildings in earthquake zones. Designing and testing a product on a

Computer-aided manufacturing (CAM)
the manufacture of products using machinery and equipment that is controlled by computers

Computer-integrated manufacturing (CIM)
a production line that is controlled by computers

Computer-aided design (CAD)
designing products with the aid of computers

computer screen is cheaper than producing expensive prototypes (samples for test purposes), at least in the early stages of production.

The Finance, Production, and Marketing Departments will all make an input to the development process at this stage. This will ensure that the finished product can be made and sold at a price that will cover production and development costs, and generate a profit for the business.

Before the product goes into full production, the Production Department will make a prototype to check the production process. The Marketing Department may test market the product in a limited area to find out the response of consumers. If everything is satisfactory, the product will then go into full production.

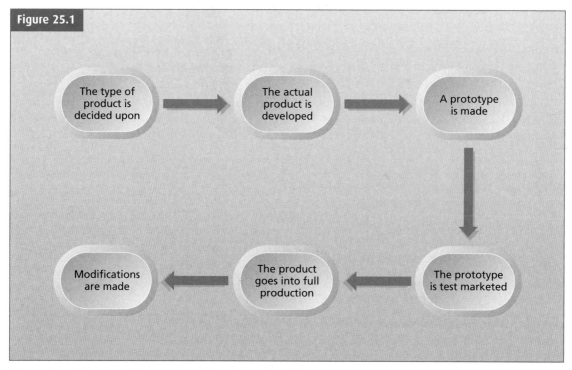

Figure 25.1

Stages of creating a product

Product differentiation

Product differentiation is where a product is given features that make it different from similar products. For example, there are many different mobile phones on the market, all with different features, although their purpose is the same. Where a feature makes a product stand out sufficiently to be a reason for customers to buy that product rather than others, it is called a unique selling point (USP). Giving a product a USP is an important element in marketing the product. A USP can be used to increase the market share of a product, or to launch it in a new market segment.

Branding

Many products are given a unique identity by giving it a special name. This is known as **branding**, and the name by which the product is known is its brand name. This enables customers to identify a particular brand when purchasing a product, and by giving their products a brand name, a business hopes that customers will ask for that particular brand by name rather than the similar products of its competitors.

Sometimes a product is identified by the name of the manufacturer, and this becomes the brand name of the product. Examples include Coca Cola (Cola drink), Kellogg's (breakfast cereals) and Kodak (cameras and photographic films). Other brand names may be made-up names. Examples are Big Mac (burgers produced by McDonald) and Pentium (computer processors produced by Intel).

The success of a brand name obviously depends on the quality of the product and how well it meets the requirements and expectations of customers. Moreover, quality and customer satisfaction must be uniformly maintained in each unit of production. Where these conditions are met, however, giving a successful product a brand name can encourage customer loyalty and repeat buying.

Branding
giving a product a unique name and identity

Packaging

Distinctive packaging gives a product an identity such that customers will look for a familiar package when buying a product. In some cases, for example household products such as washing powder, bleach and disinfectant, the style of packaging has become so much associated with the product, that customers look for a particular shape and colour of package when buying these products. Similar products in different packaging may well be at a disadvantage because they may be overlooked. It must not be forgotten, however, that packaging also serves practical purposes such as protecting the product, enabling it to be handled and used easily. The packaging of many products must carry specific instructions or notices about safety and ingredients that are required by law.

Product life cycle

Markets change and demand for some products increases while for others demand declines. There are various reasons why markets change: customers' tastes and fashions change; people change their lifestyles; new technology means that some products become out of date; demographic changes mean that the structure of the population and the needs of society change.

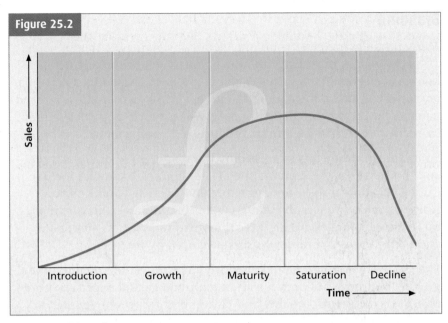

Figure 25.2

The product life cycle

Product life cycle (PLC)
the stages through which a product passes from launch to decline

All products go through a life cycle from first introduction to decline as the market conditions for the product change, although the **product life cycle** (PLC) of some products is longer than that of others. For most products the product life cycle consists of five phases (see Figure 25.2). Businesses must respond to changes in the markets for their products to maximise sales and profits: by stimulating demand through promotion, by becoming more competitive, by extending the life of a product or by developing new products as appropriate.

The introduction phase is when the new product is launched. Strong marketing stimulates demand for the product. Sales generate income but profits are low because the costs of developing and launching the product must be recovered.

Demand for the product continues to strengthen during the growth phase in response to continued marketing. Sales increase giving rise to higher profits as initial development costs are covered.

During the maturity phase demand for and sales of the product are at their highest. Costs of production are low due to economies of scale (see Unit X), so that profits are also high. Continued marketing is needed to maintain sales, but there is little further scope for increasing them.

When a product is successful similar products may be launched by other businesses. This may lead to saturation of the market – supply exceeding demand. Marketing activities such as new pricing and other policies including branding, product differentiation and special sales promotions may be needed to maintain market share.

Finally, a product will go into decline when demand falls. Consumers' tastes change and alternative products become available and fashionable. Policies aimed at extending the life of the product (extension policies), such as finding a new USP for the product, or selling it in a different market or market segment, may be introduced. If the product's life cannot be extended, however, the business that produces it may prefer to develop a new product to take its place.

Not all products go through each of these phases. Unsuccessful products for which there is little demand may be withdrawn from the market even before they reach the maturity stage.

25.2 *Activity*

Consider the following well-known products: Coca Cola; Microsoft Windows; Nike trainers; Sony Walkman.

1 At what stage is each product in its product life cycle? (>>)
2 Suggest how the product life cycle could be extended. (>>>)
3 Select one of the products listed to investigate. Alternatively you could investigate a product that you use or are interested in. How is the manufacturer of the product trying to keep the product in its growth stage? (>>>)

Summary

- The product of a business must be right for the market.
- Suitable products are designed through research and development.
- Differentiation encourages customers to choose one product rather than another, similar product.
- Products go through product life cycles, which have implications for the sales growth potential, methods of marketing that are appropriate, and current and future profits generated by the product.

26 How much is it?

In this unit you will learn about the importance and effects of the price of a product.

Pricing strategies approaches to setting the price of a product at a level that will achieve the marketing objectives of a business

People will only buy a product if they can afford it and they think it represents value for money. Getting the price right is therefore a significant factor in the success of a product. The price at which a product can be sold partially depends upon demand and supply. Other factors such as the amount and strength of competition in the market will also influence the price at which a product can be sold, however, and there are various **pricing strategies** that businesses can adopt in order to maximise the profit that is made.

Business in context

British Aerospace's Avro RJ100 aircraft is popular with many of the world's leading airlines for short-haul regional flights. It is popular because it is economical and offers features not found on similar aircraft. When considering a new aircraft, airlines consider both cost and the revenue they will receive.

For a journey of 400 nautical miles (741 km) the costs of operating the aircraft might be around $9,500. The RJ100 normally has 100 seats, although this can be tailored to the requirements of the individual airline. The average cost per seat is therefore $95. However, most airlines work on the basis of just 70% of seats occupied, and the total cost therefore has to be spread over 70 seats, rather than the full 100, giving a more realistic cost per seat of $135.71.

Air travel is very competitive, and price has a significant effect on demand for tickets. Fares vary considerably, with many cut-price offers being available, especially for standby or short-notice bookings. An average for the same 400 nautical mile trip, excluding items such as travel agents' commission and discounts, might be $160. The profit margin is therefore around $24.29 per seat, or $1,700.3 per flight of 400 nautical miles.

Demand, supply and price

The **law of demand** states that, generally, the lower the price of a product the more of that product people will buy. Reducing the price of a product, therefore, may encourage more sales. Similarly, raising the price can lead to lower sales.

Businesses that produce and sell products want to make a profit. If they can sell their product at a high price they will make more profit so, generally, the higher the price of the product the more they will be prepared to produce and sell. This is the **law of supply**.

The responsiveness of demand to changes in price varies for different products. The degree of responsiveness is called the price elasticity of demand. Knowing this can be important for a business. If costs of production increase, the business may react by putting up the price of its product to cover this increase and maintain profits. However, if putting the price up results in a significant drop in demand and loss of sales, the consequence could be even lower profits than maintaining prices and absorbing the increase in costs.

The price at which a product is sold is therefore influenced by the demand for and supply of the product. Generally, if supply is higher than demand, the price of the product will fall until both are equal, because people will not buy at the high price. If demand is higher than supply, the price will normally rise until both are equal, because businesses will raise the price of the product. The point at which demand for the product equals supply of the product at that price is called the equilibrium point, as shown in Figure 26.1.

Law of demand
the law of demand states that overall demand for a product rises as the price of the product falls, and decreases as its price increases

Law of supply
the law of supply states that the amount of a product businesses are prepared to supply increases as the price of the product increases

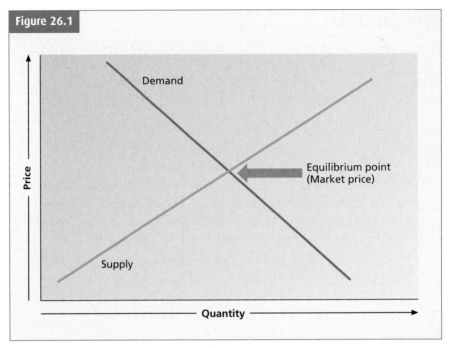

Figure 26.1

Supply and demand

26.1 *Activity*

On your way home from school or college, you see a poster for the opening of a new club tonight. You would like to go.

1 How much would you be prepared to pay for the evening at the new club? (>)
2 What is the opportunity cost of going to the club? (>>)
3 Explain how you decided on a price you would be prepared to pay. (>>>)

How do you know what price to charge?

There are various strategies that a business can use when setting a price for its product. Which strategy it chooses will depend on its marketing objectives regarding profit, competition and market share.

Competition pricing

Where the amount of competition in a market is strong, so that customers have a wide choice of suppliers to buy from, businesses must set the prices of their products competitively. In other words, the prices of products supplied by businesses in a competitive market must be closely similar or customers will simply go to the cheapest supplier. This is the nearest to the market price (see above).

Cost-plus pricing

Cost-plus pricing is the simplest form of pricing strategy and is aimed at ensuring that the business covers its costs and makes an acceptable profit. In cost-plus pricing, the business must establish the total cost of producing one unit of the product, including overheads (see Unit 11), and the required profit margin per unit. The total of these will then equal the selling price.

Penetration pricing

If the objective is to capture a share of the market, a business may decide on a penetration pricing strategy. In this strategy the business will set a low price - possibly even below the cost of production - in order to penetrate the market and attract customers by beating competitors' prices.

Price skimming

Price skimming is where the supplier of a new product is able to charge a high price in the knowledge that a significant number of customers will be prepared to pay the high price in order to buy the latest product. In this way, the supplier will obtain a high profit from these sales. Once sales at the high price begin to drop, the price can be reduced to a more competitive level.

Promotional pricing

Where the objective is to attract new customers or increase sales to existing customers, a business may adopt a strategy of promotional pricing. This is appropriate for new products that need to establish a position in the market, or existing products that need to increase demand. Promotional pricing is a short-term strategy of offering the product at a reduced price for a limited period, in the hope that the additional sales generated will be maintained when the price goes up again.

Consider the following four pricing strategies:

(a) A business launches a new mobile telephone with a built in camera that allows you to transmit moving pictures while you speak. It decides to put a high price on the product because it knows that businesses and customers who want to be the first to own one will be prepared to pay the price asked.

(b) The manufacturer of a new breakfast cereal knows that there are a lot of similar products on the market so prices the new cereal low in order to establish it

(c) The manufacturer of a perfume knows that customers are prepared to pay a high price for a quality product, so decides on the profit margin she wants and prices the product to include this.

(d) An insurance company having to pay out a large number of claims would like to quote high premiums, but knows that customers would take their business elsewhere.

1 What pricing strategy is the supplier using in each case? (>)
2 Comment on the effectiveness of each pricing strategy, and whether an alternative strategy might benefit the supplier and the customer. (>>>)

Summary

- The price of a product influences demand for that product.
- Businesses develop pricing strategies that support their marketing objectives.

27 How do businesses attract customers?

In this unit you will learn about the different ways of promoting products, including advertising and public relations.

It was sometimes said that if you produced a good enough product or service, people would beat a path to your door. This is no longer true, partly because it is no longer enough simply to produce a good product. Many other businesses also produce good products and hope that customers will beat a path to their doors too. Customers need a reason to come to you rather than a competitor.

Price may be one factor that persuades customers which product to buy. But even a very competitive price will not result in those hoped for customers if they are not aware of your business and its product. Customers need to be made aware in a way that interests them and persuades them to buy. This is the role of promotion.

Business in context

Anita Roddick is the founder of The Body Shop an international manufacturer and retailer of body and hair care products. In her autobiography, *Body and Soul* (Crown Publishing), she wrote:

'The big growth area [for the cosmetics industry] is not in fragrance or make-up, but in skin care products, yet the simple truth is that such products can do nothing more than cleanse, polish and protect the skin and hair. ... There are no magic potions, no miracle cures, no rejuvenating creams. That is all hype and lies.

The trouble with marketing is that consumers are hyped out. The din of advertising and promotion has grown so loud that they can no longer tell one pitch from another and they are becoming cynical about the whole process. They have heard too many lies. What we have tried to do is establish credibility by educating our customers, giving them intelligent information about where ingredients come from, how they are tested, and what they can be used for. It humanizes the company, making customers feel they are buying from people whose business practices they know and trust.'

How do businesses promote their products?

Methods of promotion can be above the line or below the line. Above the line promotion uses media outside the business, such as the press, television and radio. All other forms are considered below the line. Businesses will not simply use one method of promotion, however, but will use a combination of methods to achieve their aims.

Like every business activity, promotion costs money and time. Any promotional campaign therefore must be effective in increasing sales. Promotion should form part of an overall marketing plan (see Unit 25). It must be carefully monitored to check that increased income from sales exceeds the expenditure on promotion.

Reductions

Reducing the price of a product for a limited time can give a boost to sales and this boost may last longer than the period of the price reduction.

Special offers

A similar effect can be obtained by making special offers (for example, 'buy two get one free', or '25% extra free'). Like price reductions, special offers are normally available only for a limited time.

These products are being promoted by offering free gifts

Gifts

Some businesses try to attract more sales by offering free gifts with the product. These can range from toys in packets of cereals to free accessories with vacuum cleaners and electric drills. Giving free accessories with a product is intended to make the whole package more attractive to customers.

Free samples

When a new product is launched, the producer may distribute free samples, either nationally or in a local area. In this way prospective customers may be tempted to try a product that they would otherwise not have considered.

Point of sale

When a supermarket sets out stands giving away free samples of the wines and cheeses it sells, in the hope that customers may buy more of the product, the promotion is said to be at the point of sale – in other words, the product is being promoted where it is actually sold. Point-of-sale promotion can be any form of promotion that takes place where the product is sold, but the term is most frequently applied to special displays such as stands displaying Disney videos, or displays of brochures such as holiday brochures in a travel agent.

These products are being promoted by offering free samples

Competitions

Another way of attracting new customers to new and existing products is to run a competition associated with the product. A business must be careful to state that purchasing the product is not a condition of entry to, or winning the competition, however, as this is considered to be an unfair trade practice and in most countries is illegal.

Brochures and catalogues

Many businesses produce brochures and catalogues describing the business and the products it supplies. Some are glossy, expensively produced documents. A well-produced and attractively designed brochure will give the impression of a quality organisation that produces high quality products.

After sales

Continuing after-sales service is important in order to ensure that customers are happy with the product and with the response they receive in the event of any query or complaint. This includes providing guarantees against failure of the product within a certain time and honouring the guarantee promptly when necessary.

Advertising

Television

At peak viewing times, a television advertisement can reach millions of viewers. It is the form of advertising that is most easily remembered, as it consists of both sound and moving images. Television advertisements can be screened nationally or regionally. It is one of the most expensive forms of advertising, and in view of this and the fact that it also reaches a wide audience, television advertising is principally used for products with wide consumer appeal, such as cars and other consumer durables, food and household goods. Some local businesses, such as garages and stores, that have regional markets, however, may advertise on regional television.

Radio

Advertising on commercial radio can be targeted at more specific market segments, as programmes are aimed at smaller and more selective audiences. It is also cheaper, both in terms of producing the advertisement and the cost of 'air time'. Local organisations are often able to advertise on local radio networks.

Cinema

Cinema advertising uses both sounds and moving images in the same way as television advertising. However, cinema advertising reaches a far smaller local audience - the people who are in the cinema at the time the advertisement is shown. For this reason, local firms often use cinema advertising. Some national businesses, such as banks and car manufacturers, increase the size of the audience reached by advertising in cinemas throughout the country.

Newspapers and magazines

One of the advantages of advertising in newspapers and magazines is that the advertisement is relatively long lasting. In addition, the advertisement can be removed from the newspaper or magazine and kept for future reference. For this reason it is possible to include more – and more complex –information in a newspaper or magazine advertisement than in a television, radio or cinema advertisement. Advertising in newspapers and magazines is also cheaper, although prices vary, depending on the newspaper or magazine. An advertiser can **target** a specific market segment by advertising in local newspapers, national or local general interest magazines. Special interest and hobby magazines, or trade and professional magazines are even more specifically targeted, and are especially important for advertising industrial goods and services.

Target
in advertising terms, the audience at whom an advertisement is aimed

Posters

Posters may be huge images placed on large billboards in public places or smaller sheets advertising a local event such as a pop concert, fair or circus. They are mainly seen by people passing and must have enough impact to catch their attention. The message of a poster must be simple and conveyed at a glance. Posters are inexpensive, relatively long lasting, and may be seen several times by people passing, so reinforcing the message. It is impossible to target a poster, however, and most people take little notice of them as they pass. Similar to posters are electronic signboards, which use changing electric lights to give an illusion of movement, increasing the impact of the advertisement. Electronic signboards can also be seen at night, giving them a potentially wider audience.

Leaflets

Many businesses produce leaflets advertising their products. These may be available at the premises of the business, at shops and other retail outlets, in doctors' surgeries and other places. An increasing quantity of leaflets is distributed to people's homes through the post (so-called 'junk mail'). Leaflets are long lasting and may consist of a single sheet or small booklet. They often have an informative as well as persuasive purpose, and can be distributed generally or targeted at a specific market segment.

Internet

The Internet is being increasingly used as a medium for advertising. Many businesses have their own website, on which they can advertise and tell customers and potential customers about themselves and their products. You can even make purchases on-line, arranging for the goods you have ordered to be delivered to your home. Most Internet Service Providers, search engines and other Internet utilities also carry advertisements that help to pay for the services they provide.

27.1 *Activity*

The activities should be carried out in groups of four or five.
1 In your groups, decide on a product that you are going to promote. (>)
2 Plan a promotional campaign for your chosen product using whatever methods of promotion you think appropriate. (>>>)
3 Make rough drafts of any promotional material either by hand or using a computer package. (>>>)
4 Prepare a presentation of your promotional campaign in front of the other groups in your class and your teacher. In your presentation you should explain why you think your promotion will be successful. (>>>)

Public relations

Public relations (PR) promoting a business and its products through news stories and sponsorships

Many businesses use **public relations** (PR) to create a good image by issuing news stories of events concerning the business to the press, or by associating it with an event, such as a sporting event, or celebrity. Other opportunities for PR include in-house newspapers that are circulated among employees and customers; getting celebrities to endorse the business or product; and open days, when potential customers are invited into the organisation to see how it operates. Promotional materials are usually given out during the visit. Some larger companies have visitor centres, which are open to members of the general public.

You work in the public relations department of a major international oil company. The company has just signed an agreement with environmental groups in your country to create a nature reserve around one of its storage depots, so that wildlife can continue to live undisturbed in their natural habitat. Write an appropriate press release for the national newspapers. (>>>)

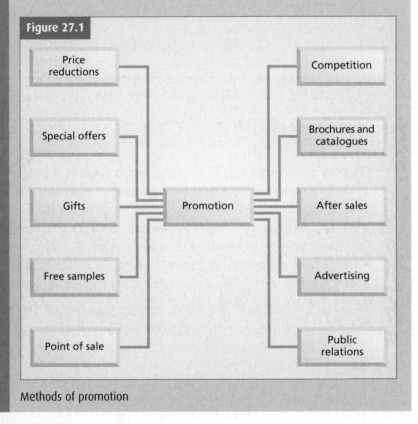

Figure 27.1

Price reductions

Special offers

Gifts

Free samples

Point of sale

Promotion

Competition

Brochures and catalogues

After sales

Advertising

Public relations

Methods of promotion

Summary

- All businesses must promote their products in order to attract customers.

  Most promotional campaigns make use of several methods of promotion.

- The effectiveness of an advertisement depends on its message, content and the medium through which it is carried.

- Public relations can be a valuable marketing tool for business.

28 How does the customer get the product?

In this unit you will learn about the importance of making a product available where customers expect to find it and the methods used by businesses to distribute their products to customers.

Channel of distribution
the system by which a product is distributed from the producer to the customer

The final element in the marketing mix is distribution. This involves both the actual place where a customer may obtain the goods he or she wants to purchase and the **channel of distribution** - the method or system used to get the goods from the producer to that place.

Business in context

Few people, when they are filling their cars or motorbikes at garages and service stations, are concerned about how the petrol got into the petrol pump. They expect to go to the garage or service station, put the nozzle into their tank, pull the trigger and the petrol will pour out. In fact, unless some of the petrol is spilt, the customer will probably not even see it. But the petrol only gets to the garage or service station, where customers go to buy it, and into the pump after a long journey.

The petrol is refined from raw oil at special refineries, perhaps close to the coast where the raw or crude oil is piped ashore. From here it is taken by tanker or pipeline to a storage depot. Major oil companies like Esso or Shell own many storage depots for storing bulk petrol in underground tanks throughout the country, and transport the petrol through their own pipelines or using their own tankers. Smaller companies may use storage depots owned by other companies.

The second stage of the petrol's journey is from the storage depots by road tanker to the customers of the oil companies – the individual garages and service stations. Here it is put into large underground tanks from where the petrol can be pumped into the petrol tanks of cars and motorbikes using forecourt petrol pumps. Some of the oil companies' major customers, however, are businesses that own large fleets of vehicles and use their own petrol storage facilities to fill up rather than going to a garage or service station. In these cases the petrol is transported directly from the oil storage depot to the customers' premises.

Questions

1 Where would you go to buy petrol? (>)

2 Is there anywhere else you might go to fill your car or motorbike? (>)

3 What would happen if people could not buy petrol where they expected to? (>>)

4 What is the difference between the sources of petrol for private motorists and owners of large fleets of vehicles with their own petrol storage facilities? (>>)

5 Explain the importance of customers being able to buy products where they expect to, using petrol to illustrate your explanation. (>>>)

Channels of distribution

Goods are distributed from the producer to customers through a channel of distribution. Traditionally, this involves a **wholesaler** and **retailer**, as shown in Figure 28.1. In this channel of distribution, the wholesaler buys goods in bulk from the producer and re-sells them in smaller quantities to a retailer. Splitting bulk purchases into smaller quantities in this way is called break-bulk.

Wholesaler
an intermediary that purchases goods in bulk from producers and re-sells them in smaller quantities to retailers

Retailer
an outlet for selling goods to consumers

Figure 28.1

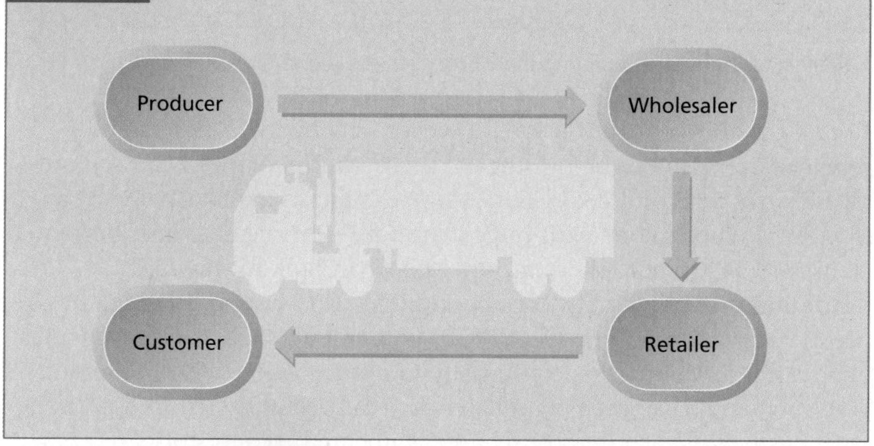

A traditional channel of distribution

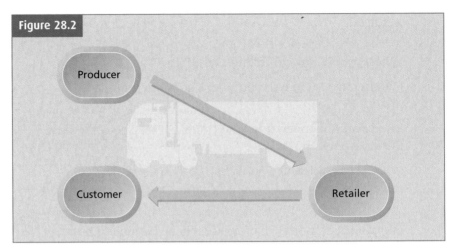

A channel of distribution omitting the wholesaler

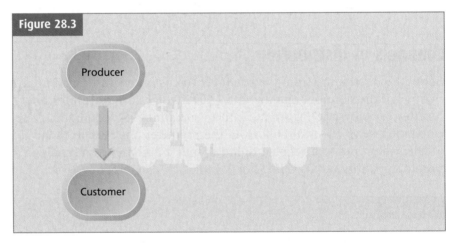

A channel of distribution omitting the wholesaler and the retailer

Not all channels of distribution, however, involve wholesalers and retailers. Sometimes one or other of these intermediaries is missed out (see Figures 28.2 and 28.3). For example, supermarkets usually act as their own wholesalers, with huge warehouses or regional distribution centres (RDC), where they can store goods in bulk for onward distribution to individual stores as required. This system is helped by the use of electronic point of sale (EPOS) equipment, such as electronic tills and scanners. Computers continually monitor stock levels of different goods: when a customer's purchases are scanned at the checkout, the level of stock of each item purchased is updated. When stocks reach a predetermined minimum level, a message is sent electronically to the regional distribution centre by electronic data interchange (EDI), and a fresh delivery of goods to the store is arranged automatically.

Other channels of distribution omit both the wholesaler and the retailer. For example, some businesses sell directly through advertisements in newspapers and magazines, inviting customers to order goods by completing and returning coupons. Other businesses sell through catalogues and mail order, where customers select the goods they want from a catalogue or an advertisement and order it by post, direct mail, telephone sales (telesales), or door-to-door salespeople. Sometimes agents may be used to sell goods and services, taking a commission on every sale they make. Estate agents, ticket agents, financial advisers and stockbrokers operate in this way. A developing method of obtaining goods is through e-commerce, where goods can be ordered direct from the producer or a wholesaler, such as Amazon, the on-line bookseller, and paid for via the Internet.

28.1 *Activity*

1. What do you think are the advantages of (a) small village grocery stores and (b) hypermarkets to (i) the retailers themselves, (ii) their customers? (>)
2. Compare buying books by mail order with a traditional bookstore as channels of distribution for books. (>>>)

Where can you get it?

Most consumer goods are purchased from retailers. There are many kinds of retailers:

- shops – such as newsagents and specialist shops
- department stores with separate departments for selling clothes, furniture and other types of goods
- chain stores, which have many branches spread throughout a country or even internationally
- discount stores, which sell a range of goods at cut prices; superstores and supermarkets, which are large stores selling a wide variety of groceries and household goods
- superstores and supermarkets, which are able to sell goods at low prices because they buy in bulk at discount and are able to pass the savings on to their customers
- specialist retailers, such as computer suppliers, photographic retailers and car showrooms, who can give expert advice about the products they sell, and are especially appropriate to high technology and similar products.

How does it get there?

Distribution involves transporting the goods from producer to wholesaler, retailer and possibly customer. Goods may be sent by road, rail, air or sea. The method chosen depends on the cost and speed of delivery required. Some goods require transporting in special vehicles or containers. For example, frozen food must be transported in refrigerated vehicles, while nuclear waste requires specially insulated containers.

28.2 Activity

Which method of transport would you use for the following? Give your reasons. (>)
(a) meat from Europe or New Zealand to your country
(b) bone marrow for transplant from America to your country
(c) bananas from the docks to the warehouse of a wholesaler.

Like everything else in business, transport costs money. If a business has its own fleet of delivery vehicles, it must pay for licences, road tax, fuel and drivers' wages. If the business does not use its own vehicles, it must pay for an outside haulier to deliver the goods on its behalf. It is also important that goods are delivered on time and when they are needed. This is particularly so with systems of just-in-time production and ordering. Efficient and cost-effective transport is vital. Computerised distribution and stock control systems can help suppliers and retailers to ensure this.

Summary

- Suppliers must ensure that their goods are available for customers to buy where and when they are required.
- Distributing goods so that they are available for customers involves distribution channels that include suppliers, wholesalers and retailers.
- Some items, such as frozen foods and petroleum products, require transporting in specialist vehicles.
- Transport must be cost effective and efficient.

29 Marketing planning and strategy

In this unit you will learn how businesses develop marketing strategies involving the marketing mix to influence consumer purchasing.

Like all business activity, marketing costs money and time. It is important, therefore, for the marketing activities of a business to be effective. This means that the revenue from increased sales resulting from the marketing activities should be higher than the cost involved. To ensure effective marketing, a business must have a clear strategy and develop a **marketing plan**.

> **Marketing plan**
> a plan of expenditure on future marketing activities

Business in context

Lerato and Nomsa both work for the same company, selling petrochemicals. In the course of their work they travel extensively. On one sales trip they might go to locations as different as Northern Europe, the Middle East, Africa and Russia, experiencing extremes of temperature within a few weeks.

The main problem is clothing. Travelling around so much, they like to travel with as little luggage as possible. But clothes suitable for hot, cold and temperate climates can take up a lot of room and be bulky and heavy.

Over the years, they tried many different types of travel clothing, and even made their own adaptations, but they always seemed to have to take too much clothing with them. Two years ago, they discovered a cloth that was lightweight and cool and yet kept them warm in colder climates. It was comfortable, waterproof, and resistant to creasing — so they did not have to press their clothes when they took them out of their cases. They made several samples of the cloth and sent them to the major clothing manufacturers.

The interest shown by the manufacturers was very encouraging. With some friends from work they set up a small workshop to produce the cloth in sufficient quantity to meet the hoped for demand.

Although the cloth was not expensive to make, Lerato thought that as it was new people would be prepared to pay a high price for clothes made from it. He thought they should charge manufacturers a high price, at least initially, until those who were prepared to pay the high price had purchased the product. Nomsa, however, thought that there was too much competition from other manufacturers, and if they were to gain a share of the market they should charge a low price, perhaps just covering their costs with a margin for profit.

The first supplies of the cloth were delivered to manufacturers in early spring, and clothes made from it were available in shops in time for summer. Lerato and Nomsa put full-page advertisements in all the main travel magazines explaining about the new cloth and the advantages it gave to clothes made from it.

Questions

1. What was special about the product Lerato and Nomsa developed? (>)

2. Who were their customers? (>)

3. How did Lerato and Nomsa use different elements of the marketing mix to influence consumer purchasing? (>)

4. Evaluate Lerato and Nomsa's marketing strategy. (>>>)

Mixing and matching strategy

Why plan?

Marketing objectives targets a business wants to achieve through its marketing activities

A marketing plan is a statement of the actions a business will take in order to achieve its **marketing objectives**. A well-constructed marketing plan will enable a business to become more competitive by:

- focusing and integrating marketing activities
- taking advantage of opportunities in the market
- protecting itself from threats in the market
- anticipating and keeping ahead of the changing needs of its customers
- identifying the right marketing mix of product, price, promotion and place.

The marketing planning process

An effective marketing plan asks three basic questions:

1 Where is the business now? This is answered by carrying out a full analysis of the business and the external and internal issues that may influence its performance.

2 What is the business aiming to achieve through its marketing activities? This requires the business to define its marketing objectives.

3 How will it get there? This relates the objectives of the business to specific marketing targets and the activities that will enable the business to achieve them.

Analysing the business

The first step in analysing the business is to look at the position of the business in the market place. This will identify reasons for current performance and the underlying causes of any trends. For example, increasing sales could be due to the activities of the business, an increase in general demand or the poor performance of a competitor. The analysis should cover external and internal issues.

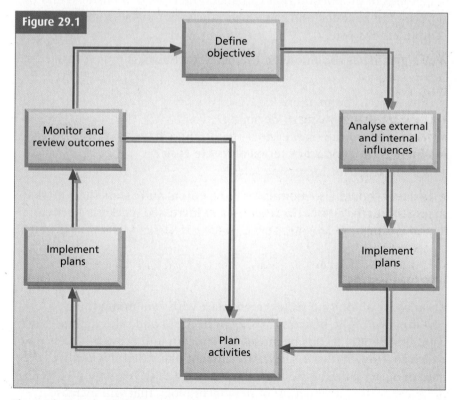

Figure 29.1

Define objectives

Analyse external and internal influences

Implement plans

Plan activities

Implement plans

Monitor and review outcomes

The marketing planning process

External issues

An analysis of external issues will look at the general business and economic climate in which the business operates, the conditions in the market, and the competition.

PEST analysis
a method of analysing
external influences
affecting a business

A good way of looking at the business and economic climate is to undertake a **PEST analysis**. PEST stands for Political, Economic, Social and Technological.

- Political: business activity is affected by government policy, such as constraints imposed by legislation on competition, advertising and consumer protection.
- Economic: economic factors affecting the future performance of a business include levels of, and trends in, consumer demand, which can be influenced by government policies on taxation and interest rates, levels of inflation and unemployment, exchange rates, which affect the prices of, and demand for, exports and imports, and the general stability of the economy.
- Social: social factors include demographic trends, which are trends in the make-up of society, such as changes in the age structure of the population, and lifestyle, such as a trend towards healthy living and organic foods. These factors affect people's buying habits.
- Technological: rapid developments in technology give rise to methods of production that can affect the costs of a business and the price of its product, and to new products that make existing products obsolete.

When looking at conditions in the market a business must consider factors such as:

- How large is the market?
- Is the market growing or declining?
- What share of the market does the business have?
- Where is the product in terms of its life cycle?
- Is there scope for increasing sales?

A business should also identify its competitors and assess their market shares, strengths and likely responses to increased marketing activity by the business.

Internal issues

An analysis of internal issues might start with examining the past performance of the business as shown in profit and sales figures. This will help identify trends or causes for concern and provide a basis on which to forecast future sales. Any current plans that might affect the marketing activities of the business, such as the development of new products or the introduction of new technology that will increase production capacity or reduce costs, must also be considered. Other internal issues include the reputation of the business and its standing in the market.

SWOT analysis

Once the external and internal issues affecting the business have been identified, the next step is to carry out a **SWOT analysis**. SWOT stands for Strengths, Weaknesses, Opportunities and Threats.

- Strengths are positive internal factors about the business and its products, such as a strong brand name or low costs of production.
- Weaknesses are negative internal factors such as a product that is in the decline stage of its life cycle, or low production capacity.
- Opportunities are external factors that have potential benefits for the business, for example the removal of trade restrictions between two countries may offer an opportunity for exporting to a new market.
- Threats are external factors that have the potential to harm the business, such as a decline in demand for a product due to a change in people's lifestyle.

Setting marketing objectives

Once a business has carried out a SWOT analysis, it is able to set its marketing objectives. These will identify what the business wants to achieve over the period covered by the marketing plan (normally a year).

Typical marketing objectives are:

- Market penetration – a typical objective of businesses that want to increase sales and market share. Going for market penetration is a relatively safe objective.
- Market development – this objective entails finding new markets or market segments for existing products. It is a step into the unknown, with customers and perhaps competitors who are unfamiliar, and therefore involves an element of risk.
- Product development – while it is important that all businesses continually develop their products to meet the changing needs of consumers, some types of businesses, such as drugs companies and high tech industries, must keep up with the latest developments in technology and science. Developing new products also involves risk as the product is unknown and may be entering an unfamiliar market.

Figure 29.2

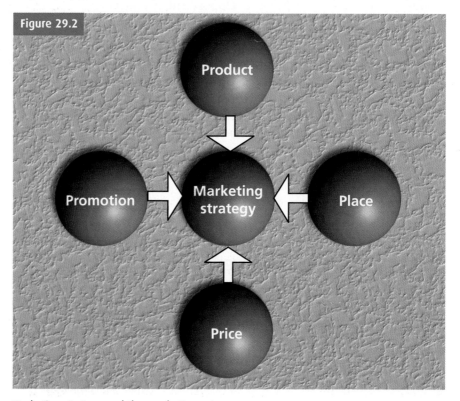

Marketing strategy and the marketing mix

Marketing planning

In developing its marketing plan, a business must consider the implications of each element within the marketing mix. However, it is the mix of all the elements that is important. It is no good getting one element right but failing with another. Together they make an integrated package, and the whole package must be attractive to customers, not just one part of it.

- Different types of product are marketed in different ways. The type of marketing methods used may depend on the market being targeted, or the product. For example, products intended for industrial markets may be marketed using methods of personal selling, where a sales executive contacts the buyer of a potential customer organisation. This may be backed up by brochures and direct mail. The product may also be advertised in the trade press. Products intended for industrial rather than consumer markets are often more expensive, and usually delivered to the customer by the supplier.

- Products intended for consumer markets may be advertised locally, nationally or internationally, depending on the size and location of the market. They may be available at a retailer, such as a shop, a specialist outlet, such as a car showroom owned by a car manufacturer, or by another method, such as mail order or via the Internet. Prices are often cheaper than in industrial markets, even for the same product, although some consumers may be prepared to pay high prices for the latest product, especially high tech products.

- Market penetration can be achieved by widening the appeal of the product to new customers who previously did not use it, attracting customers from competitors, or persuading existing customers to buy more. New customers may be attracted by increasing advertising; customers may be attracted from competitors by product differentiation or a pricing strategy such as penetration pricing.

- Market development can be pursued in two ways: repositioning a product in the existing market, perhaps by targeting a new market segment; and moving into new markets, possibly by selling in another country. Repositioning the product may involve giving the product a USP and promoting it in such a way as to appeal to the new customers. Moving into new markets may require product differentiation from other products already in that market. If the new market is in another region or country it may be necessary to create appropriate channels of distribution.

- Product development may be necessary if a product is reaching the decline stage in its life cycle (see page 207), to keep pace with new technology, or to respond to changing demand. It may involve changing an existing product to attract new and existing customers, or developing completely new products. Product development is normally accompanied by extensive advertising, public relations and other methods of promotion, such as special offers and free samples. Pricing strategies include price skimming, if the product is innovative, or penetration pricing for products facing strong competition.

Your company produces handmade bicycles. The bikes are expensive, but your company has always been able to charge high prices because there was little competition for them. Recently, however, top of the range production models of other manufacturers have presented a real threat to your company's share of the market. One model, the Challenger, is an all-round road bike and has been on the market for many years, and sales are beginning to decline. Another model, the Contender, is about to be launched in order to regain market share. It is an all-terrain mountain bike suitable for harder use than the Challenger, but light enough to be used in the city.

1 Construct a marketing plan for each model. (>>)

The marketing budget

As with every other form of business activity, marketing costs money, and the marketing plan should contain a budget so that the costs involved in carrying out the marketing plan can be calculated and actual expenditure and outcomes can be measured against budgeted expenditure and outcomes. There is little point in spending $1,000,000 on advertising that only results in an additional $500,000 in sales revenue. The marketing budget should form part of the master budget of the business.

Summary

- A marketing plan helps a business focus and integrate its marketing activities in the light of changing market conditions.
- The marketing planning process involves analysing the external and internal issues affecting the business.
- Carrying out a SWOT analysis identifies a business's Strengths, Weaknesses, Opportunities and Threats.
- The marketing plan should be based on marketing objectives and involve all elements of the marketing mix.

30 How are goods produced?

In this unit you will learn how businesses use resources to produce goods and services, the impact of technology and scale and how production can be made more efficient.

Businesses achieve their objectives by using resources to produce goods and services. The success of a business depends on the **efficiency** and cost-effectiveness with which the resources of the business are used.

Efficiency
the three main measures of efficiency of a business are productivity, average unit cost and quality

Business in context

Ahmed Hassan makes furniture. He is a sole trader and works on his own. While he has a small showroom where he displays a few examples of his work, most of his work comes from the personal recommendation of satisfied customers.

Ahmed only makes furniture to order. He prides himself on being a craftsman, and each piece he makes is unique. When he is commissioned to make something, for example a dining table and chairs, he first goes to see his customer. Ahmed finds out about their home and lifestyle, and sees where the furniture will go. Then, after discussing the customers' requirements, Ahmed sketches his ideas for the furniture before going off to carefully select the wood he will use.

Making the furniture is a slow process that Ahmed insists cannot be hurried. All his pieces are made by hand, and all bear some unique carved design for which he has become well known. There are no nails or pins in his work: all joints are carefully dovetailed and where necessary glued. This takes time, and customers must be patient. Most think it is worth it, however. In return for their patience — and money, for Ahmed's work is not cheap — they get a superb piece of furniture designed to fit the home and lifestyle of the customer.

'The proof is the amount of work I get,' Ahmed says proudly. 'I have enough orders to keep me busy to the end of next year. But, as I say to my customers, if you want something quickly and you are happy with the same sort of characterless thing as everybody else has, then go to a furniture shop or department store and buy something mass-produced. If you want something beautiful, unique and designed for you, then I will make it for you — but you will have to wait a little for it.'

What is production?

Production is the process of creating a product or service by combining the factors of production:

- Land – the natural and unrefined resources including farm and agricultural land, forestry land, quarries and mines, rivers, the sea and the atmosphere, and everything that lives and grows in or on them.
- Labour – the work that is performed by people.
- Capital – items not occurring naturally, including buildings such as offices, factories and hospitals, machinery and other equipment, materials and parts.
- Enterprise – the ability, enthusiasm, vision and skills to come up with a business idea and gather together the resources necessary to turn the idea into a successful business.

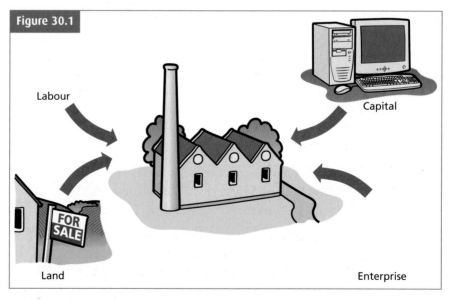

Figure 30.1

Labour

Capital

Land

Enterprise

The factors of production

Methods of production

Three methods of production are commonly found in business. The choice of method largely depends on the type of product.

Job production

With **job production**, goods or services are produced individually to customer orders. Job production is flexible, adapting to customers' individual requirements. High-quality products are often produced using job-production methods. However, job production is expensive, requiring skilled staff and specialised equipment that needs re-setting for each new job. Materials may have to be purchased specially in small quantities for each order.

Because each job is different, management of production can be difficult and complex. Employees are often highly motivated, however, since the different jobs bring variety and they are often able to see the product through from start to finish.

Job production
producing customers' special orders of goods and services

Batch production

In **batch production** a batch of items is produced at one time. The batch normally goes through each stage of the production process together before moving on to the next stage. When a batch has passed through one stage, the machinery will be re-set if necessary, ready for the next batch of items.

The main advantage of batch production is that by producing in larger quantities, unit costs are lower. Materials may be bought in larger quantities. While a business can produce different items by batch-production methods, there is no variety in each batch. Batch production allows machinery to produce goods to the same specification, but the machines may have to be re-set between batches, causing delays in production and loss of output. Work can become more repetitive.

Batch production
producing batches of different types of goods in turn

Mass or flow production

Mass, or flow, production is used where a single product passes continuously through the production process. The product might be discrete items such as screws, or continuous-flow products like coal or oil. Sometimes an entire production line is automated and controlled by just one person. Automated production processes are expensive but the cost can be spread over a large volume of units. Labour costs are low, and materials can be purchased in large quantities, so that the business can benefit from greater discounts. Mass production therefore has the lowest unit cost of production.

Mass (flow) production
the continuous production of one type of good, either as discrete units (mass) or unbroken (flow)

However, mass production is very inflexible. Automated production lines are difficult and expensive to adapt if changes to the product are needed. Mass production is most suited to products for which there is a large and stable market.

30.1 *Activity*

Look carefully at the pictures. Which type of production is involved in each case? (>)

Four different types of production

	Type of production		
	Job	Batch	Flow
Size of order	Small	Medium	Continuous
Volume of output	Low	Medium	High/Continuous
Product range	Varied	Few products	Single product
Flexibility of production process	High	Some	Low
Make to order or for stock	Order	Either	Stock

Table 30.1 Characteristics of the different types of production

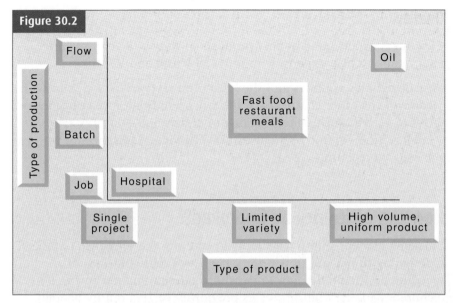

Figure 30.2

Type of production

- Flow
- Batch
- Job

Oil

Fast food restaurant meals

Hospital

Single project — Limited variety — High volume, uniform product

Type of product

The relationship between production and product

Productivity

Productivity is usually measured in terms of output per unit of labour or per item of machinery. So, for example, if a factory employing 100 workers produces 1,000,000 screws a year, the productivity per employee is 1,000,000/100 = 10,000 screws. This can be compared with expected standards, productivity in other businesses in the same industry, or productivity in previous years. Productivity measures can also highlight resources that are being under-used.

However, measures of productivity are only a guide: some units of a resource will produce more than the productivity figures show, while others will produce less. Productivity is also affected by factors such as sickness, machine breakdown and industrial action.

> **Productivity**
> the average output per unit of a resource over a given time

Average cost per unit

The average cost per unit of production is an important measure of efficiency. The calculation is:

$$\text{average cost per unit} = \frac{\text{total costs}}{\text{number of units produced}}$$

A rising figure over time may indicate falling efficiency. It will also probably mean falling profits.

Quality

Customers expect good quality products or they will go elsewhere. Poor quality is also expensive in terms of waste and lost time.

Measuring sales volumes and the level of repeat orders, together with records of customer complaints, will give an indication of customer satisfaction. Measuring usage of raw materials and other resources in relation to the volume of production will give an indication of wastage – as will average unit cost.

How can efficiency be improved?

Efficiency may be improved simply by altering the sequence of tasks, redesigning the layout of the work place to avoid hold-ups, or speeding up the production process through automation (using technology to carry out processes previously carried out by people).

Team working and cell production, organising employees into teams working together and with responsibility for meeting team targets, can improve productivity. Working as part of a team can help improve motivation.

If quality is a problem, the business must look at its systems of quality control. If there is a legal standard for the quality of the product the business must decide whether they need to provide a higher quality product than this. Responsibility for quality and systems for checking must be established, and carried out. Quality circles consist of representatives of employees actually involved in the production process who meet regularly to discuss any problems and suggest solutions.

Lean production
an approach to business that involves Total Quality Management, Just In Time production and continuous improvement (Kaizen)

Lean production is an approach to production and the management of resources. Techniques of lean production include Total Quality Management (TQM), Just In Time production (JIT) and Kaizen, or continuous improvement.

TQM involves everyone in the business, not just production operatives, checking the quality of their work. Raw materials, parts and components are checked for quality when they are received, and before they are used; the quality of the product is checked at each stage of the production process; customer service and satisfaction is checked; even the administration of the business is part of the quality process, in the belief that quality will only be achieved by an organisation in which all procedures are carried out to a high standard.

JIT production involves organising production from raw materials to finished product so that each stage of the production process is completed 'just in time' for the next stage, and ultimately the finished product is completed 'just in time' to be delivered to the customer.

In this way the business does not have money tied up in expensive stock, and there are no unnecessary storage costs to pay. Stock control becomes critical, however. Raw materials must be delivered at the time they are needed, otherwise production will stop. Good relationships between the business and its suppliers, who may have to hold stocks ready for call off by the business, are essential.

Kaizen, or continuous improvement, is an attitude that must exist throughout the organisation. It is based on continuously looking out for small improvements that can be made. While each improvement may be minor, and therefore inexpensive, their cumulative effect can be powerful.

30.2 *Activity*

You work for Excis plc, a large manufacturing company with factories in Manchester, Nottingham and Stoke-on-Trent, and a central warehouse in Derby. Your Production Director is concerned that average costs are too high, storage costs are escalating, and productivity is low. In addition, there is in increasing number of complaints from customers about quality. Write a report to the Production Director outlining the possible approaches to the problems he is concerned about, and explaining how the company might become more efficient. (>>>)

Can new technology help?

New technology can help improve productivity and quality, provide faster and more accurate information, and reduce costs through, for example, improved stock control and ordering.

In computer-aided-manufacturing (CAM), computers control machinery or equipment, reducing the need for labour and correcting faults or resetting machines. Computer-aided-manufacturing is very accurate and can produce products to exacting standards.

In computer-integrated-manufacturing (CIM) an entire production line is controlled by computers. Robots controlled in this way can perform simple repetitive or highly complex tasks accurately, reducing the need for people to undertake boring routine jobs.

With computer-aided-design (CAD) a product can be designed and displayed in three dimensions on a computer screen, tested using computer programs that will, for example, calculate the strength of the materials showing how they will react in different circumstances. Designing and testing on a computer screen saves on expensive prototypes, at least in the early stages of development.

A production line controlled by computers

New technology can also help in areas such as stock control:

- Electronic tills can update warehouse stock records with customer's purchases.
- EPOS (Electronic Point of Sale) systems scan a product's bar code to analyse sales. When stocks of a product reach a preset level an order for more goods may be sent automatically.
- Systems of Electronic Data Interchange (EDI) exchange orders and invoices by computer.

Why do businesses grow?

Economies of scale
advantages that larger businesses gain by virtue of their size

While there are limits to the size of a business — no business should produce more than it can sell – many businesses expand in order to obtain economies of scale. **Economies of scale** are advantages that businesses obtain by expanding and increasing production.

- Technical economies: large businesses can afford expensive machinery and technology to develop automated production lines. Such equipment can be operated for longer periods, increasing productivity per machine. Equipment designed for greater levels of production does not necessarily cost proportionately more to purchase.
- Managerial economies: increased production is unlikely to affect the effectiveness of managers or require an increase in their number. Larger firms, however, are in a position to employ specialist managers and other staff who can improve the efficiency of the business.

- Trading economies: larger firms enjoy greater discounts for buying in bulk. Costs of items such as research and development, advertising and distribution do not increase in proportion to increases in production and sales.
- Financial economies: large firms have access to more sources of finance than small firms, often at lower rates of interest.

Diseconomies of scale

Diseconomies of scale are disadvantages businesses can get from expanding or growing too large:

- Size: a business that grows too large becomes difficult to control and manage, leading to an increase in the number and cost of managers.
- Bureaucracy: large organisations tend to develop large and rigid administrations, or bureaucracies, leading to too much wasteful 'red tape' and inflexibility.
- The effect on employees: employees often have difficulty identifying with and feeling a part of a large organisation, leading to a drop in motivation and productivity.
- Communications: large organisations develop large structures (see Unit 15), giving rise to long communications channels; decision-making is slow.

Summary

- Goods and services are produced by job production, batch production or mass production.
- A business's efficiency can be measured by its productivity, average cost per unit, and quality of production and product.
- New technology can help improve efficiency.
- Expansion and increased productivity allow businesses to benefit from economies of scale.
- Disadvantages of expansion are called diseconomies of scale.

31 Where should a business locate?

In this unit you will learn about the importance of location on business and the factors that influence business decisions on where to locate or relocate.

The suitability of a particular location for a business is influenced by the needs of both the business and the area. Businesses must take a number of factors into consideration when deciding on a location. Some businesses may only have to consider a few of the factors described in this unit, while others may have to consider a wider range. Choosing the best location is often a matter of considering the relative importance of different factors and selecting the location that provides the best overall solution.

Business in context

A new supermarket in a prime location can cost up to $150 million. Finding the best location is therefore essential. Before selecting a new location, the supermarket's Site Research Team will look carefully at other retail outlets, customers and locations.

The first step is to estimate how much people are likely to spend in a particular area. This is based on information about customers' buying habits in the proposed location, ease of access, road networks, local competition and the attractiveness of the proposed store.

Computer programs are used to calculate distances customers might have to travel and their drive times to the store. These also display shopping patterns and competitors, in addition to the data and maps. This information, together with nationally available information (such as census data), and other research carried out by the supermarket enables the company to produce sales forecasts for the proposed store.

Potential sites are visited and photographed, and checks made on planning applications for new roads, housing developments and other food retail stores. Questions that need to be answered include:

- Is the proposed site the best size in relation to anticipated sales?
- What would be the effect on sales of competitor developments?
- Is more car parking needed?
- Is it the best site around?

Figure 31.1

Legislation

The environment

Infrastructure

Available workforce

Cost

Tradition

Customers

Suppliers

Competition

Factors affecting location of a business

Cost

When deciding where to locate, a business must consider the cost of a particular site or premises. Renting rather than buying means the business does not have to pay the whole cost at the outset. There may also be costs for additional work such as refurbishment. Building a new factory on a disused site is more expensive than renting a purpose-built unit on a modern industrial estate. Other local costs, such as rates and insurance, must also be considered.

History and tradition

Sometimes an area becomes traditionally associated with a particular industry. This is often because, in the first place, the raw materials needed were easily available in that area. Subsequently, as the industry grew, the local workforce acquired skills suited to that industry. Dedicated support services would also set up in the area to supply the main industry. Once an industry is established in an area, businesses in the industry that locate there gain a reputation for quality simply because they are located in the area.

31.1 *Activity*

Traditionally, Detroit in the United States has always been associated with car manufacturing.

1. Why do you think car manufacturing became concentrated in this region? (>)
2. Do you think that the region still has the same advantages for car manufacturers looking for somewhere to locate? Justify your answer. (>>)

The proximity of suppliers and customers

Businesses need to obtain raw materials and components from suppliers, and deliver their goods and services to customers. Heavy or bulky raw materials are costly to transport and a business may want to keep these costs to a minimum by locating close to its supplier. If, on the other hand, the raw materials are relatively easy and cheap to transport, while the finished goods are costly to transport to customers, the business is likely to locate close to its customers. Businesses providing services often also want to be close to their customers.

How does competition affect location?

If a particular area has a good reputation for a type of product, businesses locating in that area will benefit from the reputation of the area. However, a business locating in an area where there is strong competition for their product may find it difficult to win customers and sales, especially locally. On the other hand, lack of competition may indicate an opportunity for a business to supply a product for which there is a gap in the market.

What about legislation?

Building new factories and offices may require planning permission from local government authorities. This is easier to obtain in some areas where new business is encouraged, than in others where emphasis is placed on preserving the existing environment. Similarly, some types of business, for example food preparation and health services, have to be specially licensed by the local authorities.

Hotels at the seaside, a popular choice for holidays

How important is the environment?

The physical environment in which a business locates is important in several ways. Large factory complexes, for example, need many acres of flat land, while some businesses need natural resources such as water for power, or fertile land for growing crops. The proximity of a river or lake may encourage the development of boat builders, hotels and leisure services.

The infrastructure of an area includes the transport systems (road and rail networks and access to the sea and to airports). These are used to transport raw materials to the business and finished goods within a country and throughout the world. Support services such as waste disposal, power supplies and telecommunications services are other parts of the infrastructure that are also essential to business.

Infrastructure
the networks or systems of transport, communications and essential services such as power, water and waste disposal in an area or region

The effects of the business on the local community itself must also be considered. While a business may bring social benefits such as increased employment, improved services and prosperity to a community, there may also be social costs, such as pollution and noise from factories, disturbance from traffic and destruction of the environment. **Pressure groups,** concerned about the social costs of business, may be set up to bring pressure on businesses to act in a socially acceptable or ethical way.

What about suitable employees?

Businesses need employees and a business will want to know that there is a suitable supply of workers with the appropriate skills. Some areas are associated with particular industries and the local workforce tends to acquire skills appropriate to these industries. It therefore makes sense for new businesses in these industries to locate in the areas where such skills are to be found. Other businesses locating in these areas, however, may find that they have to spend considerable sums of money on retraining the workforce.

31.2 *Activity*

Find out about the workforce in your area. You will be able to find out much of this information from your careers advisor, an employment agency, local newspaper or library.

1   How many people are unemployed and available for work? (>)
2   What types of skills does the workforce in your area have? (>>)
3   What are the main kinds of industry and jobs available? (>)
4   Identify three types of businesses for which the available workforce would be an advantage if they were considering locating in your area. (>>)

Do governments help?

Governments get involved in the location of businesses for two reasons: to encourage businesses to set up in an area, or to control the development of businesses in an area.

Where a country has regions of high unemployment, perhaps because traditional industries in those regions are in decline, the government may offer grants, rent rebates or tax incentives to businesses locating or relocating in those areas. Governments also provide advice and information and practical help in finding premises, training and other business services.

Governments are also concerned with the effects of business activities, however. Where it is felt that business activities may have an adverse effect on society or the environment, a government may put restrictions on the development of new businesses in an area. For example, in most areas a business building new offices or a new factory must obtain planning permission from local government. In granting or refusing planning permission, account will be taken of matters such as pollution caused by the new factory, additional traffic, noise and inconvenience to people living nearby, the effect of the new building on the environment, and the effect on other businesses – including competitors – in the area.

31.3 Activity

You should carry out this activity in groups of three or four. Your local council wants to attract new business and industry to the area. You have been asked to produce some publicity material.

1 Research your area and find out its advantages as a location for businesses. You should find out about the factors affecting location described in this unit, and decide to what extent they apply in your area. Find out also about industries and businesses that are already located in your area. You should especially note any businesses that have set up or relocated there recently. (>>)

2 Prepare your promotional material explaining why businesses should come to your area. This can be in the form of an illustrated booklet of about sixteen A5 pages, or a presentation using audio-visual aids. If you prepare a presentation, you should give this in front of your class and tutor. (>>>)

Summary

- Businesses must consider a number of factors when deciding on their location. These include cost, history and tradition, the proximity of suppliers and customers, the effect of local competition, the environment, and the availability of a suitable workforce.
- Governments are interested in the location of businesses for various reasons and may offer financial help in the form of grants or rent rebates, practical help in the form of training and other services, or help in the form of advice.
- Governments may also place restrictions on the development of business in an area.

Revision questions

1 Give four factors that a furniture manufacturer should take into consideration when looking for a suitable site for a factory to make a new range of oak dining furniture.

2 Natasha Mackenzie is starting her own business producing handmade greetings cards, which she hopes to sell through local stationery and craft shops, and department stores. Explain the importance to Natasha of preparing a marketing plan, and what she should include in her plan.

Past examination questions

1 Why is a market-orientated business likely to be more successful than a product-orientated one? *(4 marks)*

IGCSE Paper 1, May/June 2000

2 Figure 1 shows two possible channels of production that could be used by a business. State and explain the advantages and disadvantages to a business of using Channel 2 compared to Channel 1.

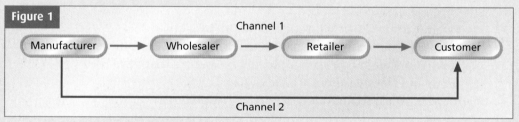

(6 marks)

IGCSE Paper 1, May/June 2000

3 Deciding how much money to allocate to an advertising budget is an important decision for all businesses. What factors should a business consider when making such a decision? *(5 marks)*

IGCSE Paper 1, May/June 2000

4 If we charge lower prices than our competitors our sales and profits must rise.' Do you agree or disagree with this statement? Give reasons for your answer. *(5 marks)*

IGCSE Paper 1, May/June 2000

5 'Product Z is at the end of the maturity stage of its product life cycle' said the marketing manager.
(a) Explain what the marketing manager meant by this. *(2 marks)*
(b) The management of the business has to decide what to do with product Z. Identify two different options that could be followed and explain their advantages. *(6 marks)*

IGCSE Paper 1, November 2000

6   A business is planning to launch a new brand of chocolate bar. Recommend a suitable channel of distribution for this product giving reasons for your choice.

(5 marks)

IGCSE Paper 1 May/June 2000

7   Figures 7a and 7b show two possible relationships between advertising expenditure and the level of sales revenue of a product.

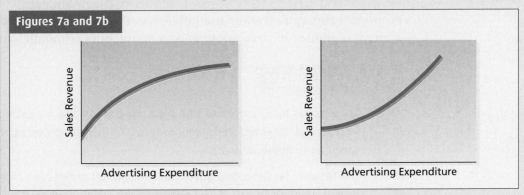

Figures 7a and 7b

(a) Explain the relationship between sales revenue and advertising expenditure as shown in each of the two graphs 7a and 7b.   *(4 marks)*

(b) Explain one way a business could increase its sales for a product other than by advertising.   *(3 marks)*

IGCSE Paper 1, November 2000

8   Joshua Mulirea runs a small business with his daughter Flo. Joshua is interested in a joint venture with another business that offers a shopping and delivery service for elderly people. 'This seems a good idea to me', he said, 'as it would be a diversification aimed at a different group of customers.'

(a) Produce a questionnaire that Joshua could use for his market research into the idea. Ask four questions that you think he should use.   *(4 marks)*

(b) Explain why you think each question is important.   *(4 marks)*

(c) How accurate are the results likely to be?   *(3 marks)*

Adapted from IGCSE, Paper 2 November 2000

32 Government and the economy

In this unit you will learn how governments can influence business activity and the economy.

An economy is the system through which a society satisfies its demand for goods and services. Governments influence their national economies through taxation and public spending, by controlling the amount of money in circulation, and by stimulating economic growth.

Business in context

The Minister for Finance has a problem. He has just had a meeting with several other ministers who want him to increase government spending in different areas.

The Minister for Defence argued that the nation's armed forces were increasingly taking part in the peacekeeping activities of the United Nations. In view of all this, the Minister said, spending on defence should be increased.

The Minister for Health complained that people were living longer and expecting better standards of health care. More spending was therefore needed on health care.

The Education Minister also pleaded for more money. A skilled workforce was vital for the country's prosperity. Employers were complaining that school leavers did not have the right skills. In addition, good teachers were leaving the profession to go to other, better-paid occupations. What was needed was more money for education.

The Minister for Public Welfare explained that social security is one of the largest areas of government spending. But increasingly more had to be paid out in benefits. Surely, said the Minister, here was the area where spending had to be increased.

Lastly, the Minister for Transport spoke. There was growing congestion on the roads. And she was concerned about pollution from vehicle exhausts as well as safety on the roads and railways. Buses and rail travel should be subsidised and the programme of road building increased. Tax on petrol and diesel could go up to help pay for it, but more might be needed.

Having heard his colleagues' pleas for more spending, the Minister for Finance sighed. Meeting their demands for increased spending would mean that he would have to put up taxes. And he was not sure that he was convinced by their arguments, anyway. He had other things to think about as well, like keeping both unemployment and inflation low.

Questions

1 What are the main areas of government spending mentioned above? (>)

2 What does the Minister for Finance think he will have to do if he is going to meet the demands of the other ministers? (>)

3 What other problems does the Minister for Finance have to deal with? (>)

4 If you were the Minister for Finance, what would you do in each case? Choose between reducing expenditure, keeping expenditure at the same level, or increasing expenditure. (>>>)

5 What do you think would be the overall outcome of your proposed actions? (>>>)

Why does the government want to influence the economy?

In this unit we will look at three areas of the economy that the government tries to influence: unemployment, inflation and economic growth.

- People who are unemployed have less to spend, this leads to a reduction in demand for goods and services and thus to a reduction in the production of goods and services. It also means that the cost of welfare benefits will increase.
- Inflation is a continuing rise in the general level of prices and leads to reduced demand, lower production and higher unemployment.
- Economic growth occurs when there is an increase in a country's **Gross National Product** or GNP (the total value of goods and services produced by a country in a year): the more goods and services a country produces, the higher the standard of living in that country.

Gross National Product (GNP)
the total value of goods and services produced by a country

Fiscal policies
government economic policies based on taxation and public expenditure

Monetary policies
policies aimed at influencing business and the economy by controlling the money supply

In this unit we will consider how governments try to influence the economy through **fiscal policies** (which are concerned with government income and expenditure) and **monetary policies** (which are concerned with the amount of money in circulation), and stimulating demand at home and abroad.

Fiscal policies

How does the government get its money?

The most important source of income, or revenue, for a government is taxation. The main types of taxes that affect business and the economy are:

Direct taxes
taxes paid directly to the government. For example, employees pay directly from income, or businesses pay directly from their profits

- Taxes on income, known as **direct taxes** because they are paid directly to the government. In most countries these are progressive, because the more a person earns, the higher the rate of tax he or she pays. They reduce the amount a person keeps out of his or her earnings.

Indirect taxes
taxes paid to the government through an intermediary. For example, purchase taxes such as VAT are added to the price of most goods and collected from customers by the businesses selling the goods. The business then pays the VAT collected in a period to the government

- Taxes on expenditure, including purchase taxes such as value added tax (VAT), which are added to the price of most goods and services, and duties added to the price of goods such as petrol and diesel, tobacco and alcohol. These are **indirect taxes** because they are paid first by the purchaser to the supplier, who then has to forward the tax collected to the government.
- Taxes on business, such as taxes on the profits made by a company.

32.1 Activity

1 Find out the present rates of direct and indirect taxes such as income tax, taxes on purchases (such as VAT), business taxes, and excise duty on petrol and tobacco. (>)
2 Were these increased in the last budget, and if so by how much? (>>)
3 If you were responsible for setting the levels of taxation and government expenditure for the next year, which rates would you change? Give reasons for your answer. (>>>)

How does the government spend its money?

Governments use the money they receive from taxation to:

- provide or purchase goods and services for the benefit of society (this includes paying the wages and salaries of government employees such as MPs, civil servants, judges, members of the armed and police forces, employees in education and the public health service)

- purchase or construct facilities such as hospitals, schools and roads
- subsidise the production of goods and services such as coal or food in order to keep the price to consumers low
- make transfer payments (money that is transferred from one sector of society to another, for example from the employed in the form of income tax to the unemployed in the form of benefits).

If a government spends more that it receives, it must borrow enough money to make up the difference. This is called the public sector borrowing requirement (PSBR) or public sector net cash requirement (PSNCR).

32.2 Activity

1 Find out how the government of your country spends its money: what are the main categories of government expenditure? (>)
2 Create a table showing the percentage of total government expenditure against each category. (>>)
3 Construct a pie chart from your table. (>>)
4 Do you think the government should change the way it spends its income, spending more on some categories and less on others? Give reasons for your answer. (>>>)

How do taxation and government spending affect the economy?

Taxation and government spending may affect the economy in several ways:

- Increasing income tax means that employees have less money to buy goods and services they want. This leads to reduced demand and lower levels of production. The result may be unemployment and a further fall in demand.
- Reducing income tax gives employees more take-home pay. This leads to an increase in demand and possibly to inflation.
- Increasing indirect taxes on some goods, such as petrol and diesel, would lead to an increase in the prices of those goods and may result in higher inflation, increased unemployment and reduced profits for business.
- Increasing the levels of taxes on business increases costs and reduces profits. This forces businesses to either cut costs in other areas such as employment costs (leading to unemployment), or to increase prices (leading to inflation).

- Increasing government expenditure on goods and services increases demand and production. This results in higher profits and increased employment

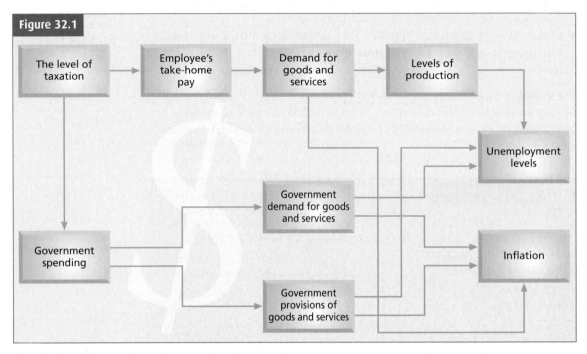

Figure 32.1

How the level of taxes affects the economy

- Increasing government expenditure on services it provides itself may reduce demand for services provided by private sector businesses. This may result in lower levels of production, profits and employment. Any increase in overall unemployment, however, might be offset by increased employment by the government.
- Changing the levels of transfer payments such as pensions, unemployment benefits and so on, mainly affect those who receive the benefits. Such changes may influence the type and amount of products purchased.

32.3 *Activity*

The government of Ruritania has decided to increase spending on the road network throughout the country. To do this it needs to raise an additional $1bn.

1. Suggest how the government of Ruritania might raise this money. (>>)
2. Explain the effect of their actions on the county's business and economy. (>>>)

Monetary policies

What is the money supply?

The **money supply** is the amount of money that is available for people and businesses to spend. It includes not only the actual cash that people and businesses have in their pockets or tills and at the bank, but also the amount that they can borrow.

Money supply
the amount of money in the economy

Why is the money supply important?

If a single person or business is able to increase their money supply, and therefore their spending power, they will always find new goods or services that they want available to spend the extra money on. That makes them better off because they have the benefit of the extra product they have purchased, and it also makes the supplier of the extra product better off because they have increased their sales.

Taking the economy as a whole, however, there is only a specific amount of goods and services available at any one time. If consumers generally are able to increase their spending power by borrowing money, some consumers will be prepared to pay a higher price to ensure they get the goods and services they want. This may lead to a general rise in the level of prices (inflation). When this happens, other consumers may be unable to afford or unwilling to pay the higher prices. Demand for goods and services will fall, causing businesses to produce less. They may make employees redundant as they are no longer needed, leading to higher unemployment. Controlling the money supply, therefore, is an important part of the government's strategy for the economy.

How is the money supply controlled?

The main way in which the money supply can be controlled is through the cost of borrowing. When a customer borrows money from a bank or other financial institution, he or she will be charged interest or commission on the loan. This is the cost of borrowing the money and is normally calculated as a percentage of the amount borrowed or the amount still outstanding at the end of each year.

If this rate is low, there will probably be no difficulty in repaying the loan plus interest or commission. If the rate is high, however, potential borrowers may be put off borrowing and having to pay back so much more than the amount borrowed.

Raising or lowering interest or commission rates therefore influences the amount people are willing to borrow. This in turn affects the amount they have to spend and, as we have seen, levels of demand, inflation, production and unemployment.

1   Find out some rates of interest charged on loans made by banks and building societies. (>)
2   Are the rates of interest charged to borrowers different from the rates of interest paid to savers? (>>)
3   Suggest reasons for any differences. (>>>)
4   If the rate of interest or commission charged was increased by 0.75%, how much more would someone have to pay on a loan of $10,000? (>>)
5   Explain the effects that an interest rate increase of 0.75% would have on inflation, production and unemployment. (>>>)

Economic growth

The total value of goods and services produced by a country is called its Gross National Product (GNP). Since one of the objectives of a government is to improve the standard of living of its citizens, it must try to increase the country's GNP. In order to do this, the government must stimulate, or increase, demand for the goods and services produced by the country. Demand for the goods and services of a country come from within the country itself and from abroad. Increasing GNP may also have the effect of reducing unemployment, since businesses will need to employ more people in order to increase production of goods and services.

Stimulating demand at home

People will only buy goods and services if they have enough money and can afford to buy them. Demand from within the country producing the goods and services can be stimulated by:

- maintaining a low level of unemployment, so that people are able to work and earn enough to buy the goods and services they want
- redistributing income through transfer payments to ensure that all sections of society can buy the goods and services they need
- keeping inflation low, so that people's incomes cover the costs of goods and services, and also so that the costs of goods and services produced by the country are not higher than similar goods and services produced abroad.

Stimulating demand from abroad

The main methods of stimulating demand from abroad are:

- encouraging international trade by providing marketing assistance and subsidies to businesses that sell goods and services abroad
- maintaining a competitive exchange rate between currencies, so that the price of goods sold abroad is attractive to foreign consumers.

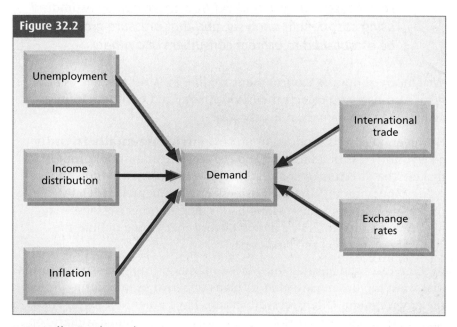

Figure 32.2

Factors affecting demand

Summary

- The government influences the economy in order to control unemployment, inflation and economic growth.
- One way the government does this is through fiscal policies, which are based on levels of taxation and public expenditure.
- Monetary policies are designed to influence the economy and business by controlling the money supply.
- Borrowing increases the money supply.
- The amount people are willing to borrow can be controlled through changes to interest rates.
- Economic growth occurs when a country's GNP grows in response to increased demand from within the country or abroad.

33 The social costs and benefits of business activity

In this unit you will learn that all business activities have social costs. You will find out how these can be estimated using cost-benefit analysis, and that pressure groups may be established to protect consumers and others.

Environmentally friendly
activities that conserve the environment or do not deplete scarce resources

We all care about the environment we live in. Most businesses also want to conserve (protect) the environment and ensure that their activities do not damage it in any way.

However, making a production process **environmentally friendly** adds to the costs of a business and reduces the amount of profit it makes. The directors or shareholders of a company may not want to spend money on making the business environmentally friendly, preferring it to continue making big profits. Another business may plan to expand by building a new factory that would pollute the atmosphere or affect the landscape.

Pressure group
a group of people formed to take action aimed at influencing the behaviour of business or government

In these cases the business may face opposition from **pressure groups** that want the business to alter its plans or activities in order to protect the environment. Other pressure groups have other objectives. These may be national or even global objectives, such as animal welfare, or local, such as to keep a factory open in order to safeguard employment.

Business in context

Friends of the Earth is an international organisation that campaigns on environmental issues such as conservation and pollution. Local groups help to bring about changes in the policies and activities of businesses and governments. These changes have helped to protect the natural environment of local and national communities.

The activities of Friends of the Earth include researching issues and providing information to interested parties, petitioning and writing to people in government and executives in businesses, and, where appropriate, demonstrating.

'Factory Watch' is a campaign that monitors pollution from individual factories, and provides information about the impact on health. The results are made available to people in the local community who are encouraged to take action.

Questions

1 What are the objectives of Friends of the Earth? (>)

2 What is the purpose of the 'Factory Watch' campaign? (>)

3 Why is information about the pollution of individual factories made available to people in the local community? (>>)

4 If you were a member of Friends of the Earth and were concerned at the amount of pollution from a local factory, what action would you take? (>>>)

5 As a class, discuss what kinds of action against individual businesses you feel are ethically acceptable. Give your reasons. (>>>)

Externalities: the social costs of business

Many business activities have effects outside the business itself. For example, mobile telephone companies spend a considerable amount of money erecting transmitters. The money they spend is a cost to the businesses. In return, they expect to get considerable revenue from subscribers to their services so that they will make a profit. This is the benefit the mobile telephone companies will gain.

However, the transmitters are a nuisance to society: they are unsightly and often spoil the environment. In effect this nuisance is a cost that is borne by society rather than the mobile telephone companies. On the other hand, society does benefit from the extra services provided by the mobile telephone companies. These are benefits to society rather than the companies. They are external costs and benefits (that is outside the businesses themselves) or **externalities**.

External costs of business activities include:

- environmental factors, such as pollution from smoke, noise, and chemicals
- spoiling the environment with buildings such as factories or the construction of roads
- damage from traffic
- the destruction of natural habitats of wildlife and flowers
- endangering species of wildlife
- global warming
- social factors, such as unemployment and loss of amenities when a factory or business closes.

Externalities
the social costs and benefits of business activity

External benefits include:

- increased employment resulting from the development and expansion of businesses, such as the opening of new factories
- economic regeneration of an area if new businesses move in
- increased training of a local workforce making the workforce more adaptable
- improved amenities and living standards.

Pollution is an external cost of business

33.1 *Activity*

Make a list of the external benefits and costs of constructing a new shopping complex on a green-field site outside a major city. (>)

Cost-benefit analysis: measuring social costs

Many businesses use a procedure known as **cost-benefit analysis** to weigh up the **social costs and benefits** of their activities. The basic procedure involves:

- identifying all costs and benefits connected with an activity or project, including future costs and benefits
- putting a financial value on the costs and benefits
- comparing the total cost with the total benefit value.

If the total value of benefits exceeds the costs of the activity or project, the business should continue. If the costs exceed the value of the benefits, however, the activity or project should be cancelled, at least for the present: circumstances change and a future cost-benefit analysis may yield a different result.

While cost-benefit analysis is helpful in making decisions about the overall costs and benefits of business activity, it does have problems.

Some business activities provide benefits for some consumers but costs for others (a new housing estate, for example, will benefit the families who will live there, but may be a social cost to others if the estate is built on land which they used to farm).

It is often difficult to put a value on some social costs or benefits, such as protecting a species of wildlife.

Cost-benefit analysis
a method of comparing the overall costs and benefits, including the social costs and benefits, of a business activity or project

Social costs and benefits
costs and benefits to society as a whole rather than to the business

What is a pressure group?

A pressure group is a group of people who come together with a common aim to try to influence the decisions and activities of businesses, local councils or the government. They may be small local groups, campaigning on a local issue, such as a chemical plant which is polluting their water supply, or they may be major national or international groups, such as Friends of the Earth, which try to influence policies and activities on a local, national and international scale.

Pressure groups try to influence the actions and policies of business and government

How do pressure groups operate?

There is strength in numbers, and members of a pressure group acting together are more effective in influencing businesses and governments than several people acting individually.

Pressure groups can take action by lobbying or contacting members of Parliament, local councillors or the Managing Director, Chief Executive or Chairman of the businesses involved. Other tactics include writing letters to local or national newspapers, holding public meetings, distributing leaflets and advertisements, organising demonstrations and contacting local or national television.

Where these tactics do not work, more direct action may be taken, such as boycotting (refusing to buy) the goods or services of a business. In extreme cases, protesters may occupy a site that is designated for development in order to stop the development going ahead.

What effect do pressure groups have?

Pressure groups have had some spectacular successes, persuading businesses to alter their behaviour. When Shell planned to scrap an obsolete oil platform at sea it met with considerable and powerful opposition from pressure groups concerned at the effect on the environment. Eventually Shell was forced to alter its plans and scrap the platform on land.

Similar protests have had considerable success regarding the disposal of nuclear waste, making fur coats out of real animal skins, and testing cosmetics on animals by companies. Longer-term campaigns have helped bring about a reduction in the use of CFCs and the burning of fossil fuels that damage the ozone layer, a change to lead-free petrol, and a far greater awareness among governments and businesses worldwide that they have a responsibility to society and the environment, as well as to their shareholders.

33.2 *Activity*

1 As a class think of all the activities of business and industry in your area that have external costs and benefits. Make one list for activities having costs and one for activities having benefits. (>)

2 Compare your two lists. Do any businesses or activities appear on both lists? (>)

3 Discuss any businesses or activities that appear on both lists. Do you think the external benefits outweigh the external costs of those businesses or activities? (>>)

4 In groups of four or five, select one business whose activities you feel adversely affect the environment. Imagine you have formed a pressure group to get the business to act in a more environmentally friendly way. What action would you take as a group? How effective do you think it would be? (>>>)

Summary

- Some activities of business are harmful to society or the environment.
- These are social costs external to business.
- Cost-benefit analysis is a method of comparing the total costs and benefits of a business activity or project, including social costs and benefits.
- Pressure groups are formed to try and influence the activities and attitudes of business.

34 *Business and the state*

In this unit you will learn how the state intervenes in the activities of businesses in order to assist businesses and protect the interests of others.

The state also intervenes in business in order to protect consumers, employees and others, regulate the production of some goods and services, and control marketing and competition. The state also aids businesses by, for example, providing assistance for exporting.

Business in context

Maria Da Costa bought a new spreadsheet package for her computer. When she got it home it would not run correctly on her computer, although the shop assistant said it was compatible, and it corrupted information already on the hard disk. Some information was work for clients, and Maria was concerned she would have to do it again, causing her financial loss.

Maria took the spreadsheet package back to the shop. The assistant apologised and said the salesman from the software company would call at the shop next week and should arrange for a replacement to be sent to Maria within a few days.

The assistant also said that although he was sorry about the information on Maria's hard disk there was nothing he could do about that. Maria said it was the shop's responsibility to replace the software and also compensate her for financial loss due to the information being corrupted.

Questions

1 Who should replace the software – the shop or the supplier? (>)

2 Should Maria be compensated for the loss of information? If so, by whom? (>)

3 What further action might Maria take? (>>)

4 Using Maria's case as an example, do you think that laws to protect consumers are necessary safeguards or a restriction on the activities of businesses that affects their ability to provide goods and services at a profit? (>>>)

Protecting consumers

Consumers have a right to expect businesses to behave fairly and honestly and to supply products that are safe, meet consumers' needs and expectations, and are of reasonable quality. While the high standards of most businesses mean that customers can deal confidently with them, legislation exists to protect consumers from unsatisfactory or unsafe goods and services.

In most countries there are many laws and organisations to protect consumers. For example in the United States, the federal Consumer Product Safety Commission together with various state consumer protection agencies regulate the safety of products, as well as advertising and sales practices. India has nearly fifty laws to protect consumers. As an example, in the UK **consumer protection legislation** includes:

Consumer protection legislation
laws designed to protect consumers

- The Resale Price Act 1964, which allows manufacturers to suggest a price for their product but not to refuse to supply any retailer who wishes to sell at a lower price
- The Fair Trading Act 1974, which established an Office of Fair Trading to provide information and advice to consumers
- The Consumer Credit Act 1974, which covers goods bought on credit
- The Consumer Protection Acts 1978 and 1987 and the Consumer Safety Act 1978, which cover the display of prices, appropriate warnings on certain items such as electrical goods, furniture and furnishings, and toys, and the clear marking of dangerous products such as medicines and solvents as hazardous, with first aid instructions given on the packaging
- The Unfair Contract Terms Act 1980, which states that all terms in a contract between a buyer and a seller must be reasonable, and any unreasonable terms, such as disclaimers as to quality, cannot be upheld.

34.1 *Activity*

David took a teddy bear back to the shop he had bought it from. He showed the sales assistant how the head could be pulled off, leaving a long length of sharp wire. 'I bought this for my three-year-old daughter', David explained. 'But it's too dangerous for a child to play with.'
'This is one of our best-selling toys', the assistant replied. 'We've not had any other complaints. Anyway, you're not supposed to pull the head off. You can't hold the shop responsible for your little girl misusing the toy.'

1. Who is responsible for what has happened? (>)
2. Is there a law that applies in this case? (>)
3. What do you think should happen now? Explain your answer. (>>>)

Protecting employees

Employees should be treated fairly and equally by their employers. **Employment protection legislation** protects employees from unfair practices. It is based on the assumption that if employees are treated fairly, and their rights respected by their employers, they will contribute more to the business, benefiting the business and the employee. Increasingly, employment protection legislation is becoming uniform throughout the world, although there are still regional and national variations. The main areas are:

- Terms and conditions of employment – all employees are entitled to a written statement of the terms and conditions of the employment, normally within a set period of commencement. Most countries require statements to give at least the information shown in Figure 34.1, but this varies from country to country.
- Wages – employees are entitled to receive a fair wage for the work they do. Many countries have a national minimum hourly wage set by the state.
- Health and safety – Workplaces should be safe and healthy and not present hazards to employees. Many businesses have formed health and safety arrangements, but employees have a responsibility to act in accordance with such arrangements and not to behave in a way that endangers either themselves or others.
- Equal opportunities – all employees should be treated equally without regard to race, religion, sex or disability. Increasingly, governments are introducing legislation to this effect.
- Unfair dismissal – dismissal of an employee is normally considered fair if it is for reason of misconduct, incapacity to do the job (including being legally disqualified, such as a driver losing his or her licence), redundancy, or some other substantial reason, such as refusing to accept a reasonable change in duties or a clash of personalities. Dismissal outside these reasons may be considered unfair and governments are increasingly introducing laws to protect employees from such unfair dismissal.

Figure 34.1

CONTRACT OF EMPLOYMENT

Name of employer ....

Name of employee ....

Job title ....

Place of work ....

Date of commencement
    of employment ....

Other employment that counts
    towards the employee's
    continuous employment ....

Hours of work ....

Rate of salary or wage ....

Sick pay entitlement ....

Holiday entitlement ....

Pension entitlement ....

Disciplinary procedures ....

Grievance procedures ....

Notice of termination of employment to be given and received (minimum: one week for each year of continuous employment up to twelve weeks)

Signed on behalf
of the company ....

Employee's signature ....

A contract of employment must include certain details

Many firms have written policies on matters such as health and safety and equal opportunities.

1 Make a list of all the points that you think should be covered by these policies. (>)

2 Write a health and safety policy and an equal opportunities policy for your school. Produce this as a short booklet. If you have access to a computer, you could use a computer desk top publishing or word-processing package. (>>)

3 Write a short account comparing and evaluating your policies and the actual policies of your school. Are there any points not covered in your school's present policies, or that you have missed? (>>)

Protecting the interests of those who lend and provide capital

As you have seen throughout this course, all business activity costs money. The capital needed by a business must be provided either by the owners or loaned to the business.

An incorporated business exists as a legal entity separate from its owners. The affairs of the business are not the same as the affairs of the owners, and any capital provided and loans made are to the business and not to the owners.

It is important that there is legal protection for those who lend and provide capital to incorporated businesses. This includes a requirement for incorporated businesses to be registered and to make their annual accounts available to all interested parties. The owners of the business (shareholders) are themselves protected by limited liability, and if the business defaults on payment to a creditor to whom it owes money, it is the business that will be sued. If the business is unable to pay the debt, the courts may appoint a receiver (usually a senior partner in a firm of accountants) to take over running the company, and if necessary sell the assets of the business in order to pay as much as possible of the amount owed. The owners, directors or other employees of the business will only be held personally liable in the event of fraud or other criminal activity.

Other reasons for state intervention

Production decisions

The amount of involvement by a state or government in the production decisions of business depends to a large extent on the political and economic climate of the country. In a controlled economy the state will intervene in the production decisions of business far more than in a market economy (see Unit 3). However, in all countries there is some state intervention in production decisions.

Most countries restrict or prohibit the production of certain goods, such as alcohol, cigarettes, drugs and pornography, because such goods are considered undesirable or harmful to society. In the case of goods such as alcohol and cigarettes, the restrictions on production may be indirect, through additional taxes that increase their price and so decrease demand for them. In the case of goods such as drugs and pornography, restrictions on production are more likely to be direct, in the form of laws making the production and sale of the goods illegal.

The state may also take action to control the production of goods that harm the environment. Sometimes this type of action is taken jointly by several governments worldwide acting together. An example is aerosol cans that use CFCs, which have been banned because of their damaging effect on the ozone layer. Similarly, there is worldwide general agreement that the burning of fossil fuels should be reduced, although at present (2001) the government of the United States is refusing to sign the agreement. Individual governments may take action against businesses in their countries that pollute the environment by, for example, disposing of effluent into rivers.

Other state intervention includes the need for some types of business to be licensed, often for consumer protection. The types of business that have to obtain a licence before they can begin operating varies from country to country, but usually involve food production and preparation, and other similar businesses.

In controlled economies, there is a greater amount of state intervention. This may even involve the state setting production targets for individual businesses, saying how many employees a business will have, and how large the business will be.

Location decisions (local, national and international)

We saw in Unit 31 how the state may become involved in the location of business. To attract businesses to its country or to a particular region, a government may offer subsidies and grants. These are often tied to a particular project or number of jobs to be created.

For example, a local government wanting to attract new business to their area in order to reduce unemployment may offer a specific grant for every new job created. Other methods of attracting business to an area or country include helping the business to find suitable premises, offering rent-free or rate-free periods, and offering practical help such as training, business planning and advice in areas such as marketing.

Besides wanting to attract businesses to some areas, however, most governments also impose restrictions on the development of others. There may be restrictions on building new factories or other business premises in residential areas, where increased industrial activity may cause disruption or inconvenience, or in areas of natural beauty, where the new building may harm enjoyment of the environment.

Marketing and trading legislation

Marketing and trading legislation laws intended to ensure that businesses behave fairly and act in an ethical manner, both towards each other and towards customers

Marketing and trading legislation is intended to ensure that businesses behave fairly and act in an ethical manner, both towards each other and towards customers. In the UK, laws covering the marketing and trading activities of businesses include: the Trades Descriptions Act, which makes it illegal to falsely describe (for example in an advertisement) any goods offered for sale, give a misleading indication of price, or make a false statement about the provision of a service; the Sale of Goods Act and the Sale and Supply of Goods Act, which state that in any sale of goods, the seller must have the legal right to sell those goods, the goods sold must be 'as described' (for example as regards to weight or size), and they must be of 'satisfactory quality' and 'fit for the purpose'; the Supply of Goods and Services, which extended the Sale of Goods Act and the Sale and Supply of Goods Act to services.

Specific legislation in other countries differs, but the substance and intent are the same.

Competition policy

Attitudes towards competition vary from country to country, according to the political climate. In countries such as China, where emphasis is placed on state control of business activity, competition is actively discouraged or even illegal. Most business activity is undertaken by state-owned monopolies – powerful business organisations that control the market for their products and are able to charge high prices and provide poor quality products simply because customers have no choice but to buy the products from the monopoly business.

Governments of more market-orientated economies are keen to encourage competition between businesses, believing that when businesses compete for customers, they have to attract their customers by offering better quality products, keener prices, a wider variety of products designed to meet what consumers want, and better customer service (such as advice and after-sales service). Competition laws exist to prevent anti-competitive practices such as price-fixing. Mergers that would lead to the merged business having a monopoly position that could be against the interest of consumers are also investigated and may be prevented.

Assistance for exporting

In Unit 32 we saw that one of the objectives of a government is to maintain or improve the balance of payments. Many governments therefore provide assistance to exporters in order to encourage exports. The main ways in which a government can encourage exports are by:

- promoting a country's products abroad through trade fairs and visits by heads of state and other government ministers
- maintaining a steady exchange rate so that prices are stable and competitive
- guaranteeing payment for goods sold abroad in the event that a foreign customer should fail to pay
- arranging and guaranteeing loans to exporters at low interest rates.

Restrictions on imports

Governments also impose restrictions in the form of tariffs and barriers on imports in order to increase demand for home-produced goods and services. Tariffs are taxes on imports that effectively make the imports more expensive and so reduce demand for them. Barriers restrict imports by, for example, imposing quotas on the amount of a product that can be imported.

The increasing need for international trade and competition has led to the formation of many alliances between countries, known as trading blocs, intended to facilitate trade between member countries and encourage exports while restricting imports outside the bloc. The North American Free Trade Agreement (NAFTA) between Canada, the US and Mexico is intended to remove all trade barriers between those countries. A similar organisation is the European Union (EU), which consists of fifteen countries within Europe.

Other international trade agreements and organisations include the United Nations Conference on Trade and Development (UNCTAD), the General Agreement on Tariffs and Trade (GATT), and the South Asian Association for Regional Co-operation (SAARC). Increasingly, international trade and the globalisation of business are leading to negotiations, such as GATT, designed to harmonise or remove tariffs in order to facilitate international trade and competition.

34.4 *Activity*

1 Find out about tariffs or barriers to imports imposed by the government of your country. (>)
2 Why do you think they have been imposed? (>>)
3 Is your country a member of a trading bloc such as the EU or SADC (the Southern African Development Community)? (>)
4 Describe the benefits and disadvantages of membership. (>>>)

Summary

- Consumers have a right to expect businesses to behave fairly and honestly and to supply goods and services that are safe and of reasonable quality.
- The high standards of most businesses mean that customers can deal confidently with those businesses.
- Codes of practice and legal constraints have been established to protect consumers from unsatisfactory or unsafe goods and services.
- The activities of businesses are constrained through legislation on marketing and trading, competition, and employee protection.
- The aim of such legislation is to ensure that businesses act in a fair and ethical way.
- Businesses that employ people must abide by employment law.
- The amount of state intervention in the production decisions of business depends on the political climate of the country.
- Governments also try to encourage exports.

Revision questions

1 Using examples to illustrate your answer, explain the difference between fiscal and monetary policies. ☉

2 What is GNP, and why might a government want to increase it? ☉

3 Pressure groups are often set up to protect the interests of consumers.
   (a) Using examples to illustrate your answer, explain what a pressure group is, and what action it can take.
   (b) Give two other groups that might set up a pressure group to protect their interests.

4 Many industries have voluntary controls on their activities; other industries are regulated by legislation. Which type of control is better? Explain your answer.

Past examination questions

1 Laws often protect employees from unfair dismissal. Under what circumstances can an employee be fairly dismissed? *(4 marks)*

IGCSE Paper 1, November 2000

2 Governments often pass laws to protect consumers. Using an example, explain how consumers may be protected by such laws. *(4 marks)*

IGCSE Paper 1, November 2000

3 Explain what is meant by a social cost. *(2 marks)*

IGCSE Paper 1, May/June 2000

4 Using an example to illustrate your answer explain why a firm is more likely to take financial costs into account than social costs when taking decisions. *(4 marks)*

IGCSE Paper 1, May/June 2000

5 In many countries governments pass laws to help protect certain groups against decisions of business.
   (a) How are the interests of shareholders protected by such laws?
   (b) State two other groups that are often protected from business activity by government laws. *(2 marks)*

IGCSE Paper 1, May/June 2000

6 The flow of imports into an economy can be limited by government action.
   (a) State two methods that can be used to restrict imports into a country. *(2 marks)*
   (b) Do you think that such methods benefit the business community of the country imposing the restrictions? Explain your answer. *(5 marks)*

IGCSE Paper 1, May/June 2000

Appendix

Example questions from paper 2

The following case studies and questions are taken from the November 2000 papers and are reprinted with the permission of The University of Cambridge Local Examinations Syndicate, from whom the full papers may be purchased.

J. M. Services

Joshua Mulirea runs a small business with his daughter Flo. It is organised on an equal partnership basis with Joshua looking after the finance, marketing and planning and Flo in charge of the workforce. The business offers a range of services to customers. It provides domestic staff who clean houses and gardeners who carry out a range of tasks outside the house. Table 1 gives some details of the business. *5*

Table 1

Number of cleaning staff employed = 20
Number of customers using house cleaning service per week = 180
Average time spent per house = 3 hours
price charged = $6 per hour

Number of gardening staff employed = 15 *10*
Number of customers using gardening services per week = 120
Average time spent per garden = 4 hours
Price charged = $5 per hour

Costs of Business
Cleaners' wages = $4 per hour *15*
Gardeners' wages = $3 per hour
Weekly oveheads of business $1000

Assume one cleaner is used per house and one gardener is used per garden.

'The market for these services is growing', said Joshua, 'because incomes are rising and more people are out at work. Our business is doing well because we employ *20* staff who are honest, relaible and hardworking. I am trying to find new costomers at the moment but I know that if we expand any more we will have to invest in more equipment. Our accountant tells us that we need to produce a detailed budget to see if expansion will be profitable and affordable. He tells us that we should also check our liquidity position.' *25*

Joshua is interested in a joint venture with another business that offers a shopping and delivery service for elderly people. 'This seems a good idea to me,' he said, 'as it would be a diversification aimed at a different group of customers.'

1 Explain the following terms used in the case.

    (a) Partnership (line 2)   *(3 marks)*

    (b) Overheads (line 17)   *(3 marks)*

    (c) Liquidity (line 25)   *(3 marks)*

    (d) Diversification (line 28)   *(3 marks)*

3 (a) Complete the profit and loss statement for the business as a whole for a year (assume a 50 week year).

	$
Sales Revenue	....
Less Wages	180 000
Overheads	....
Net profit before tax and interest	....
Less interest	15 000
Net profit before tax	....
Tax at 25%	....
Net profit after tax	....

                                                                      (8 marks)

    (b) (i) What do you understand by the term 'budget'?   *(2 marks)*

        (ii) Explain why a budget might be useful to J. M. Services.   *(6 marks)*

4 In order to gain more customers, J. M. Services may need to change their marketing mix. Describe a suitable marketing mix that J. M. Services could use. *(10 marks)*

5 As a business grows it can become more difficult to manage.

    (a) How do you think the employees of J. M. Services might react to any growth in the business? Explain your answer.   *(5 marks)*

    (b) What other problems do you think that Joshua and Flo might have if their business grows?   *(5 marks)*

    (c) How might they try to overcome these problems?   *(5 marks)*

Answers to Business in context, Activity, Revision and Past examination questions

Note: the answers to many of the Activity questions depend on the student's home country.

Unit 1

Business in context

1   Shell produces oil products such as petrol and diesel.
2   Shell's products can be purchased at garages and gas or petrol stations.
3   Shell's products are made from raw or crude oil.

1.1 Activity

1   Bread is made from flour; an oak coffee table is made from wood; this book is made of paper.
2   Flour is made from wheat that is grown on farms; wood comes from trees that grow on the land; paper is made from wood and other fibres.
3   Wheat and trees are renewable in that as they are used to make products, new wheat and trees can be grown. However, while a new crop of wheat can be grown every year it takes many years for trees to grow. If these resources are used to make products faster than they can be replaced, supplies will run out.

Unit 2

Business in context

1   Neptune Shipping Agency's mission statement is the only one that states the service the company provides. However, students may know that local government provides public services for the local community. Neptune Shipping Agency Ltd provides shipping freight forwarding services. International Energy plc provides energy such as electricity.
2   In each case, students should be able to identify consumers or customers (the people who buy or use the products of the organisation), and employees or workers. They may also identify for local government: the community; for Neptune Shipping Agency and International Energy plc: owners and those with a financial interest.
3   Answers should refer to purposes mentioned in the mission statements, such as providing customer service, developing employees and preserving the environment.

4 Local government seeks to provide public services (a non-profit-making activity), while both Neptune Shipping Agency and International Energy seek to make a profit.

5 Local government is set up to serve the local community; Neptune Shipping Agency was established to provide a profit for its owners; International Energy was set up to make a profit by providing a service needed by its customers.

2.1 Activity

Answers will depend on the business selected.

2.2 Activity

Answers should reflect the conflict in objectives between profit and environmental protection.

Unit 3

Business in context

1 The problem facing the minister is that smoking-related diseases are causing a drain on the country's health services. There is pressure on the government to reduce the level of smoking, but this would upset other sections of society who work in the tobacco industry or value the freedom to choose whether to smoke or not.

2 The government has to deal with the problem because it affects the health and welfare of various groups of people in society, which is the concern of government.

3 Option 1 is to increase tax on cigarettes and tobacco products; option 2 is to educate people about the dangers of smoking; option 3 is to do nothing, but leave the decision to people in society.

4 Student's own answer.

3.1 Activity

1 Arguments for include: freedom of choice for consumers; low taxes due to little government intervention mean that employees keep more of their wages or salaries; competition between suppliers leads to better goods and services at lower prices. Arguments against include: if there are no public services provided by the government, services such as education and policing will only be available to those who can afford to pay – or not at all, while undesirable or harmful goods and services such as drugs and pornography will be available to all those willing to pay; without government intervention economic factors such as unemployment and inflation might get out of control; the drive for profits might reduce the choice of goods and services available to consumers.

2 Student's own answer.

3.2, 3.3 and 3.4 Activities
Answers will depend on the country.

Unit 4

Business in context
1 The bus service was owned and run by the state, but is now privately owned.
2 The main problems are that the service is mainly used in one direction, and higher costs.
3 The problems for users are: unreliability; lack of comfort; and the unfriendly attitude of drivers.
4 If the private company is more concerned with profit than running a service it may be keen to reduce costs.
5 Student's own answer.

4.1, 4.2, 4.3 and 4.4 Activities
Answers will depend on the country and the area.

Business in context
1 9
2 5
3 Answers should reflect the fact that no stage of production can take place unless prior stages have been completed.

Unit 5

Business in context
1 Korea.
2 165.
3 At least 10.
4 Daewoo grew by diversifying and taking over other businesses.
5 Student's own answer.

5.1 Activity
Answers will depend on the country.

5.2 Activity
Vertical; horizontal; vertical; conglomerate; lateral.

5.3 Activity
Answers will depend on the businesses selected.

Revision questions

1 Specialisation is the tendency of an individual, business, region or country to concentrate on producing those goods and services in which they have an advantage, such as special skills or an abundance of raw materials. Division of labour refers to the breaking down of processes into specialised activities that are undertaken by different employees. Exchange refers to the ability to exchange one type of foods or services for another, usually with money as a means of exchange and allowing employees to exchange their labour for the goods and services they want.

2 Any three from: consumers; workers; managers; owners; those with a financial interest; the community; the government.

3 Non-profit-making enterprises are set up to fulfil a perceived social need, while one of the main objectives of private enterprises is to make a profit.

4 The priorities of a business may change over time as the business grows or there are changes in stakeholders and their objectives.

5 Features of a market economy include freedom of choice for consumers and suppliers; lack of intervention by the government; competition between businesses.

6 Most economies are mixed because, while private enterprise and competition can benefit consumers, some public goods and services are most effectively provided by the government.

7 Examples should reflect the distinction between primary sector business activities which are concerned with producing raw materials, while secondary sector activities are concerned with manufacturing.

Past examination questions

1 (a) The main methods of measuring the size of a business is by output of goods and services; turnover; profit; number of employees; capital employed; number of outlets.

   (b) Problems arise because it is difficult to compare businesses in different industries, and different methods may give different measures.

2 (a) (i) An objective of most private sector businesses is to make a profit, while public sector organisations are established to provide services for the community.

      (ii) Answer should compare the benefits of a state-owned service with those of a privately owned business.

   (b) (i) Tertiary business activity consists of providing services.

      (ii) Any service.

3 (a) (i) A private sector business is one that is set up, financed and managed by private individuals or groups of individuals.

(ii) A public sector organisation is one which is financed, owned and controlled by local or national government.

(b) Because of their different ownership structures their aims and objectives differ. A public sector business is financed largely by the state and hence aims at achieving targets determined by the state. These might include providing an adequate level of service at affordable prices accessible to all people. Private sector businesses will aim to achieve the objectives of their owners, including making a profit.

Unit 6

Business in context

1 Advantages put forward by Sofia include: being her own boss; being responsible for her own success; keeping the profits of her business.
2 Disadvantages put forward by Tina include: lack of shared responsibility for the business; long hours of work; responsibility for all aspects of the business; no previous experience either of running a business or of the type of business Sofia wants to set up; high risk if the business is not successful.
3 Student's own answer based on an evaluation of advantages and disadvantages.

6.1 Activity

Answer will depend on the business selected.

6.2 Activity

Student's own answer. The advice given must cover the advantages and disadvantages of being a sole trader, including liability, and the ease of setting up in business.

Business in context

1 Taleni, Jatura and Namene.
2 The Design Partnership offers architectural and interior design services.
3 Taleni decided to join the Design Partnership because she felt limited in her previous business as a sole trader and felt that becoming a partner in the larger business would enable her to develop her career and offer her clients a wider range of services.

4 Being a partner in a larger organisation will give Taleni access to a wider range of clients and enable her to gain greater experience. Her clients will also be able to benefit from the services, skills and experience of the other partners.
5 The partners must discuss their different objectives and agree how they will take the business forward.

6.3 Activity

Student's own answer, depending on the type of business selected.

6.4 Activity

1 Forming a partnership will enable Meka and Delyth to share responsibility for the business and getting clients, and provide their clients with a greater range of services than either could provide individually.
2 There may be a disagreement between Meka and Delyth, or one of the partners may not put as much effort into the business as the other.
3 Principal sources of finance for a partnership are the partners' own funds, personal loans, or loans and grants from local or national government.
4 Delyth must discuss the matter with Meka. If things cannot be resolved and Delyth is unhappy about the situation, the partnership must be dissolved.

Unit 7

Business in context

1 Tesco started as a partnership between Jack Cohen and T. E. Stockwell.
2 50.
3 Several reasons may be given, but important ones are shared responsibility and finance.
4 If it had remained a partnership, Tesco would have had limited scope to develop as a business: the partners would have found it hard to control and limited sources of finance would have hampered growth.

7.1 Activity

1, 2 and 3 Answers will depend on country.

4 Incorporated businesses are required by law to have a Memorandum and Articles of Association in order to register with the Registrar of Companies or other responsible body, and be given a certificate of incorporation.

7.2 Activity

The report should draw on features mentioned in the text and the advantages and disadvantages which are discussed.

7.3 Activity

Answers will depend on the shares selected.

7.4 Activity

Student's own answers based on the advantages and disadvantages discussed in the text.

Unit 8

Business in context

1 Each advertisement is offering the opportunity to open a business trading under the name and offering services developed by the franchisee.
2 Energy Efficiency Inc.: between $12,000 and $25,000; Kitchen Solutions for Any Budget Ltd: between $16,500 and $21,500; One-Stop Home Services Ltd: between $8,400 and $20,600.
3 Energy Efficiency offers services designed to improve energy efficiency in the home; Kitchen Solutions offers kitchen restoration services; One-Stop Home Services provides comprehensive service, repair and maintenance services.
4 It is difficult to judge the success of each company on the basis of information in the advertisements but Kitchen Solutions for Any Budget Ltd is the longest established and already has by far the largest number of franchises worldwide.
5 Based on the answer to question 4, Kitchen Solutions for Any Budget Ltd does seem the safest franchise opportunity. However, far more research into each company is needed to justify opening a franchise. Choice also depends on personal preference and the experience and skills of the person taking out the franchise.

8.1 Activity

1 The most appropriate type of business in each case is probably a sole trader due to the size of business involved.
2 Applicants who are sole traders will probably raise the necessary finance from their own resources, perhaps from savings or a 'windfall' such as a redundancy payment, or by taking out a personal bank loan.

8.2 Activity

Student's own answer.

Business in context

Answers will depend on the country.

8.3 Activity

Answers will depend on the country.

Unit 9

Business in context

1 Tandi needed to start her own business because she had been made redundant and had to find a new source of income.
2 Tandi's main source of finance was her redundancy payment.
3 Sole trader.
4 If Sipho became more involved in the business it may be appropriate to form a partnership. A limited company would only really be appropriate if the business grew, perhaps with several employees.
5 Student's own answer. It is important that the advantages and disadvantages of different types of business are explained with reference to Tandi's business.

9.1 Activity

Student's own answers, based on the business idea chosen.

9.2 Activity

Student's own answer. Important factors affecting Luisa's choice are the finance that would become available and the loss of control and vulnerability to takeover.

Unit 10

Business in context

1 $20,000.
2 $8,000.
3 20%.
4 $30,000.
5 $10,000.
6 Most likely sources are: owner's capital or bank loan.

10.1 Activity

Appropriate sources of medium-term to long-term finance are: internal – profits and reserves, owners' capital; external – bank loans; debentures and corporate bonds; venture capital; shares.

10.2 Activity

Answers will depend on type of business.

(b) Likely sources of finance include: owners' capital; bank loans; hire purchase of equipment; leasing of premises.

(c) Profits and reserves; owners' capital; bank loans.

Unit 11

Business in context

1 Typical costs Zebada will have to meet include: wages for the part-time assistant; rent; insurance; equipment; maintenance; heating, lighting and power; other costs such as postage, printing, stationery, telephone and advertising.

2 Zebada can get the money to pay her costs by selling the decorative mirrors she makes.

3 If Zebada does not pay for the resources she uses she will be unable to obtain further supplies to make more goods to sell and so go out of business. In addition suppliers to whom Zebada owes money will probably sue her.

4 She might be able to reduce her costs by now paying wages for an assistant, but she would be able to make fewer mirrors to sell, so her income would also be less.

5 Zebada is probably aware that there are many costs, such as wages, rent, insurance, heating and lighting that have to be paid whether she makes and sells any mirrors or not.

11.1 Activity

1

Level of production	Total costs of production
0 mirrors	$4,500
50 mirrors	$4,800
100 mirrors	$5,100
150 mirrors	$5,400
200 mirrors	$5,800
250 mirrors	$6,500

2

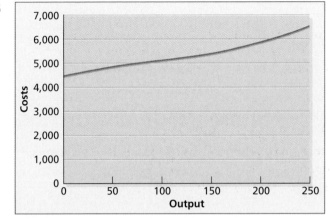

The relationship between Zebada's output and cost

3 Answers should recognise that total costs increase with increases in the volume of production because variable costs increase. It should be noted that variable costs increase at the rate of $300 for every additional 50 mirrors produced, up to 200 mirrors. When production is increased from 200 to 250 mirrors, however, variable costs increase by $700. A possible reason for this may be the need to take on an additional employee to achieve this level of production.

11.2 Activity

1

Level of production	Cost of production	Average cost per unit
5,000	$300,000	$60
7,500	$375,000	$50
10,000	$450,000	$45
12,500	$525,000	$42
15,000	$690,000	$46
17,500	$840,000	$48

2

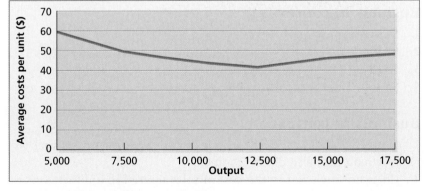

The relationship of output to average cost

3 12,500

4 At this level average cost per unit is lowest, producing highest profit per unit.

11.3 Activity

1 Contribution = $7.5 − $3 = $4.5;
Break-even point = $750 ÷ $4.5 = 167

2 $750 + $100 = $850 ÷ $4.5 = 189

3 Only if the donation to school or college funds is to be reduced or abandoned.

11.4 Activity

1

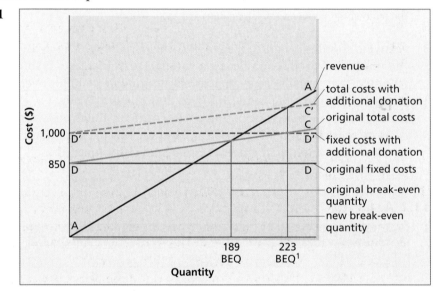

Break-even chart for end-of-term disco

2 223 tickets

Unit 12

Business in context

1 $7842

2 $53

3 $5157

4 $4968

Business in context

1 Costs included in the cost of sales figure are direct costs such as raw materials and direct labour.

2 Costs not included in the cost of sales figure are indirect costs or overheads.

3 Answers should include items such as rent and rates, maintenance, insurance, indirect wages and salaries, power, marketing expenses such as advertising, and other administrative costs.

12.1 Activity

1 Fixed assets will include items such as premises, machinery and equipment, fixtures and fittings.

2 Debtors are people and businesses that owe the company money; these will mainly be customers who have not yet paid their accounts.

3 Creditors are people and businesses to which the company owes money, for example in respect of loans and goods supplied but not yet paid for.

4 The figure for stocks represents goods made but not yet sold, and parts and materials not yet converted into finished goods. This may appear to be rather high.

Unit 13

Business in context

1 No: the bank balance shows how much cash the business has, not how much profit it has made.

2 The amount of money in the bank account represents the cash the company has available to pay its bills and creditors; the profit the business has made is the amount by which income has exceeded expenditure, regardless of whether the income has actually been received or the expenditure actually paid for or not.

3 Other useful information is: how easily could the business pay its creditors? Is the business making a reasonable profit on money invested in it?

4 The business could decide, for example, if it needs to improve its profitability, by increasing sales while maintaining costs, or if it should improve liquidity, by getting payment from customers more quickly and reducing the amount it is owed, or by delaying payments to suppliers (a more risky method).

5 Other interested people would be other shareholders, employees, banks and other financial institutions that have lent the business money, suppliers and customers. The business would be interested in other companies' final accounts in order to check the performance of the other companies and compare their own performance with this.

13.1 Activity

1 Gross profit margin = $2,738,000/7,842,000 x 100 = 34.91%

2 Net profit margin = $1,038,000/7,842,000 x 100 = 13.24%

3 ROCE = $1,038,000/1,641,000 x 100 = 63%

4 The company's figures are very healthy. The figure for ROCE is high, representing a good return on capital, however this could indicate that the business is in fact undercapitalised and ready for further investment and expansion.

13.2 Activity

1 Current ratio = $60,000:$4,000 = 15:1

2 Acid test = $7,000:$4,000 = 1.75:1

3 Again, the current ratio is very high indicating that some assets could be used more profitably. The high figure for stock we have identified in Activity 12.1, question 4, is largely responsible for this. This is confirmed by the acid test at 17.5:1. The business should reduce its stock level and consider investing in expansion.

4 and 5 Answers depend on the companies selected.

Unit 14

Business in context

1 Daniela's start-up costs include: rent on the property; fittings; initial stock. FURNITURE.

2 Daniela used her own savings, a loan from her parents, and a bank loan.

3 The bank manager wanted to see that Daniela had thought about her business carefully and had calculated her costs, likely sales and the profit she anticipated. This information would tell the bank manager whether she would be able to repay any bank loan.

4 The principal source of finance for running costs is income from sales.

5 Daniela should plan her future spending by forecasting sales, expenditure and cash flow.

14.1, 14.2 and 14.3 Activities

Answers depend on the business idea chosen.

Unit 15

Business in context

1 Three.

2 Newsha Nazari and Darren Campbell.

3 Two.

4 Go through Mohammed Al-Gharibi and Newsha Nazari.

5 Student's own answer should reflect the channels of communication and having to pass communications through different levels.

15.1 Activity

1 No.
2 Various factors may be identified including the personalities of the manager and the people managed, as well as the complexity of the tasks.

15.2 Activity

Answers will depend on the organisation.

15.3 Activity

1 Student's own answers based on the departments identified in the text.
2 Answers should include examples such as the production department being dependent on the sales department for forecasts of levels of production.
3 The main advantage is that people in departments are able to specialise. This means that they can develop skills in and knowledge of their work which will help them to contribute more to the organisation. The main disadvantage of working in departments is that people may feel their department is more important than others; there may be competition between departments and employees may work for the good of their department rather than the organisation.
4 By enabling employees to work in specialised groups.
5 A newspaper has departments such as editorial and advertising; a hospital has departments such as casualty and nursing; a bank has departments such as savings and investment.

Unit 16

Business in context

1 Typical resources both companies use are: buildings; land; employees; heating and lighting; equipment. Various other resources may be identified.
2 and **3** Student's answers should reflect the importance of the entrepreneur in setting up a successful business.

16.1 Activity

1 Factors include: land (the site on which the school or college is built); labour (teaching and administration staff); capital (the school or college building; equipment and furniture).
2 The head or principal may be considered an entrepreneur in some regards.
3 Student's own answer.

16.2 Activity

Role	Example
Allocating work to members of the department	Allocating individual jobs to production workers
Ensuring targets are met	Telling production workers about new range and overtime involved; checking production levels
Solving day-to-day problems	Showing two production workers how to construct the joint
Managing people	Meeting production workers unhappy about learning new skills
Managing finance	Completing returns for the finance department

16.3 Activity

1 The steps are:
   (a) Identify the problem – a decline in demand for Sun's products.
   (b) Decide what you want to achieve – Sun must increase its level of sales or reduce costs.
   (c) Consider possible alternatives – reduce production facilities and staffing levels; undertake an advertising campaign; develop new products.
   (d) Take action – Sun must decide which alternative to choose and carry it out.
   (e) Monitor effectiveness – once the action is underway, Sun must check that it is achieving the desired results: for example, if Sun decided to undertake the advertising campaign, it must check that this results in the required increase in sales.
   (f) If necessary make changes – if the advertising campaign does not produce sufficient increase in sales, Sun may decide to develop new products to stimulate demand.
2 Other courses of action Sun may consider include: reducing costs in other areas; finding new outlets for the range of products; exporting.
3 Student's own answer.

Unit 17

Business in context

1 10.

2 and **3**

Method of communication	Objective of communication
Discussion with foreman	To agree targets
Written report	To give information and recommendations
Meeting with departmental managers	To discuss and exchange ideas
Telephone conversation with Sales Manager	To obtain information
Talking individually to staff	To motivate staff, resolve any problems and give information
Letter to customer	To deal with an enquiry or complaint
Letter to supplier	To resolve a problem
Demonstrating how to put a joint together.	To give information
Forms	To give information
Says 'goodnight'	Motivating staff

4 Answer should reflect the need for speed and complexity of information communicated.

5 Student's own answer.

17.1 Activity

Student's own answer.

17.2 Activity

Student's own answer should be in correct report format.

Revision questions

1 An incorporated business is one that has been established as a legal entity separate from its owners; an unincorporated business does not exist as a separate legal entity. Owners of incorporated businesses have limited liability, while the liability of owners of unincorporated businesses is unlimited.

2 The principal differences are: partnerships have more owners who can share responsibility and decision-making, access to greater finance, and can bring different skills to the business.

3 Advantages: greater access to finance; opportunities for growth. Disadvantages: greater divorce of ownership from control; danger of company being taken over.

4 A joint venture is a business project that is undertaken by two or more businesses acting together. The advantages to the businesses involved include sharing the risks and the finance of the project.

5 (a) fixed costs do not vary in response to the level of production;
   (b) variable costs do vary in response to the level of production;
   (c) direct costs are incurred in the actual production of goods (materials, parts, direct labour);
   (d) indirect costs are overheads that are incurred in running the business.

Past examination questions

1 (a) Governments may give financial aid to start-up businesses in order to reduce unemployment, increase competitiveness and strengthen the economy.
   (b) New businesses often fail because the business planning has not been effective enough or monitored efficiently. A business that does not meet its sales targets, has too high expenses, has a poor cash flow or over-extends itself is in danger of failing.

2 (a) The main items found in a balance sheet are: current assets; liabilities; capital employed.
   (b) A cash-flow forecast shows anticipated cash coming into and going out of the business over a period, and the business's bank balance; the profit and loss account shows the difference between income and expenditure over a period, regardless of whether the cash has actually been received or spent.

3 (a) Net profit margin for 1998 = $20,000/100,000 x 100 = 20%
      Net profit margin for 1999 = $30,000/125 x 100 = 24%
      ROCE for 1998 = $20,000/150,000 = 13.33%
      ROCE for 1999 = $30,000/150,000 = 20%
   (b) These ratios show that the business has a healthy profit margin and is using its capital effectively. Both ratios have shown an improvement over the two years. It would also be useful to compare the figures with those of other businesses in the same industry.

4 (a) Effective communication occurs when a message from a sender is received, correctly interpreted and understood, and appropriately acted upon by the intended receiver.
   (b) Problems occur due to barriers to effective communication. 1 mark for each barrier identified.
   (c) 1 mark for each solution to a barrier identified.

5 Generally accepted management functions are: goal (objective) setting; leadership; organisation; co-ordination; monitoring and control; decision-making. Some development of points is required for 4 marks.

Unit 18

Business in context

1 Carmela is a computer operator, inputting information; Mohammed is an electrician who works on motor cars.

2 Carmela's job title may be 'computer operator' or 'accounts assistant'; Mohammed's job title is probably 'electrician' or 'motor engineer'. In both cases other suitable job titles may be suggested.

3 Carmela likes the contact with other people and the knowledge that the work she does is important to the company. Mohammed likes working with others and the money he is paid.

4 Carmela dislikes the occasional monotony; Mohammed dislikes the lack of responsibility, getting all the 'boring' jobs and the lack of opportunities for promotion.

5 If Carmela's and Mohammed's employers listened to their comments they might be able to change their jobs so that they got more satisfaction out of them. This would encourage them to contribute more in their work. Carmela's employer might try to make her job more varied, while Mohammed's employer could give him more responsibility and help him develop his career.

18.1 Activity

The main needs identified by Maslow that are satisfied by each factor are as follows (other needs may be identified, however, as most factors satisfy more than one need):

- money: physiological needs; needs for safety and security
- job satisfaction: need for self-fulfilment
- challenge: need for self-fulfilment
- promotion: need for recognition and esteem
- training: need for self-fulfilment
- social contact with colleagues: social needs
- opportunities for career development: need for self-fulfilment.

18.2 Activity

Answers will depend on the job advertisements selected.

Unit 19

Business in context

1 The group Nangolo belongs to consists of employees who work for the same employer but do not work together. They do not meet in the course of their work but get together once a week at college, where they are able to discuss work-related and personal matters.

2 Nangolo calls it an informal group because it has not been formally organised by Coldstore Appliances and has no official structure or purpose.

3 Nangolo's department can be considered as a workgroup.

4 The informal group supports Nangolo by enabling him to find out more about what is happening in the company and to discuss any problems he may have. Being a member of the informal group also gives Nangolo a sense of identity.

5 Coldstore Appliances gains because the informal group helps to motivate Nangolo and give him an interest in his work and employer, which will make him work better.

19.1 Activity

1 Fatima is a member of the works committee. She is also a member of her department.

2 The works committee is a formal group, because it has been set up and given a structure and purpose by the company.

3 The group's objectives are to discuss the concerns of the workforce and senior management of the company, improve motivation, solve problems and help management and workforce to work towards the same ends.

4 Fatima's objectives are to get noticed by senior management and improve her chances of promotion.

5 Sometimes members bring personal agendas to a group. In Fatima's case, her ambition to improve her chances of promotion through membership of the works committee means that she may be unwilling to put forward the views of those she has been elected to represent.

19.2 Activity

1 If they feel that Juan is considering their motivation, morale and welfare, his workers are likely to support Juan and put in extra effort to complete the order on time.

2 Answers should consider ways of gaining the support of workers by discussing the situation with them, listening to their views and responding to their needs. Juan should also show leadership by being prepared to support and help the workers.

19.3 Activity

1 Zuriada adopted a more autocratic style of management for the current situation.
2 By adopting this management approach Zuriada was able to give positive leadership and direction to her inexperienced team. This helped the team fulfil what was expected of them.
3 By responding effectively to the situation and adapting her management style, Zuriada probably adopted the best course.
4 Other group members will respect Zuriada's positive leadership and management ability, while appreciating her naturally democratic style. They may therefore be happier to work for her and follow her leadership. Zuriada could have tried to maintain her democratic style by negotiating targets with individual team members either at the meeting or later, but their lack of experience may have led to them suggesting unrealistic targets.

Unit 20

Business in context

1 The dispute is over tea and coffee breaks.
2 Juanita Cortes is representing the staff in negotiations with the management of the company.
3 Student's answer must be logical, fair and the conclusions must be justified.
4 Adequate breaks are necessary for motivation. The attitude of management might also serve to demotivate staff. Answer should refer to motivation theory, including Herzberg.
5 Student's answer should mention that any action must be aimed at resolving the dispute through negotiation and improving the motivation of staff.

20.1 Activity

Answer will depend on the trade union selected and also the country.

20.2 Activity

Answers will depend on the country.

Unit 21

Business in context

1 The vacancy is for a Trainee Recruitment Administrator.
2 The successful candidate will be required to use a word processor and computer keyboard, answer the telephone, organise and confirm interviews, keep and file records, and read CVs and applications that are received by the agency.

3 Skills and aptitudes needed by applicants include: keyboard and word processing skills; good telephone manner; good organising skills; methodical approach to record keeping and filing; analytical reading skills. While the advertisement does not specifically require experience, some working clerical and keyboard experience is implied.

4 Student's own answer. The advertisement does not tell prospective applicants much about the agency or about benefits such as salary.

21.1, 21.2, 21.3 and 21.4 Activities

Student's own answers.

21.5 Activity

Answer should outline different types of training mentioned in the text, including induction, on-the-job and off-the-job training. The benefits of training for the employee and the employer should be explained, together with their costs in terms of finance, time and resources.

Revision questions

1 Work satisfies people's needs in various ways: money received in wages or salaries enables employees to purchase necessities such as food and clothing as well as luxuries such as radios and televisions. Work also satisfies people's social and other needs, such as the needs for security, belonging, recognition and esteem, and personal fulfilment.

2 A formal group is established by the employer and has a set hierarchy and purpose; an informal group arises naturally, may serve a variety of purposes and leaders are elected or appointed by group members.

3 In business, groups undertake tasks and procedures that cannot be undertaken by one person, bring together different skills of group members, increase motivation and commitment, and aid management and control.

4 Being a member of a group can give a person an identity, establish relationships, give a sense of belonging and enable a person to exert more influence through the combined efforts of the members of the group.

5 Induction training; on-the-job training; off-the-job training.

Past examination questions

1 Protection in case of dispute with employer; help and advice if unsure of their rights; financial assistance in certain circumstances; comfort in numbers! 1 mark per benefit; maximum 2 marks.

2 **(a)** A fixed weekly wage is a set amount per week regardless of
        work done. The amount of a performance-related weekly wage
        is dependent on the amount of work done. Paying a
        performance-related weekly wage can therefore motivate
        employees to work harder, although this can result in cutting
        corners in order to get more done, leading to a drop in quality.

   (b) Paying a performance-related wage may increase motivation, as
        long as performance can be fairly measured and improved
        performance is equally possible by all staff. A fixed weekly
        wage may increase motivation if staff feel that they are being
        more fairly treated.

   (c) Non-financial rewards can also increase motivation.

3 Payment by results (piece rate); bonus payments; commission;
   profit sharing.

4 **(a)** A motivated employee is one whose attitude is positive so that
        they work effectively for a business. This can be developed
        further by examples of employee motivation.

   (b) Answers should refer to things like better communication,
        improved working conditions, enhanced management
        methods. Reference to motivational theorists is not required,
        but may be rewarded.

5 Generally accepted management functions are: setting objectives;
   leadership; organisation; monitoring and control; decision-making.
   Some development of these points is required for full marks.

Unit 22

Business in context

1 A luxury sports car, a tractor, a mobile phone, a bottle of perfume.
2 Sports car: private individual; tractor: business; mobile phone:
   private individuals and businesses; bottle of perfume: private
   individuals.
3 Sports car: car showroom; tractor: agricultural machinery outlet;
   mobile phone: retailer; bottle of perfume: chemist, drugstore,
   department store or similar retail outlet.
4 Sports car: wealthy young person; tractor: farmer; mobile phone:
   almost anybody of any age, depending on the cost and availability
   of mobile telephone services and reception; perfume: women. All
   the products illustrated may be bought by other types of
   customers.
5 Both mobile phones and perfume are bought by customers who
   will give the product to someone else as a present.

22.1 Activity

1 **(a)** The market for holidays may be segmented on the basis of, for example: age; marital status; personal interest or hobby.
   (b) Examples of segments in the clothing market are: age; gender; taste.

2 A supermarket may make use of market segmentation to identify who its customers are and tailor its products to them, or to enter a new market segment and attract new customers.

Business in context

1 Elizabeth and Thismanya run an instant printing business.
2 They use a computer to keep their customer records.
3 They compile a marketing database to send regular mailings to customers.
4 Regular mailings inform customers of special offers, and prompt customers to think about re-ordering.
5 The main disadvantage is that it only uses information about existing customers.

22.2 Activity

1 Customers do buy benefits rather than the product for its own sake, even if the benefit is only the satisfaction of knowing that one has the product.
2 The implication of customers buying benefits rather than products is that market orientation becomes even more important to ensure that the product provides the benefits that customers want.

22.3 Activity

Answers will depend on the advertisement selected.

Unit 23

Business in context

1 The most profitable part of Lucy's business was beauty treatments.
2 Lucy asked her customers to complete a questionnaire.
3 Lucy also researched the services offered by other local salons.
4 Lucy's research provided a good foundation for the future of her business, although she could have been surer if she had also researched people who were not currently her customers.

23.1, 23.2, and 23.3 Activities

Student's own answers.

Unit 24

Business in context

Answers should reflect the impact and ease of comparing statistics presented graphically rather than as simple figures in the text. In this example, the bar chart is probably easiest to understand and has most impact. Another way of presenting the figures may have been in the form of a map of the world with relevant sales figures on each country.

24.1 Activity

1 Frequency distribution:

Value	Frequency
5	1
6	1
7	2
8	5
9	10
10	3
11	2
12	1

2 Arithmetic mean = 8.76.
3 Mode = 9.
4 The arithmetic mean gives a representation of the number of units sold per day spread over the 25 days. The mode shows the most frequent number of units sold on any one day.

24.2 Activity

1

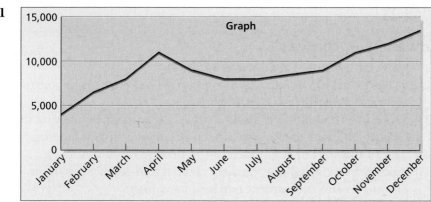

Number of accounts opened each month

2

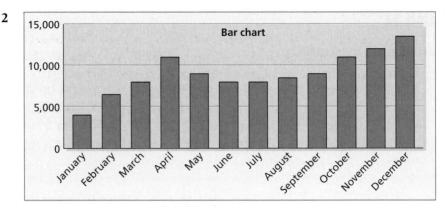

Number of accounts opened each month

3 Student's own answer based on impact and ease of understanding the charts.

24.3 Activity

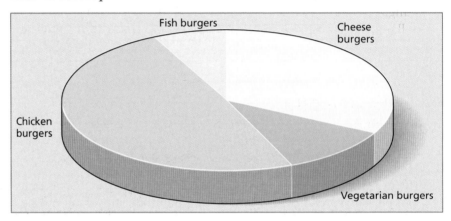

Sales volume of different burgers

Unit 25

Business in context

1 SA Fruit Farms Ltd produces fruit drinks.
2 Reasons for the decline include: competition; changes in consumer taste and demand; changes in packaging.
3 SA Fruit Farms Ltd gave their drinks a new image by making them healthy and energising, and altered the style of the packaging.
4 SA Fruit farms Ltd responded to the decline in sales of their product by carrying out market research and redesigning their product to suit the current needs of consumers.

25.1 Activity

1 Objective features include those that are an essential part of each product, such as a responsive sole or free-flowing, non-drip nib.
2 Subjective features are those that fulfil the personal wants of customers, such as colour, shape and style.
3 Answers should emphasis that although the design of a product must include objective features in order to fulfil its purpose, customers will only buy it if it has appropriate subjective features.

25.2 Activity

1 Coca Cola is at its maturity phase; Microsoft Windows is still in its growth phase; the market for trainers, in which Nike operates, is in its saturation phase; Sony Walkman is in its decline stage.
2 Student's answer may suggest a variety of extension strategies.
3 Coca Cola extends its life cycle through marketing; the market for Microsoft Windows is extended by continually updating the product; Nike extends the life cycle of its trainers by continually changing the designs and functionality; Sony extends the life of its Walkman by bringing out new products under the Walkman name.

Unit 26

Business in context

1 Although the aircraft has 100 seats, on an average flight only 70 seats are expected to be occupied.
2 The level of demand for a product is affected by its price. As its price rises, the demand for air travel declines.
3 Cut-price offers make standby and short-notice bookings more attractive to customers. In this way airlines can fill seats that would otherwise be left empty.
4 20 seats at an average price of \$160 = \$3,200; 16 seats at an average price of \$320 = \$5,120; \$5,120 − \$3,200 = \$1,920; new profit margin = \$1,700.3 + \$1,920 = \$3,620.3, assuming all the new Business Class seats are occupied.
5 Cutting profit margins, especially on Business Class, may encourage demand for the airline's seats.

26.1 Activity

1 Student's own answer.
2 The opportunity cost is whatever else you would have liked to spend your money on.
3 Student's own answer.

26.2 Activity

1 **(a)** Price skimming; **(b)** penetration pricing; **(c)** cost-plus pricing; **(d)** competition pricing.

2 Each pricing policy is likely to prove successful, at least in the short term. The mobile phone company is likely to face strong competition soon and may be forced to adopt a competitive pricing strategy. If the breakfast cereal has a strong brand name or is given a unique selling point which makes it more attractive to customers, the manufacturer may be able to adopt a cost-plus pricing strategy. The perfume manufacturer could increase market share, or enter new market segments by pricing more competitively. The insurance company probably has no realistic alternative pricing strategy.

Unit 27

Business in context

1 The Body Shop sells body and hair care products.
2 Anita Roddick believes that the growth area is in skin care products.
3 She means that consumers are tired of exaggerated claims by manufacturers for their products.
4 Student's own answer.

27.1 Activity

Answer will depend on the product selected. It should show an awareness of different types of promotion.

27.2 Activity

Answer should show an awareness of how a good press release can provide effective publicity for the business.

Unit 28

Business in context

1 Petrol is purchased at a garage, or service station.
2 Gas stations and filling stations.
3 People would be confused and unable to buy the petrol when they wanted it.
4 Private motorists purchase the petrol from a retailer, while businesses that have their own storage facilities may buy the petrol in bulk from the oil storage depot.
5 Answer should highlight the difficulty in making purchases and satisfying needs if customers do not know where they can obtain the product.

28.1 Activity

1

	Advantages		Disadvantages	
	Village stores	Hypermarkets	Village stores	Hypermarkets
To retailer	Independence Knowledge of customers Can respond quickly to changing needs and tastes	Purchasing in bulk enables low prices which attracts more customers Business may grow, leading to greater profits	Cannot buy goods in bulk Few opportunities for growth Small customer base	Lack of knowledge of individual customers Slow to adapt to changing needs and tastes
To customer	Local Useful for buying small quantities Convenience	Large range of products Inexpensive Useful for bulk shopping	Small range of products Expensive	May have to travel Requires transport to carry bulk shopping

2 Mail order is quick and easy, but products cannot be examined. Delivery is often an additional cost and may take time. In traditional bookshops customers can examine books they are interested in, easily compare them with alternatives, and take their purchases away with them.

28.2 Activity

Answers will depend on the country. Meat must be chilled or frozen and requires bulk transport. Bone marrow is small but must be transported urgently under sterile conditions. Bananas may be transported by road or rail in large trucks.

Unit 29

Business in context

1 The product Lerato and Nomsa developed was lightweight and cool, yet warm in colder climates. It was also comfortable, waterproof and crease-resistant.
2 Their customers were clothing manufacturers, particularly manufacturers of lightweight travel clothing.
3 Lerato and Nomsa promoted their product by sending samples to clothing manufacturers and advertising in travel magazines.
4 Lerato put forward a policy of price skimming, while Nomsa was in favour of penetration pricing. Lerato's strategy, if successful, would produce a larger profit in the short term. This might help cover the costs of developing the product. Nomsa's policy would establish the product in the market place. Once established it may be possible to increase the price and so obtain greater profits.

29.1 Activity

Answers will depend on the product selected. It is important that the use of all elements of the marketing mix (product, price, promotion, place) in marketing the product is described.

29.2 Activity

Answers should be a well-formatted marketing plan that establishes marketing objectives and sets out appropriate marketing activities to achieve these.

Unit 30

Business in context

1　The main advantages are that Ahmed is able to make furniture to meet the specific requirements of individual customers. As a craftsman, Ahmed produces individual pieces of furniture to a high standard.

2　The main disadvantage is that Ahmed is only able to produce on a small scale, thus limiting numbers of customers and the scope of his business.

3　Ahmed's main competitors are large furniture manufacturers making mass-produced items. The main advantages they have are that they are able to produce a large quantity of furniture at a low cost which customers can purchase easily and conveniently at a furniture store.

4　Ahmed could increase his production by taking on more labour and producing by machine.

5　Answers should reflect that there would be a trade off between producing more and satisfying more customers quickly, and reducing the individuality, and possibly the quality, of the furniture.

30.1 Activity

Making toys: batch production
Car manufacturing: mass production
Oil production: flow production
Building a factory: job production

30.2 Activity

Reports should cover approaches such as improving efficiency through altering the sequence of tasks; redesigning the layout of the work place; automating processes; methods of lean production, and introducing methods of team working or cell production and quality circles. Quality can be improved by introducing methods of quality control and developing a TQM approach.

Unit 31

Business in context

1   A supermarket gathers information about customers and their level of spending in an area, ease of access, road networks, local competition and attractiveness of the proposed store.

2   Sources of information include: computer programs; nationally available information such as census data; research carried out by the company.

3   The main factors include: planning applications for new roads, housing developments and other stores; size of site; proposed competitor developments; availability of car parking; suitability of other sites.

4 and 5 Answers should show judgement and evaluation of all factors.

31.1 Activity

1   The main reasons for car manufacturing becoming associated with Detroit were availability of suitable labour, ease of access to parts and materials, and ease of distribution of cars.

2   As Detroit has become a centre for car manufacturing, it is probably still advantageous for US car manufacturers to locate there in view of the availability of skilled labour and the support services that have become established.

31.2 and 31.3 Activities

Answers will depend on the area.

Revision questions

1   Factors include: cost; legislation; ease of access and distribution; availability of skilled labour; any government incentives.

2   Preparing a marketing plan will help Natasha define her objectives and decide on marketing activities that will help her achieve them. She will be able to monitor the plan and check that the marketing activities she undertakes result in increased sales. Her marketing plan should include: objectives; analysis of the strengths and weaknesses of the business; results of market research; marketing strategy based on the marketing mix; budget.

Past examination questions

1   A market-orientated business will take account of the specific requirements of its market and develop a product to meet these.

2   Advantages include: direct contact with customers; increased profit margins due to selling direct; easier control over production and stock. Disadvantages include: goods purchased in smaller quantities; higher cost of distribution to individual customers; higher administrative costs.

3   A business must consider: the type and cost of the proposed advertisements; the anticipated outcomes in terms of increased sales and profits; and the available financial resources of the business.

4   Lower prices will result in lower profit margins. These may be offset by increased demand, and sales of the product; however, if the increase in demand is not strong enough, profit will fall.

5   (a) A product that is at the end of its maturity stage is likely to face strong competition and declining sales.

   (b) The business may try an extension strategy or allow decline to set in and withdraw the product from the market, replacing it with another. Answers should identify and explain advantages of options.

6   The most suitable channel probably involves both wholesalers and retailers. Answers should give reasons.

7   (a) In both cases sales revenue and advertising expenditure are positively related. However, in A the rate of increase in sales is declining while in B it is increasing. This implies that in A advertising is having a diminishing impact on sales, while in B the opposite is true.

   (b) Answers should explain and give advantages of methods such as finding new markets; a new pricing strategy; product differentiation.

8   (a) One mark per question asked. To be acceptable the question must be clearly relevant and answerable.

   (b) Answers must justify each question by showing that the information it generates is of value to Joshua.

   (c) Accuracy of results will depend on size and composition of sample – a larger sample will produce more reliable results if sample composition is representative of total population.

Unit 32

Business in context

1   The main areas of spending are: national defence; health care; education; social security; and transport.

2   Meeting the demands of the other ministers would mean increasing taxes.

3   Other problems include keeping unemployment and inflation rates low.

4 and 5 Answers must be based on an evaluation of factors involved.

32.1 and 32.2 Activities

Answers will depend on the country.

32.3 Activity

1 Answers should identify different types of tax.
2 Effects must relate to the types of tax involved and include effects on spending power and demand, inflation, unemployment and business activity.

32.4 Activity

1, 2 and 3 Answers will depend on the country.

4 $138.75
5 If the increase led to reduced borrowing, demand might fall. This would result in lower inflation but might also lead to reduced production as fewer goods and services are demanded, and increased unemployment as less labour is required.

Unit 33

Business in context

1 The objectives of Friends of the Earth are to encourage conservation, reduce pollution and bring about changes in the policies and activities of businesses and governments in order to protect the environment.
2 The purpose of the 'Factory Watch' campaign is to monitor pollution from factories and provide information about the impact on health.
3 Information is made available to local people to encourage them to take action.
4 and 5 Student's own answers.

33.1 Activity

External benefits include: employment; availability of shopping services; and economic development of a rural area.

External costs include: destruction of a site of the natural environment; pollution; increased traffic; possibly also the loss of an area previously used for leisure and recreational purposes.

33.2 Activity

Answers will depend on the area.

Unit 34

Business in context

1 Since the shop supplied the software, the shop is responsible for replacing it.
2 Maria has no right to compensation.
3 If Maria does not receive satisfactory action then she should take legal action against the shop.
4 Student's own answer.

34.1 Activity

1 The shop is responsible for selling a dangerous toy.
2 This case comes under consumer protection legislation. Laws may vary in different countries.
3 If David does not receive satisfactory action he may take legal action against the shop.

34.2, 34.3 and 34.4 Activities

Answers will depend on the country.

Revision questions

1 Fiscal policies are concerned with government income and expenditure; monetary policies are concerned with the amount of money in an economy.
2 Gross National Product represents the total value of goods and services produced by a country. Increasing this increases the amount of goods and services available and the standard of living of the population.
3 **(a)** Pressure groups are set up to influence the behaviour of businesses and governments through direct and indirect action. Consumers may, for example, lobby a business or take their custom elsewhere.
   (b) Any group of stakeholders. Answers should give reasons for setting up a pressure group.
4 Voluntary controls may be more effective, easier to implement and accept, but only if they are effective.

Past examination questions

1 Answers should identify circumstances where dismissal may occur, such as: breach of contract of employment; inability to do a job correctly even when trained; ignoring company rules regarding things like health and safety; damaging an employer's reputation.

2   Consumers need protection against exploitation by businesses. This could take the form of being overcharged, being sold goods which are not fit for their purpose, mis-selling or misrepresentation etc.

3   A social cost is the cost of a business activity to society as a whole.

4   Financial costs affect the business directly, are more easily identifiable, and have a more immediate impact on the activities of the business.

5   (a) Shareholders are protected against businesses acting in ways that may jeopardise their investment in them.

   (b) Employees (employment legislation) and consumers (consumer protection).

6   (a) The government can impose tariffs and barriers, such as quotas on imports.

   (b) Restricting imports reduces competition and may lead to retaliation by other countries. This harms the ability of businesses to export.

Index

Please note that references to activities or examination questions and answers are in italics.

Acknowledgements

We are grateful to the following for permission to reproduce photographs:

Corbis page 175; Daewoo website page 37; Eye Ubiquitous pages 217, 247; Hardlines page 148; Impact pages 63, 242; Popperfoto pages 23, 264; Robert Harding 262; Spectrum 177, 188 ; Yiorgos Nikiteas pages 174, 205, 216

We would like to thank the following for permission to use their material in either the original or adapted form:

Barclays Bank plc, pages 105–110; The Body Shop, pages 123, 215; Cadbury's Trebor Bassett, page 33; Cambridge International Examinations Publications, page 276; Civil Aviation Authority, page 210; Daewoo, page 37; Friends of the Earth, page 260; Neptune Shipping Agency Ltd, page 13; Tesco Stores Ltd, page 54; Virgin plc, page 123

The past examination questions are reproduced by permission of the University of Cambridge Local Examinations Syndicate.

Every effort has been made to reach copyright holders. The publishers would be pleased to hear from anyone whose rights they have unwittingly infringed.

The publisher has used its best endeavour to ensure that the URLs for external websites referred to in this book are correct and active at the time of going to press. However, the publisher has no responsibility for the websites and can make no guarantee that a site will remain live or that the content is or will remain appropriate.